virgin film

COEN BROTHERS

Eddie Robson

This book is dedicated to Mum, Dad, Helen and Gran – because it's a family thing.

First published in Great Britain in 2003
by Virgin Books Ltd
Thames Wharf Studios
Rainville Road
London
W6 9HA

A catalogue record for this book is available from the British Library.

ISBN 0 7535 0797 8

Typeset by TW Typesetting, Plymouth, Devon
Printed and bound in Great Britain by Mackays of Chatham PLC

Contents

Acknowledgements

Thanks to my editor, Kirstie Addis, and muchas gracias to Scott Andrews, Mark Clapham, Adrian Cooper, Ben Felsenburg, Steven Gardiner, Simon Guerrier, Stephen Lavington, Daniel O'Mahony, Jim Smith and Andy Thatcher, all of whom assisted with research materials and/or readthroughs.

Thanks also to the BFI Library, Camden Libraries, Goldsmiths College, Neil Corry at *Film Review*, Garth Franklin at *Dark Horizons* (http://www.darkhorizons.com), Stephen Thompson at *The Onion AV Club* (http://www.theonionavclub.com), Paul Tweedle at *You Know, For Kids!* (http://x-stream.fortunecity.com/fleetst/71/index.html) and the Internet Movie Database (http://www.imdb.com). Box office data courtesy of The Numbers (http://www.the-numbers.com), with thanks to Bruce Nash.

All material from *American Cinematographer* is reprinted with permission of *American Cinematographer* C1985, 1996, 2000, 2001, 2003, 2004. More information about the American Society of Cinematographers (ASC) can be found at http://www.theASC.com. Many thanks to Jim McCullaugh.

Finally, very special thanks to Catherine Spooner who has put up with the whole thing magnificently, especially considering she doesn't like the films.

Picture Credits

The following pictures are from the Ronald Grant Archive:
Page 1 (top) courtesy of River Road Productions; Page 1 (bottom) courtesy of Embassy/Renaissance Pictures; Page 2 (top and bottom) and Page 3 (top) courtesy of Circle Films; Page 3 (bottom) courtesy of Working Title/Silver Pictures; Page 4 (top and bottom) courtesy of Working Title/Polygram/Gramercy Pictures; Page 5 (top) courtesy of Working Title/Polygram; Page 5 (bottom) courtesy of Naked Man Productions/October Films; Page 6 (top) courtesy of Buena Vista Pictures/Mike Zoss Productions/Studio Canal/Touchstone Pictures/Universal Pictures/Working Title.

The following pictures are from the Kobal Collection:
Page 6 (bottom) and Page 7 (top) courtesy of Kobal Collection/Working Title; Page 8 (top) courtesy of Kobal Collection/Circle Films; Page 8 (bottom) courtesy of Kobal Collection/Working Title/Polygram.

The picture on page 7 (bottom) is copyright Universal/Everett/Rex Features.

Introduction

It's difficult not to feel self-conscious when embarking upon a critical assessment of the work of Joel and Ethan Coen. This is precisely the kind of analysis which they tend to resist: they appear puzzled by the existence of critics and bemused by any attempt at an intellectual reading of their work. Their interpretation of the journalist's activity is that 'they have to write a certain number of words, so they indulge in all sorts of things that will justify that number.'

At this point, therefore, I feel that I must apologise to Joel and Ethan, and warn them that there are rather a lot of words about their movies in this book.

It sometimes seems that the brothers' reluctance to talk about their work stems from the fact that they too are afflicted with a degree of self-consciousness, to the point where they'd really rather just get on with their work and refrain from analysing it too much. Sometimes, in order to get anything done, you have to let go and just *do* it. The Coens were also some of the first filmmakers to have grown up with movies as part of everyday life, consuming film indiscriminately from the television during their early years. Cinematic technique seems to be instinctive to them and this is perhaps because their formative experiences made it a second language. That said, they have sometimes been enticed into explaining the thought behind certain aspects of their movies and, on these occasions, they have revealed the level to which they conceptualise before they start (check their comments on lines and circles in **The Hudsucker Proxy**, for example).

So, what is this book and how does one go about using it? Well, in the format established by previous entries in the Virgin Film series, information and criticism are ordered under category headings to aid the reader in locating what they want to know. Each of the ten films the Coens have directed (from *Blood Simple* to *Intolerable Cruelty*) has its own chapter and there are also shorter chapters for *Crimewave* (which they co-wrote with the film's director Sam Raimi) and *The Naked Man* (which Ethan co-wrote with J Todd Anderson). Each chapter is headed with the title of the film and year of release, followed by the main production credits (transcribed in the order that they appear on-screen, whether at the beginning or end of the movie) followed by the credited cast. From there on, the following headings are used as appropriate:

TAGLINE: The one-line sell for the movie used in contemporary publicity materials. Sometimes there's more than one.

SUMMARY: The plot. Best to watch the film before reading this, for obvious reasons.

DEVELOPMENT: How Ethan and Joel initiated each project, concentrating on the scripting process. While they usually work from an original concept, they do have a tendency to 'borrow' from other sources. In some cases they even draw upon real events – and no, I'm not talking about *Fargo* . . .

REFERENCES: Throwaway references to books, films and so on. This section also notes references to other Coen films.

CASTING: A rundown on who's in each film and how they ended up there, including their previous work and what you might have seen them in since. Also, since the Coens like to work with tried and trusted colleagues on their films, this section will make note of any Coen regulars the first time they appear.

PRODUCTION: An account of the film's production process, focusing mainly on the shoot and post-production.

DELETED SCENES: Details of scenes that were either scripted but never shot or shot but never used, along with the reasons for cutting them.

MUSIC: The original music on every Coens movie has been written by Carter Burwell, whether on his own or in collaboration with others (in the case of *O Brother, Where Art Thou?* most of the work was done by T-Bone Burnett). This section will cover his score as well as any stock music that has been used on the soundtrack.

CRITICAL RECEPTION: What the critics thought of the film on its original release. Some love the Coens' movies, some hate them: I will include as wide a variety of comments as possible.

BOX OFFICE: A note on how much money each film made from its primary market, its first run in American cinemas.

AWARDS: A rundown of the awards garnered by each film, from the Oscars to Cannes. It must be said that, given the sheer number of prizes that are awarded these days for excellence in the field of anything you care to name, it would be impossible to give *complete* information on which film has won what, but the most significant ones will be listed.

DIALOGUE TO SKIP BACK FOR: Every script that Joel and Ethan have written is a finely wrought piece of work, with the dialogue as not so much the icing on the cake as the thick layer of custard on the trifle. This section is for quoting standout lines from each film.

ANALYSIS: This section looks at structure, character, camerawork, cinematography, themes – whatever seems pertinent, really. Other critical standpoints on the brothers' work will also be examined.

GENRE: 'There's no point in making a genre movie *unless* you use that knowledge somehow as a kinda device of the storytelling,' says Joel. 'But then you can change or subvert that, and that's what's nice.' The Coens love to play tricks with genre: most of their movies are film noir to a greater or lesser extent, but other genres make appearances. Further discussion of the influences on each film may also be appropriate here.

EVER AMERICA: Every Coens film thus far has been set in the twentieth century and most have been period pieces looking back to the recent past, whether that involves skipping back a few years (*The Big Lebowski*, *Fargo*) or doing a full-on costume drama like *Miller's Crossing*. 'We tend to do period stuff,' Ethan says, 'because it helps make it one step removed from boring everyday reality.' They have also situated all of their movies in their home country: 'Strangely, the subjects that come to mind are always situated in America,' says Joel. 'That's what seems to interest us.' A distinctive view of twentieth-century America has therefore emerged across their work (moving into the 21st with *Intolerable Cruelty*), and this section looks at how the Coens' homeland is depicted in terms of the period and location selected for each film.

AVAILABILITY: This section lists whether, at the time of writing, the movie is commercially available on DVD. (All of them are available on VHS unless otherwise stated.) Where a DVD is available, it'll note whether it's on Region 1, Region 2 or both, and what extras you get on the disc.

THE COENS' VIEW: A comment from the Coens that sums up their feelings about the movie in question.

VERDICT: Enough beating about the bush – how *good* is it? This is the place for assessing the film's merits and how it rates against the Coens' other works.

Early Life

The advantage of dealing with a creative partnership between two siblings is that one can deal with both their childhoods at once without having to recount the historic circumstances of their meeting. Ethan has known Joel all his life, while Joel has known Ethan all of Ethan's life.

Joel Coen was born on 29 November 1954 and Ethan arrived just under three years later, on 21 September 1957, in Minneapolis, Minnesota. Their parents were middle-class Jewish academics: though born in New York, their father Edward was brought up in his parents' home town of London and earned his qualifications at the London School of Economics. He later took a teaching job at the University of Michigan. Joel and Ethan's mother Reba came from an orthodox Jewish Latvian family and she went on to become a professor of art history at St Cloud State University. Neither parent made a particular effort to impress their interests on the boys: 'My mother once wrote an article, "How to Take Children to an Art Museum",' Joel says, 'but I don't recall her ever taking us.' The brothers also have an elder sister, Deborah Ruth. They have claimed on many occasions that their childhood years, spent in the Minneapolis suburb of St Louis Park, are of no interest whatsoever.

'There's three years difference in age and that's important when you're a child,' Joel says. 'It was only after leaving school that we really got to know each other.' Even so, both of the boys were frequently at a loose end during their teens and Joel hit upon the idea of buying a Super-8 camera and making their own movies. They mowed lawns to earn the cash and purchased the equipment, then they began shooting. Many of their early efforts were remakes of bad movies they had seen on TV: notable titles include *Lumberjacks of the North*, *Ed . . . A Dog* and *The Banana Film*. Evidently Joel enjoyed the filmmaking process because when he went to New York University in 1974 he enrolled to study film. What he did there, it seems, was much the same as what he had done with Ethan during his teenage years, only with better facilities and a diploma at the end. He claims not to have learned anything – apparently he spent the majority of his time sitting at the back of the class looking cynical – but he appreciated being able to concentrate on moviemaking for a few years. His thesis was a thirty-minute film called *Soundings*, in which a woman fantasises out loud during sex with her deaf boyfriend. The subject of her fantasies, however, is not her boyfriend but his roommate, who is next door.

Meanwhile, Ethan went to Princeton University in nearby New Jersey in 1977 and studied philosophy. He acknowledges that he chose the subject because he didn't really know what he wanted to do with his life and his attitude to the course was casual. On one occasion he was ordered to see a psychiatrist after submitting a faked doctor's note to the effect that he had fallen victim to a freak hunting accident and lost an arm. Joel married his first wife during this time, whose identity he has admirably managed to keep from the public. On graduating from NYU Joel started to look around for movie work and in 1980 he scored an assistant editing gig on *The Evil Dead*, the debut feature by a 21-year-old independent director called Sam Raimi (see **Crimewave**). He also did editing work on *Fear No Evil* (Frank Laloggia, 1981) and *Nightmare* (Romano Scafolini, 1981), and got himself fired from the latter.

Ethan had moved to New York by this time and was working as a typist at Macy's department store, which at least taught him valuable skills for his writing career. (He also did some writing for the cop show *Cagney and Lacey*.) The brothers had re-ignited the creative partnership from their teens, in a more structured way this time. 'We started writing scripts for other people, for people who were coming in to work on projects I was working on,' says Joel. 'It was at that point we realised: this works out pretty well.' When they saw what Raimi had achieved with *The Evil Dead*, they saw the possibility of making a movie of their own.

Blood Simple (1984)

(Colour – 97 mins)

Directed by Joel Coen
Produced by Ethan Coen
Written by Joel Coen and Ethan Coen
Executive Producer: Daniel F Bacaner
Associate Producer: Mark Silverman
Director of Photography: Barry Sonnenfeld
Production Designer: Jane Musky
Music: Carter Burwell
Editing: Roderick Jaynes and Don Wiegmann
First Assistant Director: Deborah Reinisch
Casting: Julie Hughes and Barry Moss

CAST: John Getz (*Ray*), Frances McDormand (*Abby*), Dan Hedaya (*Julian Marty*), M Emmet Walsh (*Private Detective*), Samm-Art Williams (*Meurice*), Deborah Neumann (*Debra*), Raquel Gavia (*Landlady*), Van Brooks (*Man from Lubbock*), Señor Marco (*Mr Garcia*), William Creamer (*Old Cracker*), Visser Bivens (*Strip Bar Exhorter*), Bob McAdams (*Strip Bar Senator*), Shannon Sedwick (*Stripper*), Nancy Finger (*Girl on Overlook*), Rev William Preston Robertson (*Radio Evangelist*)

TAGLINE: 'Breaking up is hard to do.'

SUMMARY: The scene is contemporary Texas. An unhappily married woman named Abby commits adultery with a man named Ray who works in the bar owned by her husband, Marty. Marty has hired a private detective named Loren Visser to get proof of the infidelity. Abby moves out of their house, and when Marty fails to force her to come back, he pays Visser $10,000 to kill her and Ray. Visser breaks into Ray's house, steals the pistol that Abby keeps in her bag, then takes photographs of the sleeping Abby and Ray. Visser doctors the photographs to make it look like the lovers are dead, then presents this to Marty in his office at the bar. Marty pays Visser and hides one of the photographs in his safe, but Visser kills him using Abby's gun and leaves the weapon on the scene of the crime.

Ray discovers Marty's body and assumes that Abby has killed him. He tries to clean up the scene and, with tremendous difficulty, disposes of the body. Marty isn't quite dead and Ray buries him alive in a shallow grave. Ray then drives to Abby's new apartment and they speak at cross-purposes, with the result that each believes the other has killed Marty. Meanwhile Visser has realised that his lighter is missing and so is one of his faked-up photographs of Abby and Ray. He breaks into the bar to look for them and Abby walks in when he's trying to crack the safe: she doesn't see him but she does discover his tampering. Visser realises that he is not secure with Abby and Ray still alive and heads for Abby's apartment. He succeeds in killing Ray, but after a lengthy game of cat-and-mouse, he is outmanoeuvred and shot by Abby.

DEVELOPMENT: 'The inspiration [for *Blood Simple*] was these movies that Joel had been [editing],' Ethan remembers, 'which had been done mostly by young people like us who didn't have any credentials or credibility in the mainstream movie industry.' These young people had written scripts with obvious selling points – exploitation films – and raised the money themselves. Sam Raimi was happy to give the Coens advice on getting their first feature together, drawing on his experience of making *The Evil Dead*, and he wound up collaborating with the Coens on a script called *Crimewave*, which he decided to make his next project after *The Evil Dead* was released. While Raimi was securing distribution for his debut feature (the film was finally released in 1983), the Coens started work on a new screenplay with a view towards rolling it into production under their own steam.

'When we did *Blood Simple* we were influenced by the novels of James M Cain,' Ethan says. 'They're the same sort of thing: overheated, domestic melodramas.' This was partly because of the brothers' great admiration for the writer described by the critic and novelist Edmund Wilson as 'the poet of the tabloid murder', but also because they felt it was within their means. Ethan notes that Cain's brand of murder narrative 'seemed tailor-made for something you might be able to do successfully on a small budget, in real practical terms'. Their contemporaries like Raimi were doing horror films because the genre had a young, strongly defined audience, but the Coens wanted to do something, well, simpler. 'These types of stories are about a small group of people doing very non-special effects-type of stuff to each other; it's really that simple,' says Ethan. 'They're even simpler than horror films.' However, as Joel notes, the script 'was also very much inspired by' horror, particularly in its closing sequence (see **GENRE**).

The germ of the story was an inversion of Cain: his novels *The Postman Always Rings Twice* and *Double Indemnity* both feature a married woman getting her lover to murder her husband, so the Coens wanted to write a story where the cuckolded, jealous husband plots to murder his wife and her lover. (As in *Postman*, the husband is of Greek extraction, although the novel's influence is stronger on **The Man Who Wasn't There**.) The film's title derives from another pulp crime novelist, Dashiell Hammett, who described the confused, paranoid, guilt-ridden state of mind a person falls into after committing a murder as 'going blood-simple' in his novel, *Red Harvest* (see **Miller's Crossing**).

The other element that the Coens threw into the mix was Hitchcock, whose influence is strongest during the chain of events in which Ray tries to cover up Marty's murder. The sequence is an extrapolation from the lengthy murder scene in *Torn Curtain* (1966), a five-minute sequence that sees Paul Newman awkwardly dispose of a body, finding it trickier and messier at every step. The Coens decided to prolong their corpse disposal for even longer – twenty minutes – as the centrepiece of *Blood Simple*. (Hitchcock's quote on the matter – 'It is very difficult, very painful, and it takes a very, very, long time to kill someone' – appeared at the beginning of the *Blood Simple* trailer. See **ANALYSIS**.) Furthermore, Ray's attempt to clean up Marty's blood from the floor of his office recalls *Psycho*, something which the Coens kept in mind when writing it. 'What we asked ourselves was: How could we make it different?' Ethan says. 'So, instead of making it an efficient cleanup like [*Psycho*] does, we made it inefficient. There's blood everywhere.'

REFERENCES: Marty's death sequence isn't the only segment influenced by Alfred Hitchcock. Visser leaving his lighter in the office is reminiscent of *Strangers on a Train* (1951), in which one character tries to frame another for a murder by placing a monogrammed lighter at the scene of the crime. However, in *Blood Simple* the lighter is never found (it's under Marty's fish) and is, in the end, of no consequence.

The opening sequence is similar to that of *Kiss Me Deadly* (Robert Aldrich, 1955), with the credits progressing over the screen as a man drives a woman along a straight, featureless road.

The character of Helene Trend, who leaves a message on Abby's answering machine, originated in the Coens' own *Crimewave*, written before *Blood Simple* but produced afterwards.

CASTING: The most notable actor to work on the Coens' first film is Frances McDormand, although the role of Abby almost went to another actor destined for a successful career. They needed an actor from the southern states and found one performing on the New York stage in a play entitled *Crimes of the Heart*. 'We met Holly Hunter and liked her,' remembers Ethan, 'but she wasn't available because she was doing [another] play in New York.' Joel picks up the story: 'But she and Fran were roommates at the time, in the Bronx.' The two aspiring actors had met at Yale Drama School, where McDormand had enrolled as a graduate student after her years as a theatre major at Bethany College in West Virginia. 'Holly went back and told Fran, "I can't do this movie but you should go and get an audition".' (Hunter did make a small appearance in the movie, uncredited, as the voice of Helene Trend.)

'I went in and they were my age,' McDormand recalls of this meeting, which was the first time she had ever auditioned for a film. 'They were chain-smoking with a huge ashtray full of cigarette butts in the middle.' Her first impression of the Coens was that Hunter had been right about them being slightly odd. 'I thought they were weird, geekish, intellectual. I asked Joel a question about the character and he went into a twenty-minute monologue from a writer's point of view.' She won the role and went on to appear in roles of varying scale in *Raising Arizona*, *Fargo* and *The Man Who Wasn't There*, plus an uncredited role in *Miller's Crossing* and a small part in *Crimewave*. She also has an enviable reputation as a character actress outside of the Coens' work, with notable credits including *Short Cuts* (Robert Altman, 1993), *Wonder Boys* (Curtis Hanson, 2000) and *Almost Famous* (Cameron Crowe, 2000). She also became Joel's second wife in 1985.

Unlike McDormand, the other principals all had some screen experience when they came to *Blood Simple*. However, the only one specifically sought out by the Coens was M Emmett Walsh, who had over thirty film roles to his credit including parts in *Serpico* (Sidney Lumet, 1973), *Slap Shot* (George Roy Hill, 1977), *Ordinary People* (Robert Redford, 1980) and *Blade Runner* (Ridley Scott, 1982) as well as numerous TV appearances. Joel and Ethan had seen him in *Straight Time* (Ulu Grosbard, 1978) and he stuck in their minds while they were writing the character of Visser. They sent Walsh the script and although he didn't rate the film's chances of success he liked the character enough to accept. His intention was to construct a performance around the character and make use of it in one of his later roles, 'because nobody was going to hear about this movie,' he said. 'At best, it would be the third bill at an Alabama drive-in.' Walsh continued to be sceptical of the film's chances of success until he arrived in Austin and met the Coens. While he assumed at first that the brothers were being bankrolled by rich parents, that changed when 'I saw the storyboards and the shooting schedule, and I realised they knew exactly what they were doing.' Even so, Walsh would often ground Joel and Ethan in reality during the shoot, pointing out that they were doing the moviemaking thing for real this time. He also made one further appearance with the Coens, taking a small role in *Raising Arizona*.

While *Blood Simple* was only John Getz's third film role, he came to the production with plenty of TV experience, having appeared in a number of TV movies and regular roles in series such as *Another World* and *Rafferty*. The exposure he received from playing Ray in *Blood Simple* launched him into further film roles, including *Born on the Fourth of July* (Oliver Stone, 1989) and *Requiem for a Dream* (Darren Aronofsky, 2000). Dan Hedaya came to the film from supporting roles in films such as *The Seduction of Joe Tynan* (Jerry Schatzberg, 1979) and *True Confessions* (Ulu Grosbard, 1981). Afterwards he took a semi-regular role in *Cheers* as Carla's good-for-nothing ex-husband Nick Tortelli: the character was one of the leads in a short-lived 1987 spin-off, *The Tortellis*. In the cinema he has often been cast in police roles, notably in *Running Scared* (Peter Hyams, 1986) and *The Usual Suspects* (Bryan Singer, 1995). Samm-Art Williams had worked with Hedaya on *Night of the Juggler* (Robert Butler, 1980) prior to *Blood Simple*, and although he had done some acting before the film his career moved behind the cameras afterwards. He was a producer and writer on the highly successful sitcom *The Fresh Prince of Bel-Air* and has taken similar roles on a number of other TV series.

PRODUCTION: In early 1982, having decided to press ahead with the *Blood Simple* script they'd written, Joel and Ethan set about raising the cash to make it. 'We knew no one would buy it,' Ethan says, 'particularly since we wanted to make it ourselves.' The brothers estimated that they would need somewhere in the vicinity of $1.5 million if they were to make the film. Movies have since been made for much less – *Clerks* (Kevin Smith, 1994) had a budget of $27,000 while *El Mariachi* (Robert Rodriguez, 1992) cost just $7,000 – but at the time of *Blood Simple* there was no model for low-budget independent filmmaking and the Coens had to do things in more or less the conventional way.

'We followed the example of Sam Raimi,' Joel says. 'Sam had done this trailer, almost like a full-length version of *The Evil Dead*, but on Super-8. He raised $90,000 that way.' Raimi's promo version, entitled *Within the Woods*, was about thirty minutes long, but the Coens decided to adapt his method and shoot a two-minute trailer on higher grade film. Joel got a friend of his from NYU, Barry Sonnenfeld, to assist them. They had no equipment of their own and only enough money to hire a camera and lights for a day or so, so they waited until the Thursday before the four-day President's Weekend holiday. This meant that they were allowed to keep hold of the equipment for five days rather than one, which gave them enough time to shoot a selection of arresting scenes from their script: a revolver being loaded, a man being buried alive and bullets tearing through a wall in a darkened room. They performed in the scenes themselves, with Ethan taking the part of Marty as he was buried. 'The trailer was our selling tool,' says Sonnenfeld. 'It showed prospective investors that we could make something that looked like a real film.' (When it came to putting together a trailer to promote the completed film, the bulk of it was made up of the re-shot versions of these scenes.)

Ethan and Joel found a lawyer who was willing to defer half of his fee until the film made some money back and they set up a limited partnership. They then took their trailer back up to Minnesota, because they had been told that potential investors would be more sympathetic to a pair of local boys. They got in touch with as many local philanthropists as possible, most of whom came from a list of a hundred names supplied by Hadassah, the Zionist women's charity. In the end, most of the investors were 'small business people [who] related to the entrepreneurial aspect of it,' according to Joel. One substantial investor was Daniel Bacaner, who not only put money into the project but became its executive producer and introduced the Coens to other potential backers. Others were less interested in getting directly involved in the project. 'A lot of [the investors] said they didn't know anything about films or scripts, so why should they read it?' Ethan says. 'They were just interested in whether it was a good deal or not.'

The trailer, intended to make them look like pros, caused some problems. 'We couldn't get people to come to a screening room to see it in 35mm, so we made a 16mm reduction, got a projector, and took it around to people's homes or where they worked,' says Joel, estimating that around 95 per cent of these meetings were completely fruitless. On one occasion they were pulling into a potential investor's drive and accidentally rammed his Cadillac.

'We had a short discussion on whether to tell him before or after we asked for the money,' says Joel. 'We decided to do it after,' remembers Ethan, 'so he'd already turned us down when we told him about his car.' It took almost a year of canvassing to raise the necessary $1.5 million. 'You've got to *really* want it,' says Ethan, 'because there are plenty of opportunities along the way for you to throw up your hands and say, "Hey! Why am I doing this?" ' They got their cast together and, with Barry Sonnenfeld on board as cinematographer, they were ready to head off to their location – Texas.

'I'd lived in Texas for a little while,' says Ethan. 'We actually went down there because we were familiar with it, having spent time down there and knowing people there . . . I went to UT for a semester and lived down there for about a year, so I knew people who I knew would work on the movie. I knew what the production climate was like down there.' Equally important was that Texas was a right-to-work state, where crewmembers could be hired for sub-union wages. The brothers were keen to employ inexperienced but adept crew who would be looking to get a movie on their CV, so that the money they'd raised could be spent elsewhere. Joel notes that, when shooting your first movie, having time on your side is more important than surrounding yourself with experience. 'Essentially, don't pay [the crew] very much and shoot longer. Time is the most important thing in terms of getting what you want and having to compromise less – regardless of the skill of the crew.'

One crewmember who was able to bring some experience to the set was key grip Tom Prophet, who had moved to Austin from Los Angeles because of his wife's concerns that LA was not geologically sound. 'Tom taught us a lot of Hollywood high technology with his pipe dolly and other rigging devices,' Sonnenfeld recalls, 'and we taught him some low technology as well.' The Coens began to develop their fluid, drifting camera style in this film, having decided at an early stage that they wanted a lot of camera movement. 'Joel and I decided early on that we wanted to move the camera a lot,' Sonnenfeld adds, 'and when the camera wasn't moving, we sometimes would dolly or raise or lower lights during the shot, so there was always some kind of apparent movement.'

The shoot was scheduled for 48 days, for which all involved were grateful as it made for a less pressurised set. The Coens and Sonnenfeld storyboarded the film in advance and in detail, and stuck to their plans throughout the shoot. They have carried this discipline through all of their films, but because of the tight budget on *Blood Simple* they were aware that it was even more important to plan ahead. 'We had to be able to tell the designer so the designer would then be able to come and say, "We need to see this wall and this wall or just this wall",' says Joel, noting that their storyboards meant that they could always answer such questions. (The Coens' economical attitude seems to be something else they learned from Raimi: even when making the huge-budget *Spider-Man* in 2001 he shot almost nothing he didn't need.)

'The first day of shooting on *Blood Simple* was the first time I'd ever been on a feature movie set in any capacity,' says Joel. 'I remember we were both very impressed by the number of trucks.' This isn't as facile a comment as it might seem. To watch *Blood Simple* you wouldn't think that the crew would have much of a presence, but the production base was pretty huge, 'even on this little low budget movie,' Ethan says. 'The real surprise was that it's such an ungraceful thing in terms of manipulation because of its size,' adds Joel. 'It's so hard to pull it from here to there.' However, they did have the advantage of knowing their material intimately. 'The one thing we did have experience with,' says Joel, 'which is good for a first time director I think, was having written a script as opposed to being given a script that we were interpreting.'

The Coens continued to draw on what Raimi had told them about filmmaking. One of the most celebrated technical aspects of *The Evil Dead* was its use of 'shakicam', although it was apparently invented by director Caleb Deschanel while making *More American Graffiti* (1979). Raimi showed the Coens how to use one, and according to Sonnenfeld it 'cannot be beat at any price'. A camera is mounted at the centre of a twelve-foot plank of wood with a handle at either end. Two grips grab a handle each and run with the camera low to the ground, while the cinematographer runs behind to get an idea of what angle the camera is seeing (obviously it isn't possible for him to put his eye to the viewfinder). The purpose of the board is to smooth out the bumps as the grips dash at full speed: by the time they reach the middle the bumps are less dramatic and the camera seems to float rather than bounce over the ground. On *Blood Simple*, the device was used to create the shot outside Ray's bungalow as Marty forces Abby outside: Sonnenfeld fitted the camera with a wide-angle lens to achieve the maximum zoom effect, as the view switches from a wide shot to an extreme close-up. 'It was a very enjoyable shot to watch being made,' he says, 'since it looks like such a stupid idea.'

Other experiments were attempted during the shoot. For the shot where she moves from Marty's office to her bedroom in a dreamlike manner, McDormand was strapped to a sort of pivoting flatbed with the camera in a fixed position in front of her. The bar-room wall and the bed in her bedroom were constructed as two backdrops at ninety degrees to each other. By moving the flatbed McDormand appeared to 'fall' from one scene into the next. Other shots were achieved with Sonnenfeld lying on a sound blanket and holding a handheld camera while the grips dragged him across the floor, a technique which allowed them to achieve a slow, smooth close-to-the-ground shot. The 'skip' over the sleeping drunk on the bar was almost abandoned when Joel declared that it was 'too self-conscious'. Ethan countered, 'This whole *movie* is self-conscious,' and the shot stayed in. Ethan was right: it's the one shot everybody remembers.

'For *Blood Simple* the lighting was used as a psychological tool,' says Sonnenfeld. 'For the film to be effective, the film had to be dark and contrasty. In fact, at the end of the film, the lighting itself becomes a character.' This refers, of course, to the sequence in which Visser shoots holes in the wall. Light floods through these holes into the darkness at a variety of angles, for no reason other than that it looks great: they originate from a rig of twenty lights set up by Sonnenfeld behind the wall. It creates an effective sense of chaos in the frame and, in a film dominated by darkness,

Roderick Jaynes and Coen credits

One question that pops up time and again in interviews with the Coens is who does what on the movies. How did they wind up with Joel directing and Ethan producing? Well, as they have explained on numerous occasions ('I'd be perfectly happy never to have to answer anything again about how I work with Ethan,' Joel commented in 2001), the credits don't actually have much to do with the way that they work.

'The fact that we separate the two credits is fairly arbitrary to a certain extent,' Joel has said, and when it has come to winning awards such as Best Director at Cannes, he and Ethan have shared the credit. Ethan notes that there is a degree of specialisation – 'Joel talks to the actors more than I do and I probably do production stuff a little more than he does' – but confirms that 'it's largely overlapping'. While they have suggested that it is less confusing for the cast and crew to know who is nominally in charge, many people who have worked with the duo say that they can guarantee the same answers to their questions no matter which brother they ask. So why spread the credit? 'Psychologically, it's sort of important to us to realise that Ethan produces the movie and I direct,' says Joel, 'so, in a sense, we don't want another producer – or another director.' After *Blood Simple* they were somewhat cautious that they might be assigned a producer by a studio, on the pretext that it would free them up to be more involved with the direction. 'That's sort of why we keep it separate that way, but it doesn't really reflect what happens on the set.'

The Coens also realised when putting together *Blood Simple* that the credit 'Directed, Produced and Written by Joel Coen and Ethan Coen' overemphasised their brotherly dominance over the film in a slightly freaky way and might scare audiences off, and this also contributed to Joel becoming the 'official' director and Ethan the producer. For the same reason they decided not to credit themselves as editors of *Blood Simple* when they took that job on as well, and created a pseudonym for themselves: 'Roderick Jaynes'. Practical jokers that they are, they didn't just leave it at that, and Jaynes started to develop a personality of his own.

It's hard to pinpoint just when this started. It may have been with the foreword for the screenplays of *Miller's Crossing* and *Barton Fink*, published to coincide with the release of the latter. The Coens had delegated editing duties on *Raising Arizona* and *Miller's Crossing* but, when they returned to the editing suite for *Fink*, the pseudonym was pressed into service again. When it came to providing a foreword for the scripts, the Coens wrote one themselves and credited it to Jaynes. In this, Mr Jaynes was revealed to be a survivor from the golden age of British cinema, now retired except for his work on the Coens'

films and living in Haywards Heath, Sussex. A fictitious filmography began to emerge here, as Jaynes claimed that at the time of *Blood Simple* he hadn't worked in film since editing the Basil Radford-starring *The Mad Weekend* (not actually a real movie: Jaynes claims 'almost thirty years' separate his work on those two pictures, yet he worked on *Blood Simple* in 1983 and Radford died in 1952). The Coens allegedly contacted him after admiring his work on *Beyond Mombassa* (which *is* a real movie), although Jaynes had to inform them that it was comprehensively recut by Jack Tuttle and none of his own work remained, although he was still credited owing to union rules (this becomes a running theme of Jaynes's stories).

The Coens have used the Jaynes device on a number of occasions to poke fun at themselves. Jaynes is an irascible figure who is rude about nearly everybody he's worked with (*The Mad Weekend* director George Milestone is described as 'a small man both in stature and talent') and the Coens are no exception. In Jaynes' introduction to the screenplay for *The Man Who Wasn't There* they are seen expressing their keen admiration for the work of Steve Guttenberg while their editor is 'struggling to make simple match cuts in footage shot by people patently ignorant of the simplest mechanics of film construction'. His working relationship with the Coens is rather terse, due in part to Jaynes's contempt for directors and screenwriters (he refuses to read the script before starting work) and his old-fashioned attitude (he commends *Miller's Crossing* because 'the actors had been issued proper suits').

However, when Jaynes was nominated for an Oscar after his fine work on *Fargo*, the Coens were finally forced to admit that he didn't exist. Refused permission to send up a delegate if Jaynes won, the Coens had to accept credit for their own editing. Nevertheless, they continue to talk about their veteran editor as if he was real (it clearly amuses them still). On the DVD commentary for *The Man Who Wasn't There*, Billy Bob Thornton claims that he bumped into Jaynes in an LA supermarket and was surprised at how tall he was, and on a visit to Cannes Joel was asked if Jaynes would be in attendance and responded, 'He's probably at some BAFTA event. He's a member of BAFTA. He was nominated for an award, and every nominee automatically becomes a member. So we have his membership card.'

this became another memorable shot. Sonnenfeld achieved solid darkness throughout by overexposing the film stock slightly. 'Joel, Ethan and I felt strongly that we wanted our blacks to be rich, with no milky qualities.' When the film was being developed and printed back in New York at Du Art Labs, Sonnenfeld sent them camera reports with the instruction, 'Print it too dark!'

Inevitably there were also some lessons to be learned. '[Something] which we had no idea of at the time but knew much better with our second movie is just walking into a space and knowing whether you can shoot there,' Ethan says, noting that they discovered a great deal about the demands of setting up lights and manoeuvring a camera within a space. 'It's weird, if you have no production experience you can walk into a room and say "oh this is great, we'll shoot here and it will be great," but there is a reality about shooting.'

DELETED SCENES: One scene from an early draft is noted in the published version of the script. In this, Ray stops off at a motel shortly after burying Marty and tries to check in, but is frustrated by the two surreal characters who work there, Dusty Rhodes and Kyle. After a lengthy explanation of the various options from Rhodes, with frequent interruptions from Kyle, Rhodes reveals that the motel is booked up anyway.

The brothers considered this scene too lengthy and replaced it with a more basic scene in which Ray stops at a traffic light: this was shot but was itself omitted from the finished film for the sake of getting to the thrilling climax more quickly. In later years, the Coens realised that farcical non-sequitur scenes like this were actually one of their strengths, and they have become a Coen trademark (the Mike Yanagita scene in *Fargo* and Ann Nirdlinger's abduction story in *The Man Who Wasn't There* are good examples).

MUSIC: Before *Blood Simple* Carter Burwell was a fine-arts major at Harvard who had never considered trying to get into the movie business. 'Their sound editor, Skip Lievsay, asked me if I would be interested in working on a film,' Burwell explains. 'He knew my music from playing in clubs in New York. So he introduced us.' In his first effort as a movie composer, Burwell's background as a classically trained pianist is evident, as is his experience as a blues improv player. The score is downbeat and minimal, based around a simple, stark piano figure that Burwell twists and repeats endlessly. It's one of his subtler scores: while it undoubtedly makes a contribution to the tone of the film, you can almost forget it's there at times.

As a result of his continuing work with the Coens – he has worked on all of their films – Burwell has found himself increasingly in demand, working on the soundtracks for numerous left-field movies and occasionally straying into the mainstream. His work can be heard on films such as *Buffy the Vampire Slayer* (Fran Rebel Kuzi, 1992), *Kalifornia* (Dominic Sena, 1993), *Wayne's World 2* (Penelope Spheeris, 1993), *Gods and Monsters* (Bill Condon, 1998), *Velvet Goldmine* (Todd Haynes, 1998) and *Being John Malkovich* (Spike Jonze, 1999). He continues to work with the guys who gave him his break, however. 'We have an informal, maybe even slightly formal agreement, that we're going to work with each other until we die . . . I'd be happy to do their films the rest of my life.'

The stock music used in the film is sparse but eclectic, taking in genres from reggae to country. The most noticeable of these is 'It's The Same Old Song', written by Motown's mighty Holland-Dozier-Holland team and a hit for The Four Tops in 1965. (The title is an ironic reference to the fact that it is a skilful but shameless rewrite of Holland-Dozier-Holland's previous hit for the group, 'I Can't Help Myself'.) The record is used at three key points: first, as a theme song for Meurice, who is from Detroit and prefers the soul sound patented in his home town to the country music favoured by the patrons of Marty's bar; as an inappropriate soundtrack to Ray's attempts to cover up Marty's death; and over the final shots of the movie, as Visser lies dying in Abby's apartment. The winding backwards and forwards of the film as the droplets of water seem about to drip from the pipe makes them appear to dance with the music. All of this was completely spoiled in the American video release when copyright problems meant that the song had to be removed and substituted with Neil Diamond's own version of the song he wrote for the Monkees, 'I'm a Believer', something which Joel says 'really disturbed us'. Thankfully, the Four Tops record was cleared for use in the Directors' Cut and has been reinstated on the DVD (the commercial UK releases, incidentally, have never suffered this problem).

CRITICAL RECEPTION: Not all of the critics were sure what to make of *Blood Simple*, but most of them seemed to enjoy it all the same. Pauline Kael rather bizarrely described it as 'a splatter-movie art movie' in the *New Yorker*, but went on to do a reasonable job of pinpointing the brothers' strengths and weaknesses. 'Joel Coen doesn't know what to do with the actors,' she suggested, but the framing of each shot 'makes the audience feel knowing and in on the joke.' One performance that did receive praise was that of M Emmet Walsh: 'There hasn't been a creepier screen menace since Robert Mitchum's mad minister in *Night of the Hunter* [Charles Laughton, 1955] 30 years ago,' declared the *People* on 4 February 1985.

Variety went a little further, hailing it as 'An inordinately good low-budget film noir thriller' in its 23 May 1984 issue. It also generously praised the 'subtle performances' and delighted in the film's technical achievements in spite of its cheapness. 'Every cent, and then some, is up there on the screen.' The tone of the review exudes excitement at these new arrivals on the scene, and since *Variety* is so widely read in the industry this must have been a substantial boost when trying to secure backing for *Raising Arizona*. Roger Ebert, writing in the *Chicago Sun-Times*, was also highly enthusiastic: 'The movie has been shot with a lot of style, some of it self-conscious, but deliberately so.' Again the review bears the hallmarks of a critic keen to encourage new talent, noting the film's lack of complacency and eagerness to make an impression. Ebert gave the film his maximum mark of four stars and described it as 'violent, unrelenting, absurd and fiendishly clever.'

Europe also took an interest when the film made it there in 1985. 'Joel and Ethan Coen here demonstrate that well-worn private eye plots involving unfaithful wives and murderous husbands can be polished to gleam as sparkling new,' Marjorie Bilbow wrote in *Screen International* on 19 January 1985, lauding the brothers for their 'remarkable' confidence. She predicted that *Blood Simple*'s primary appeal would be for movie buffs 'and other discriminating regulars' and went on to suggest that the film 'may attain cult status'. For Steve Jenkins, writing in *Monthly Film Bulletin*, the film's 'strikingly detached' style had great appeal: 'Coen mobilises his camera around the characters, rather than on their behalf, creating a fatalistic sense of space in which they are all trapped.' Despite giving the film a strongly theoretical reading, Jenkins also pointed out that 'the formalism never strays into "artiness", since it reinforces the film's overall design which, it should be stressed, always maintains its humorous edge.' Like so many others, he declared *Blood Simple* 'a strikingly assured first feature'.

Rather more restrained in its praise was the much-respected *Cahiers du Cinéma*, as Stephané Braunschweig anticipated what would come to be the American media's standard critical line on the Coens. While Braunschweig appreciated the 'formidable construction of a fool-proof script', the 'systematic editing process' was felt to produce, 'in the long run, an impression of monotony and boredom,' with the effect of 'turning this exemplary script into an exercise in style'.

BOX OFFICE: With the film completed, the Coens faced one final hurdle – distribution. They offered *Blood Simple* to just about every major studio, all of whom turned it down. In the end, Ben Barenholtz and Ted and Jim Pedas, owners of a chain of cinemas in the Washington DC area called Washington Circle Theaters, paid the Coens a substantial cash advance for the rights and put it out under their distribution wing, Circle Releasing, in 1985. It had a limited run in various art-house cinemas and scooped around $3 million. While this would have represented a failure for most Hollywood product, for a wholly independent movie that cost $1.5 million it was an unqualified success.

AWARDS: The film did well at the indie awards ceremonies, scooping Best Dramatic Feature in 1985 at the hugely respected Sundance festival. It also won the Grand Jury Prize at the United States Film Festival in 1984 and took two belated Independent Spirit Awards in 1986, for Best Director and Best Actor (the latter for M Emmet Walsh's performance). This represented the Coens' best haul until *Barton Fink*'s extraordinary performance at Cannes.

DIALOGUE TO SKIP BACK FOR:

Visser: (as Marty looks over the photos of Abby and Ray in bed) 'I know a place you can get that framed.'

Abby: 'I'm not afraid of you any more, Marty.'

Visser: (dying, but laughing) 'Well ma'am, if I see him, I'll sure give him the message.'

ANALYSIS: Since *Blood Simple* was not widely viewed on its original release, it's probably safe to say that this was not most people's introduction to the Coens. In fact, most of the people who have seen *Blood Simple* probably investigated it after watching and enjoying later Coen movies, and the first thing that will strike somebody who comes to *Blood Simple* after watching the likes of *Raising Arizona*, *Fargo* or *The Big Lebowski* is that it isn't particularly funny.

Actually that's not entirely fair. It just suffers by comparison with the Coens' later films and their acutely observed dialogue. There is humour in *Blood Simple* but it's muted and dark, coming from small ironies and a sense of the ridiculous creeping into ostensibly serious situations rather than from character-based wit. There aren't many jokes in *Blood Simple*. In fact, there isn't a lot of dialogue full stop. Whereas their later scripts are packed with memorable lines, *Blood Simple* is economical to say the least: the film's two most memorable sequences (Ray's cover-up of Marty's death and Visser's hunt for Abby in her apartment) are almost entirely dialogue-free.

To its credit, however, the film takes this on as a theme and runs with it, rather than simply using it as a stylistic conceit. 'We don't seem to be communicating,' Marty tells Debra when failing to chat her up and indeed many of the problems suffered by the characters result from lack of communication. The film is based around a marriage that has broken down and two lovers who appear to have little to say to each other. In fact, the communication problems between Abby and Ray become the driving force of the plot later on: Ray believes too readily that Abby is capable of murder when he finds Marty's body and when he speaks to her later, their conversation convinces her that he has murdered Marty while failing to dispel his impression that she committed the act. Ray believes that his suspicions are confirmed because Abby says 'I haven't done anything funny' – the exact line that Marty warned Ray that she would use when trying to deceive him. The film even ends with a misunderstanding: Abby believes that Marty is still alive because she has had another of those silent telephone calls from his office, with the sound of his fan in the background. In fact, the call came from Visser at Ray's home, where there is a similar fan. Visser is only trying to kill her because of his mistaken belief that she knows he killed Marty, but Abby doesn't even know that her husband is dead and because she never sees Visser during the climax, she assumes that the man trying to kill her *is* Marty.

The use of misunderstandings to drive the plot reappears in the Coens' later work, but it is rarely as central as it is to *Blood Simple*. In this film no single character is ever in possession of all the facts and this leads them all to make mistakes, while the viewer, who has been granted omniscience by the Coens' camera, takes voyeuristic pleasure in their full knowledge of the situation. Sheer incompetence also plays a part, of course. The situations in most Coen films are generic in nature, even if they are original stories in themselves (the inversion of the Cain stories for the *Blood Simple* script is a great example of this). However, while most of the heroes and villains in crime fiction and film noir are brought down by a fatal flaw in their character or some piece of regrettable bad fortune, the Coens are more interested in out-and-out losers who tend to fail because they aren't up to the task they've set for themselves.

Marty is a good example of this type of character. Right from the outset, he's completely useless. His early threat towards Visser is needless and Visser laughs it off easily. His attempt to pick up Debra in the bar is clumsy. His gambit to take Abby back by force only results in his complete humiliation. This is despite his relative affluence, which should enable him to wield the power in this situation (the fact that money ultimately can't tempt Abby to stay with him is the first hint of the Coens tackling themes of social inequality: see **Raising Arizona**). When Marty decides to use his money to resolve the situation he steps completely out of his depth, and in hiring a murderer he only succeeds in getting himself murdered. In his final act before he is buried alive, he draws the pistol which was used to shoot him and levels it at Ray, but in a final pathetic reflection on his character, the little gun won't fire (there is a bullet left in one of the chambers but Marty doesn't get to it before Ray takes the gun from him). In Marty are the seeds of many Coen characters: Jerry and Carl in *Fargo* particularly come to mind, and *The Big Lebowski*'s Dude is an example of a positive character who doesn't fit in with the narrative in which he finds himself.

'Realistic' is too often used as a byword for 'good' (see also **The Hudsucker Proxy**), but the Coens use a realistic approach to good dramatic effect here. Murders are so common in fiction that one could almost forget how difficult it must be to successfully carry one off. This is why Marty gets out of his depth so easily and it's also why it takes Ray so long to hide Marty's body. 'The idea is that it's very difficult, and takes a very long time to kill someone,' the Coens commented, echoing Hitchcock's sentiments on the matter. 'It's not necessarily just bang, and the character keels over dead.' This confounds the audience's expectations because they are used to seeing murders committed more easily, particularly in crime thrillers, with bodies dumped off-screen (as Visser tells Marty he has done with Abby and Ray). This also creates for the audience the sense that they too are out of their depth, that they are getting more than they bargained for. The greatest illustration of this is the sheer quantity of blood that spills from Marty: at first there's just a little, pouring through his gunshot wound, but by the time Ray arrives there's a pool of it. Ray tries to mop it up and only succeeds in spreading it around even more. It starts to drip from Marty's nose. After Ray takes him out to a deserted spot, at which point Marty turns out to be alive still, Marty throws some up on Ray as Ray tries to drag him off the road. Later, Ray finds that Marty's blood has filled the back seat of his car and it keeps seeping up. Ray can only look on in horror, like Lady Macbeth trying to wash her hands.

The script's finest character is Visser, and M Emmett Walsh puts in a performance to match. While the other characters come across as relatively straightforward and uncomplicated people, Loren Visser is an oddball character who can sink to unexpected depths. (The Coens have since noted that giving him a Volkswagen Beetle was a deliberate attempt to make him more surreal, plus the fact that they find fat men in little cars amusing.) For most of the first half-hour he seems like a buffoon, chuckling to himself and drawling casually, but then he agrees to murder two people for $10,000. Visser then wavers in a moral grey area, as he fakes Abby and Ray's deaths rather than killing them, before coming down firmly in the dark as he kills first Marty and then Ray (see **GENRE**). By the end of the film he's become a fully fledged gun-toting maniac, although he never loses his sense of humour. He may have a bullet-tear in his guts and his blood may be draining away but he can still appreciate good irony.

While the murder plotline is strongly realised, some critics have noted the lack of chemistry between Abby and Ray. Indeed, it's hard to pin down any of Abby's characteristics – Marty says she's manipulative, for example, but there is no evidence of this in the film. All the audience is told is that she's unhappy with Marty (but who wouldn't be?), she's mentally healthy and she likes to live well. Too often she comes across as simply taking a role in a plot. McDormand has taken some of the responsibility for this, citing her inexperience: 'When you look at the movie now, where other people think I made the choice of looking dumb – that was me. I stood paralysed until they told me what to do.' However, the character doesn't exactly leap off the page and onto the screen: John Getz suffers similar problems when playing Ray.

Furthermore, while it's often a pleasure to find a film that rewards repeated viewing, *Blood Simple* is so subtle in its unfolding of the plot that it's difficult to catch all the details first time around, and it's often the smallest details that are vital. For example, if you haven't realised that Visser has used Abby's gun to kill Marty, you'll wonder why Ray is even trying to cover up the murder. It's easy to miss the presence of Visser's lighter under the fish, too (see **THE DIRECTORS' CUT**). A couple more viewings reveal the intricacies of the plot: the very first line after Visser's opening narration is Abby talking about the gun given to her by Marty for their first anniversary. On first sight this simply appears to be a statement about what kind of man Abby is married to and the viewer forgets it within a few minutes. When seen in the context of later events, it's a well-crafted irony. The Coens' ability to construct an airtight plot is signalled here before it really comes to the fore in their later noir-ish escapades, *Miller's Crossing*, *The Big Lebowski* and *The Man Who Wasn't There*, but only when you look at it really closely. As time has gone on they have learned how better to tell a story visually and, of course, to increase the dialogue.

GENRE: *Blood Simple* is the Coens' first stab at shooting a film noir in colour, although they claim that wasn't really their intention. 'We never really thought of it as film noir, although it is,' Ethan says. 'It's plain, mean, ordinary people doing bad things to each other in the dark, so I guess that qualifies it as film noir.' The Coens always claim that they don't set out to try and do film noir, but that sensibility is clearly built into the way that they shoot a movie, whether intentional or not. The fact that they are so influenced by the crime fiction of that era – in this case, Cain – is also a big part of it.

In 1983, shooting in black and white was not an option because no distributor would have gone anywhere near it. During the 1990s black and white became more accepted as an artistic choice, with films such as *Schindler's List* (Steven Spielberg, 1993) and *Ed Wood* (Tim Burton, 1994) and when Kevin Smith made his no-budget teen comedy *Clerks* (1994) in black and white, it was mistaken for an art-house movie and subsequently championed on those grounds. Would that the Coens had been allowed to do this, but they cope well with the problems of shooting in colour while using the noir tradition: in noir you shoot for maximum contrast, giving the picture a stylised look. In lieu of white, the Coens frequently swamp the screen with red, blue or yellow and contrast this with the blacks. They also make use of extreme and unusual angles, a technique which sits well with their habit of keeping the camera in motion even on the most innocuous shots. The shots that really stand out are the sweeps behind Marty's fan (which swoops loudly as the camera passes) and the downward-facing tracking shot as Ray clears up the blood from the floor (a highly ambitious shot for two rookie filmmakers to attempt).

In this light, the choice of Texas for the setting was an interesting one. Aware that their story was very much in the noir style, the brothers played their first genre-twisting trick in a career of genre-twisting tricks by setting the film in a place that's almost the exact opposite of the traditional locations for such films. Noir is usually oppressively urban (although there are examples to the contrary, such as *Out of the Past* (Jacques Tourneur, 1947) or *Touch of Evil* (Orson Welles, 1958)), taking place in cities where overcrowding means that danger can lurk anywhere, and the proliferation of people makes the world more alienating because there are so many strangers around. *Blood Simple* goes to the opposite extreme, isolating its characters in a sparsely populated place. The flat nature of the landscape leaves the characters exposed, and the fact that there's nowhere to hide is frequently a problem: Ray is nearly spotted disposing of the semi-dead Marty by the side of the road and when the sun comes up the next morning over the plains he and his car have become all too visible. The camera style also makes a substantial contribution, contriving a sense of claustrophobia even when the environment does not. And, even in the middle of the desert, there's always the night – the time when Visser, the film's most threatening character by some margin, does his work.

There is one final twist of genre in the closing sequence: Visser lays siege to a house with a single female occupant and the film morphs into something quite different. It's far more reminiscent of the horror genre and the slasher flick in particular, bringing to mind the likes of *Halloween* (John Carpenter, 1978) and, of course, *The Evil Dead*. The villains of slasher movies tend to prove remarkably difficult to kill and so it is with Visser, even though he doesn't have the advantage of supernatural powers (one assumes). The moment when Abby pins his hand to the windowsill with a knife, and Visser has to punch through the wall in order to pull it out, is the most visceral event in any of the Coens' movies. They never stray this close to horror again, which perhaps suggests that the inclusion of this sequence was mainly for the purpose of selling the film and not because it was something that they were particularly keen to do. Sam Raimi has noted that he was not initially interested in making a horror movie when considering what to make as his debut feature, but at the time there was no real 'indie' film scene. If you were going to make a self-financed film, better follow the Roger Corman model: an exploitation picture was something you could sell around the drive-ins and, sure enough, Raimi built a cult reputation from there. That wasn't how it worked out for the Coens, but it worked out all the same.

EVER AMERICA: Visser's opening narration, comparing communist Russia with Texas, immediately sets him apart from the Coens themselves. While Ethan had spent a year living in the area before they went there to shoot *Blood Simple*, the younger Coen concedes that, 'I think maybe part of the attraction of going was the fact that it's a very different place and somewhat exotic, having grown up in Minnesota.' The Coens were not, at this time, terribly interested in covering their home ground. Minnesota was somewhere they were working to escape from. (It's worth noting that there is one representative from the north in the form of Meurice, who is only tangentially related to the plot and usually appears for the purpose of commenting on the other characters' actions.) Visser notes that in Texas, 'you're on your own': in America, the rights of the individual are prized above all else, but that means that you may well find that there's nobody to protect you when you need it most. Abby, who seems to have spent her life in the shadow of one man or another, finds herself fighting for survival at the end of the movie and the psychological battle she fights with Marty in this sequence is as important as the physical battle with the man she has mistaken for him: Visser.

While most of the Coens' movies have been period pieces, this would not have been an option with *Blood Simple* because of the budget and facilities that were available. The contemporary setting does, however, suit the story, not least because under Reagan it seemed to be accepted that the 1940s and 1950s had been a golden age, and here the Coens delve into the more pessimistic literature of that time to show that it wasn't all rosy. The Cain-style narrative contains an appropriate act of greed, with Visser agreeing to murder Abby and Ray despite his misgivings. It's as if he feels that he should take advantage of the fact that he lives not in Russia, where everybody has to work for the collective, but in Reaganite America, where it is possible to earn $10,000 in a day as long as you're willing to murder people for it. If you wanted to be *very* generous to Visser at this point you could suggest that he's not entirely cold-hearted because he decides to kill one man of dubious character rather than two people who don't deserve it, but later it's confirmed that he only does this because it's less risky: he has the money and he's killed the only man who knows anything about their deal. His attempt to frame Abby and his willingness to kill her and Ray when they get too close proves this. Visser is very much a 1980s man, entirely motivated by the pursuit of material wealth.

THE DIRECTORS' CUT: On preparing a restored print of *Blood Simple* for DVD release, the Coens realised that they would have to reconstruct the movie from the original sound and celluloid masters. 'Because it's our only movie that wasn't released by a studio, the elements for it weren't archived anywhere,' Ethan says. 'They weren't housed anywhere, so we had to go back and find the print and sound elements. It was impossible to find a good print of the movie, and we were afraid that if any more time passed, we wouldn't be able to find the original elements to make new prints.' Joel notes that, as they were working on remixing the sound into stereo anyway, 'we figured we might as well cheat a little bit and fix up the picture.' In any case, when they returned to the film they weren't terribly satisfied and became keen to do further work on it. 'The impression that we had of the film,' Ethan says, 'was that it seemed very clumsy and we thought it would be interesting to try and solve some of those problems.'

'It was an interesting editing exercise as we didn't have the resource of any trims or outtakes,' Joel says. 'We were dealing only with the material in the printed film.' This meant that they didn't have the option of using alternative takes if they found that the recut scenes matched up poorly. This accounts for the overall shortening of the film, which has been quoted as one minute shorter by some sources and five minutes by others. Although Joel has claimed five on some occasions, one minute seems to be closer to the mark (the American DVD runs to 95 minutes and 48 seconds). The trims are mostly small cuts made to the beginnings and ends of scenes and rearrangements of shots. One sizeable cut comes in Meurice's introductory scene over at the jukebox, which now moves from him preventing the Lubbock guy from playing his own choice straight to the Four Tops blaring out across the bar, missing out the exchange regarding what night it is. This is possibly because the shot features none of the four protagonists and is therefore not relevant to the plot. There are a couple of odd fade-out cuts which don't quite work – one just after Abby wakes up and one after Visser sweeps a pile of objects into a bag – but these are minor distractions.

The sound is a massive improvement on other commercially available versions, being far cleaner and better mixed (noises actually sound like they're *coming* from somewhere in a way that they didn't before). The *crack* of Marty's finger breaking comes through a treat. The superior picture is also welcome, not only because it's easier on the eyes but also because it greatly improves those elements of the story that are told visually. The glint of Visser's lighter under the fish is more visible on this print: on the original version, with the shine dulled by a murky picture, the lighter looks grey and blends with the fish. There are a number of shots which might as well be new to this cut, since their impact is much greater on the cleaned-up print. The scenes set at night are also substantially clarified.

In addition, the film has a spoof introduction from Mortimer Young, head of Forever Young Film Preservation, played by George Ives (Lloyd Garroway in *The Man Who Wasn't There*). Young is an elderly cliché sitting behind a large wooden desk, reading a heavy book, smoking a pipe and obviously reading off cue cards. The intro is full of lies: Young claims that *Blood Simple* broke box-office records around the world, although 'filmographic techniques were in their infancy' at the time. This re-release supposedly uses digital technology and Ultra-Ultra Sound ('a Lucas process'), and as a bonus 'the boring parts have been cut out'. This comical attempt to mythologise *Blood Simple* continued with the commentary recorded for the DVD of this edition (see **AVAILABILITY**).

The film was released in its revamped form to American cinemas on 7 July 2000 and, while it was never showing in more than 68 theatres at any given time, its performance was impressive for a sixteen-year-old film with a modest cult following. Over the course of sixteen weeks it grossed $1,690,913, which is more than it originally cost to make and fully justified the work that Joel and Ethan put into recutting and remastering it. However, when asked if they were tempted to recut any of their other films, Joel said, 'Yes, but it's cheating. We decided only to cheat on this first one . . . It's not an issue with our other movies.' Ethan agreed, stating that once a movie is completed and released, 'You've got to stand by it.'

AVAILABILITY: *Blood Simple* is available on DVD in both the USA and Europe, but rather oddly you can only buy the original version on Region 2 DVD while it has only been released on Region 1 as the 2000 Directors' Cut. The Region 2 features no extra material while the Region 1 includes a contemporary trailer, filmographies, production notes and a commentary. Rather than recording a commentary themselves, however, Joel and Ethan put together a spoof of film historian commentaries. This ties in with the Mortimer Young introduction shot for the theatrical re-release, as it purports to have been recorded by the British film historian Kenneth Loring on behalf of Forever Young Films.

There is nothing on the packaging to indicate that the commentary is a complete fabrication, which may have puzzled some people less familiar with the Coens. Among other things, Loring claims that Marty's dog is animatronic, that the opening scene with Abby and Ray in the car was shot upside down, that a lengthy sub-plot set in Bulgaria was dropped after previews, in which it would have been revealed that Visser is the son of that country's dictator, played by Gene Kelly (the opening narration was supposed to read, 'In Bulgaria Dad's got it mapped out . . .'). Loring repeatedly claims that apparently simple shots were in fact achieved with model work, stop-motion or CGI before concluding portentously, 'Movie . . . magic.' It *is* funny, not least because Loring's English reserve contrasts so bizarrely with the brutality of the movie and its Texas setting. Loring doesn't think much of the finished movie, regarding it as 'butchered' (he was one of the few to see the Bulgaria material at the preview, material that has since been lost in a warehouse fire in New Jersey and hence could not be re-instated for the Directors' Cut). However, ninety minutes is a long time to spend listening to wilful gibberish: you have been warned.

The commentary antagonised many of Joel and Ethan's fans, who demanded to know why they resisted the conventional director's commentary. 'I don't know,' said the ever-articulate Joel in 2001. 'Generally speaking, it's not something I listen to. Usually, I don't want to sit down and listen to the director gas on about his movie.' That said, he and Ethan were enticed to record one a few months later for *The Man Who Wasn't There.*

THE COENS' VIEW: 'I really think our film has been blown up out of proportion. [The press was] hungry for something else. It looks like we're it. Now they're reviewing each other's reviews. Let's face it: it's only a movie.' (Joel in 1985)

VERDICT: 'I don't know what the hell you two thought you were gonna pull off.' One probable reason why *Blood Simple* provoked such interest on its emergence in the mid-1980s was that it isn't an easy film to categorise. It seems highly original, yet it operates within (and exploits) generic boundaries. It offers visceral thrills, yet its subtleties emerge on repeated viewing. It carries emotional punch, yet maintains an ironic distance.

While the story isn't anything that hasn't been done before, the Coens invest *Blood Simple* with very solid filmmaking values. The

Hollywood marketplace was becoming more and more crowded in the 1980s and this led to the rise of the 'high-concept' movie, where the central idea can be summed up in a sentence and therefore ensnare an audience before they even have time to consider the alternatives. *Blood Simple* takes the opposite approach: it has no obvious hook or selling point, but it draws the viewer in with a well-constructed script and a camera style that involves the viewer in the action (much the same qualities that made Hitchcock's films so successful). While it may be generic, the film is not formulaic, which means that the viewer can't work out what's going to happen ahead of time. Above all, it's very cinematic. While the Coens undersell one of their greatest talents by writing a script with so little dialogue, this does mean they have to tell the story visually and in the process demonstrate how well they appreciate the possibilities of the medium.

It's difficult to judge *Blood Simple* separately from the circumstances of its production. Considering it was made for very little money by two newcomers to the film industry working with no outside support, it's an incredible achievement, and it was undoubtedly considered as such when the world's critics encountered it for the first time. When judged in the context of the Coens' later work it seems a little rough around the edges, not only in terms of its production values but also in terms of its technique, and while its roving, inquisitive camera is effective the visual subtleties don't always come across. Nevertheless, you could give most other filmmakers all the facilities in the world and they couldn't come up with a film as good as this.

Crimewave (1985)

(Colour – 86 mins)

Embassy Films Associates Presents
A Pressman/Renaissance Production
Directed by Sam Raimi
Produced by Robert Tapert
Co-Produced by Bruce Campbell

Executive Producers: Edward R Pressman and Irvin Shapiro
Written by Ethan Coen, Joel Coen, Sam Raimi
Director of Photography: Robert Primes
Supervising Film Editor: Michael Kelly
Music Composed & Conducted by Arlon Ober

CAST: Louise Lasser (*Helene Trend*), Paul L Smith (*Faron Crush*), Brion James (*Arthur Coddish*), Sheree J Wilson (*Nancy*), Edward R Pressman (*Ernest Trend*), Bruce Campbell (*Renaldo 'The Heel'*), Reed Birney (*Vic Ajax*), Richard Bright (*Officer Brennan*), Antonio Fargas (*Blind Man*), Hamid Dana (*Donald Odegard*), John Hardy (*Mr Yarman*), Emil Sitka (*Colonel Rodgers*), Hal Youngblood (*Jack Elroy*), Sean Farley (*Jack Elroy Jr*), Richard DeManincor (*Officer Garvey*), Carrie Hall-Schalter (*Cheap Dish*), Wiley Harker (*Governor*), Julius Harris (*Hardened Convict*), Ralph Drischell (*Executioner*), Robert Symonds (*Guard #1*), Patrick Stack (*Guard #2*), Philip A Gillis (*Priest*), Bridget Hoffman (*Nun*), Ann Marie Gillis (*Nun*), Frances McDormand (*Nun*), Carol Brinn (*Old Woman*), Matthew Taylor (*Muscleman*), Perry Mallette (*Grizzled Veteran*), Chuck Gaidica (*Weatherman*), Jimmie Launce (*Announcer*), Joseph French (*Bandleader*), Ted Raimi (*Waiter*), Dennis Chaitlin (*Fat Waiter*)

TAGLINE: 'A fast, gory cliffhanger full of suspense and excess!'

SUMMARY: Security systems installer Vic Ajax is dragged to the electric chair, protesting his innocence of murder charges. In a flashback, Vic's employer Ernest Trend is plotting to sell his store to a man named Renaldo. Trend knows that his business partner Odegard won't agree to the deal and hires two psychotic vermin exterminators, Faron and Arthur, to murder Odegard. Unfortunately, the overzealous exterminators kill both Odegard and Trend, and then set about taking out any possible witnesses.

Vic and Renaldo vie for the attention of a girl called Nancy: she doesn't like either of them, but Vic is the more persistent and he offers to help clean her dress when it is splashed with mud by a passing car. Nancy's apartment is in the same building as Trend's, where Faron and Arthur are trying to eliminate Trend's wife. Vic and Nancy become embroiled in the situation there, as the

Sam Raimi

Born in Franklin, Michigan on 23 October 1959, Sam Raimi's introduction to the world of filmmaking was not unlike the Coens'. Raimi was shooting amateur movies with his father's Super-8 camera from the age of eleven and he received a camera of his own for his thirteenth birthday.

In his high school drama class Raimi met Bruce Campbell and the two became close friends. During his time at school and later, at Michigan State University, he also hooked up with Josh Becker, Robert Tapert and Scott Spiegel, and it was this team that he took to the woods of Marshall, Michigan in 1979 to make a short horror film called *Within the Woods*. The short helped them to secure funding for a feature, which became *The Evil Dead*. As well as bringing Raimi and the Coens together, the film was an impressive sleeper success and performed very well on video.

After *Crimewave* Raimi's career faltered a little, but with the help of Stephen King he secured the funding for 1987's *Evil Dead II: Dead By Dawn*. He then had a modest hit with *Darkman* (1990), which featured a leading role for Frances McDormand, before making a final *Evil Dead* film, *Army of Darkness* (1992). His impressively varied career later took in the western *The Quick and the Dead* (1995) and the baseball movie *For Love of the Game* (1999), while he also executive produced the TV show *Hercules: The Legendary Journeys*. *Fargo* inspired him to make *A Simple Plan* (1998), the story of two geeky brothers who stumble across a fortune in an abandoned bag. His film of Billy Bob Thornton's script *The Gift* (2000) did poorly at the box office, but Raimi was able to put that behind him when his slick, confident *Spider-Man* became the biggest box-office hit of 2002, grossing over $400 million. He had to fight hard for the gig but, with a collection of over 25,000 comic books, he was a popular choice with the character's many fans.

Raimi has overcome the disdain that critics often reserve for schlock-horror pictures and comic-book movies because his camera style is genuinely innovative. The 'Ram-o-cam' rush is a celebrated invention, for example, and he loves to experiment with different shutter speeds. These ideas have filtered through into the work of many directors, not least the Coen brothers.

exterminators kidnap Nancy. Vic chases after them, battling Arthur on the roof of the exterminators' van. Arthur is killed by a low bridge. Vic struggles with Faron and they fall in the river. Nancy assumes them both dead and joins a convent, but Vic has survived. Unfortunately he is wrongly arrested for all of the murders and the only person who could have corroborated his story was Nancy. The film returns to Vic in the electric chair. He is saved at the last minute when Nancy arrives and proves him innocent. The two of them get married.

DEVELOPMENT: The Coens have rarely talked about their experience of writing *Crimewave*, since the film was barely promoted at all and they disowned it soon after its release (see **PRODUCTION**). The script dates back to before *Blood Simple*: the Coens were looking for a way into moviemaking and Raimi was looking for a follow-up project to *The Evil Dead*. The three of them put together a script called *The XYZ Murders*, which aimed to be fast and funny, with influences from 1930s and 1940s Hollywood. Elements of the crime thriller and the romantic comedy were thrown into the script, along with the likes of Laurel and Hardy and the Keystone Cops.

The title remained *The XYZ Murders* until previews, for which it was renamed *Broken Hearts and Noses*. *Crimewave* was intended to be the overseas title, but by the time the film made it to full release this had been adopted as the American title as well (see **BOX OFFICE**).

REFERENCES: Vic is incarcerated at the Hudsucker State Penitentiary, the first use of the name that would form the title of the Coens' second collaboration with Raimi. Apparently this was not intended to suggest that Hudsucker Industries extend into running prisons: they just liked the sound of the word.

PRODUCTION: The Coens were scarcely involved in the production of *Crimewave*, which was probably just as well from their point of view. Bruce Campbell describes the whole affair as 'a fiasco'. Interference from the studio, Embassy Pictures, meant that all of the parts were recast one week before filming, and while Campbell had been set to play the lead role the studio disagreed. As a result, Raimi and the Coens returned to the script and 'beefed up the Heel role'. (Indeed, Renaldo seems to be two characters combined into one, as there is no plot reason for Vic's love rival and the prospective buyer for Odegard & Trend to be the same person.) 'It was a blessing in disguise,' Campbell says, since this permitted him to play *Crimewave* down in later years. The movie did see a rare appearance from Joel in front of the cameras, as he took a small uncredited role as a newspaper reporter at Vic's execution.

Embassy, who had insisted on a great deal of control over *Crimewave* from the beginning, substantially recut the movie before release, which Raimi was deeply unhappy with and which prompted the Coens to insist on final cut for *Raising Arizona*. The end product of *Crimewave* fell a long way short of what its writers had hoped for and they simply decided to put the experience behind them, although this was somewhat easier for the Coens, who had invested less time and effort in the project than Raimi. 'It's no big deal for us,' Ethan says, 'but Sam wasn't thrilled with it.' Raimi has rarely spoken of *Crimewave* since. Joel notes of its current obscurity, 'We like it lost.'

CRITICAL RECEPTION: *Crimewave* was barely noticed by critics, although of course *Variety* gave its overview of the film, which was generous. 'A boisterous, goofy, cartoonish comedy in the *Airplane* [Jim Abrams, David Zucker, Jerry Zucker, 1980] mould,' the reviewer declared in the 22 May 1985 issue, singling out Paul L Smith for particular praise: 'a fabulously enjoyable comic performance that single-handedly keeps the film afloat'. They added that '[The picture] gives the impression of having been storyboarded rather than directed and, despite good execution all around, production looks pretty cheap,' concluding that 'laughs are abundant enough to make this a passably funny entertainment.'

The British reception was somewhat harsher. Tim Pulleine of *Films and Filming* was disappointed that the film did not live up to its billing as the work of the people behind *The Evil Dead* and *Blood Simple*. 'Both of those films displayed a sense of humour, but it was implicit in the treatment,' he wrote in April 1986. '*Crimewave*, however, represents an attempt at overt comedy and, sad to say, comes badly unstuck.' *Screen International*'s Marjorie

Bilbow agreed. 'Overacted and overwrought, *Crimewave* is a hotchpotch assortment of sketches which give the impression of having been ad-libbed by the cast while the director was out at lunch.'

Steve Jenkins, writing in *Monthly Film Bulletin*, wasn't impressed either, suggesting in April 1986 that, while its creators had brought a variety of promising elements to the piece, they had failed to gel them together. The whole, he considered, was less than the sum of its parts. 'Occasionally, *Crimewave* hits the genuinely bizarre note to which it frantically aspires . . . but these moments merely suggest the movie which Raimi has ultimately failed to deliver.'

BOX OFFICE: Embassy eventually gave up on *Crimewave* without giving it the courtesy of a full theatrical release. They let it go to Columbia, who gave it a very limited release on 25 April 1986. It was screened in just seven cinemas for one week, grossed $5,101 and closed again. One wonders why they bothered.

DIALOGUE TO SKIP BACK FOR:
Nancy: 'I'm not that kind of girl.'
Renaldo: 'Well, with a little practice you could learn to be.'

ANALYSIS: It doesn't come as a massive surprise to discover that *Crimewave* is closer in spirit to *The Hudsucker Proxy* than any other Coen brothers movie. The two were written around the same time and their nature as collaborations between the Coens and Raimi produce a distinctive combination of concerns and influences. While the Coens and Raimi do overlap substantially in their thinking, the plundering of 1940s Hollywood and the preoccupation with crime stories seem to come more from the Coens, while Raimi enjoys comic-book aesthetics and wacky violence. The result is a retro-styled living cartoon. While the story must take place in the 1980s because of the modern security systems, the clothes and characters come straight out of the 1940s and 1950s. This is also a simplified world where people live across the road from their workplace and exterminators have three settings – 'RATS', 'MEN' and 'HEROES'. It's no more than a rough approximation of the real world and it operates by the rules of cartoons. Just as Anton Chekhov once identified that a gun seen mounted on the wall in act one of a play must be used in act three, so the shelf of bowling balls seen early on in *Crimewave* must eventually fall on somebody's head.

While a direct comparison with *The Hudsucker Proxy* is hardly fair, since *Crimewave* clearly had a much smaller budget and the Coens had complete control over *Hudsucker*, it's interesting to see what a Coen script looks like when it's been produced by somebody else. Both Raimi and the Coens have been influenced by each other, and so the visual stylings aren't wildly different: the zoom into Helene Trend's mouth, for example, was appropriated by the Coens for *The Hudsucker Proxy* as well as *Raising Arizona*. Raimi's style is a little more disjointed and unsettling (he often uses rapid cutting, where the Coens' camerawork tends to be more fluid) but they're not a million miles apart. Where you really notice the difference is in the contribution of others to the film. The music, composed by Arlon Ober, is more intrusive than Carter Burwell's. It successfully emulates music from cartoons and classic Hollywood scores but it merely feels like pastiche where Burwell's scores are distinctive, and Ober uses obvious cues to stress the humour in a way that Burwell never does (note the military theme that accompanies the Colonel). Also, the Coens have traditionally used actors with whom they are comfortable, but in this case Raimi's cast was largely imposed upon him by the studio and their responses to the material vary. Since *Crimewave* is primarily a comedy, this causes problems and jokes that should have been hilarious fall rather flat.

On occasion the jokes do work, and in these Raimi and the Coens play with the audience's expectations in the way that both have since become notable for. The narrative performs an ingenious double back flip when Nancy prepares to leave the club. Renaldo has paid $40 towards the $76 bill, leaving Nancy to find the other $36. She doesn't have enough and neither does Vic. 'So where on Earth am I gonna get thirty-six dollars?' wails Nancy. Cut to the club's compere, who announces that the club is holding a dance contest tonight and the first prize is thirty-six dollars. The film is completely open about the contrivance of this device and uses it to comic effect, only to subvert it straight away. The introduction of the dance contest can only serve two purposes: firstly it gives Nancy the cash she needs for the bill, and secondly it will bring Vic and Nancy closer together. They get up and start to dance, and of course the audience assumes that they will win because, otherwise, why would any of this be happening? The film then abruptly cuts away to Vic and Nancy washing dishes in the kitchen. They didn't win and they have to pay off their bill the difficult, and less romantic, way. (See also the scenes with Mussburger's tailor in **The Hudsucker Proxy**.)

GENRE: While the Coens are constantly analysed in terms of film noir, the one element of the genre that they rarely make use of is the flashback narrative. This tends to operate in one of two ways: either the movie begins near the end of the story and the central character then narrates the story for the viewer (examples are numerous but include *D.O.A.* (Rudolph Maté, 1950) and *Double Indemnity* (Billy Wilder, 1944)), or another character investigates events that have already happened but which may have a bearing on the present (pioneered in *Citizen Kane* (Orson Welles, 1941) but also used very effectively in *The Killers* (Robert Siodmak, 1946)). While *The Hudsucker Proxy* starts at the end of the story it isn't Norville who relates it to us, and while there are Coen films where the central character narrates (*Raising Arizona*, *The Man Who Wasn't There*), these don't open with a point near the end of the story, so neither is a true flashback narrative. *Crimewave*, by contrast, opens with Vic being strapped into the electric chair and telling his story, which means that in narrative terms it is closer to film noir than any of the Coens' directorial efforts. The device is a hallmark of noir cinema rather than the literature that inspired it, which seems to confirm what the Coens have always said about their own films. The noir influence on their films comes more from the novels of Cain and Chandler than the movies.

AVAILABILITY: *Crimewave* has been released in the UK on VHS but this was deleted long ago. The US video is still available but it isn't easy to find in shops these days. Second-hand copies pop up fairly regularly on eBay and this remains the best chance of locating one. With Raimi's reputation increasing following the colossal success of *Spider-Man*, it seems likely that his complete works will make it to DVD fairly soon.

THE COENS' VIEW: 'We've always let Sam make these mistakes for us. "Sam," we tell him, "you go do a movie at a studio and tell us what happens." ' (Joel in 1987)

VERDICT: 'Lady, you ain't seen nothin' . . . yet!' *Crimewave* slipped by virtually unnoticed on release and despite being the work of three filmmakers with a highly enthusiastic following it is rarely talked about now, least of all by the filmmakers in question. This does, however, mean that it is infrequently seen and the film seems to be gaining a certain mystique as a result.

This is not a lost classic, but an interesting failure. While it would be wrong to completely absolve Raimi and the Coens from blame for the film's problems, *Crimewave* has a very idiosyncratic style that would have needed careful and thoughtful handling at every stage. Unfortunately it was taken out of Raimi's hands after shooting and it seems likely that whoever produced the final edit did not have an affinity with the film's aesthetic, with the result that it doesn't flow very well despite its frenetic pace. The performances are also at fault, with the majority of the cast delivering the peculiar dialogue in a rather stilted way. Only Bruce Campbell carries it off – he's a master at making this kind of material sound natural and Raimi should have been allowed to retain him in the lead.

As a consequence, *Crimewave* is largely of interest to fans either of the Coens' work or of Raimi's, since despite its problems it still fits into their development as filmmakers. While the Coens remained very good friends with Raimi and evidently do not blame him for the movie's failure, neither of them permitted another director to make one of their scripts until Ethan collaborated with J Todd Anderson on *The Naked Man*. On this evidence it is easy to see why. The Coens' films are usually elegant in execution: *Crimewave* is a bit of a mess.

Raising Arizona (1987)

(Colour – 94 mins)

Circle Films presents
A Ted and Jim Pedas/Ben Barenholtz Production
Directed by Joel Coen
Produced by Ethan Coen
Written by Ethan Coen and Joel Coen
Co-produced by Mark Silverman
Executive Producer: James Jacks
Associate Producer: Deborah Reinisch
Director of Photography: Barry Sonnenfeld
Production Designer: Jane Musky
Edited by Michael R Miller
Music by Carter Burwell
Costume Designer: Richard Hornung
Supervising Sound Editor: Skip Lievsay
Associate Editor: Arnold Glassman
Casting by Donna Isaacson CSA and John Lyons CSA

CAST: Nicolas Cage (*Hi*), Holly Hunter (*Ed*), Trey Wilson (*Nathan Arizona, Sr*), John Goodman (*Gale*), William Forsythe (*Evelle*), Sam McMurray (*Glen*), Frances McDormand (*Dot*), Randall 'Tex' Cobb (*Leonard Smalls*), TJ Kuhn Jr (*Nathan Junior*), Lynne Dumin Kitei (*Florence Arizona*), Peter Benedek (*Prison Counsellor*), Charles 'Lew' Smith (*Nice Old Grocery Man*), Warren Keith (*Younger FBI Agent*), Henry Kendrick (*Older FBI Agent*), Sidney Dawson (*Moses*), Richard Blake (*Parole Board Chairman*), Troy Nabors (*Parole Board Member*), Mary Seibel (*Parole Board Member*), John O'Donnal (*Hayseed in the Pickup*), Keith Jandacek (*Whitey*), Warren Forsythe (*Minister*), Ruben Young (*Trapped Convict*), Dennis Sullivan (*Policeman in Arizona House*), Dick Alexander (*Policeman in Arizona House*), Rusty Lee (*Feisty Hayseed*), James Yeater

(*Fingerprint Technician*), Bill Andres (*Reporter*), Carver Barns (*Reporter*), Margaret H McCormack (*Unpainted Secretary*), Bill Rocz (*Newscaster*), Mary F Glenn (*Payroll Cashier*), Jeremy Babendure (*Scamp with Squirt Gun*), Bill Dobbins (*Adoption Agent*), Ralph Norton (*Gynaecologist*), Henry Tank (*Mopping Convict*), Frank Outlaw (*Supermarket Manager*), Todd Michael Rodgers (*Varsity Nathan Jr*), M Emmet Walsh (*Machine Shop Ear-Bender*), Robert Gray, Katie Thrasher, Derek Russell, Nicole Russell, Zachary Sanders, Noell Sanders (*Glen and Dot's Kids*), Cody Ranger, Jeremy Arendt, Ashley Hammon, Crystal Hiller, Olivia Hughes, Emily Malin, Melanie Malin, Craig McLaughlin, Adam Savageau, Benjamin Savageau, David Schneider, Michael Stewart (*Arizona Quints*), And Featuring the Amazing Voice of William Preston Robertson

TAGLINE: 'A comedy beyond belief.'

SUMMARY: Feckless armed robber HI McDonnaugh (known to all as 'Hi') is repeatedly caught, imprisoned and released: every time he is incarcerated, his mugshot is taken by the same officer, Edwinna. When he is released for the third time, he proposes to Ed and they marry. Their attempts to have a child are thwarted by Ed's infertility, and they are turned down for adoption because of Hi's criminal record. When they hear that the wife of local furniture-store mogul Nathan Arizona has given birth to quintuplets, Hi kidnaps one of them – Nathan Junior. Two of Hi's friends from prison, Gale and Evelle, escape incarceration and turn up at Hi and Ed's, unaware that a biker named Leonard Smalls is on their trail.

After a couple of days, Hi begins to wonder if he is cut out for family life. He punches his boss, Glen, for suggesting that they indulge in some wife swapping and steals a pack of nappies from a convenience store. He and Ed seem set on divorce. A $25,000 reward has been posted for Nathan Junior's return: Smalls wants the reward and Glen wants Nathan Junior for himself, but then Gale and Evelle kidnap the baby. At first they intend to get the $25,000 but then decide to keep him. Smalls then captures the baby, but Ed takes him back and Smalls is killed when Hi accidentally pulls the pin from one of his hand-grenades. Hi and Ed decide to give Nathan Junior back to the Arizonas. Nathan realises that Hi and Ed are the kidnappers, but he forgives them and tells them to stay married.

Hi dreams of the future. He sees Gale and Evelle return to prison; sees Nathan Junior's progress, influenced by Hi and Ed, to becoming a football star; and finally he sees an elderly couple – himself and Ed, perhaps – being visited by their children.

DEVELOPMENT: 'Essentially, after having finished *Blood Simple*, we wanted to make something completely different,' Ethan says. 'We didn't know what, but we wanted it to be funny, with a quicker rhythm.' As their prime motivating factor, this set a pattern of making each movie distinctly different from the previous one. (They would carry this maxim throughout their career until it was forcibly broken with *O Brother, Where Art Thou?*) Holly Hunter was also a significant factor. Having been unable to use her in *Blood Simple* they started to write a character around her personality and Ethan notes an image that motivated them to take the script in a particular direction: 'Holly in uniform hurling orders at the prisoners. It might appear secondary, but that image had great importance in setting the writing in motion.'

'We weren't that interested either in the problem of sterility or the desire for having a child,' says Joel. Rather, they worked from 'the idea of a character who has that desire and at the same time feels outside the law'. The idea for the kidnapping evolved as the character of Hi developed. While *Blood Simple* emerged from a story idea and the Coens developed their characters as necessary to fulfil the plot functions, the plot of *Raising Arizona* 'was a way of talking about the characters' as Joel puts it (this is often the main difference between the process of writing drama and that of writing comedy). This is evident in that the Coens' first act during the three-and-a-half month writing process was to put down on paper the ten-minute montage sequence that precedes the opening credits. This sets up the back-story for Hi and Ed and tells us who they are, and eventually arrives at their inability to have children:

the Coens accelerate the development of their characters until a plot emerges from them.

The influences of *Raising Arizona* are less palpable than in the Coens' other movies. 'I guess you can detect our admiration for Southern writers like William Faulkner and Flannery O'Connor,' says Joel. 'Most of what we know of the place, in fact, comes from what we've read,' adds Ethan. It was literature, rather than experience, that tended to dictate the characters' speech patterns – not only novels about the region but also the characters' probable reading matter, such as the Bible. The stylised mode of speech, in which simple words are mixed with grandiose ones, drew criticism to the Coens, who were accused of patronising the inhabitants of the Deep South. Others criticised them for giving the film too happy an ending, by showing Hi's projected future. The Coens' answer to both was that the characters were not intended to represent anything outside of the characters. 'There are people who find the conclusion too sentimental,' says Joel. 'Once again it doesn't reflect our own attitude to life. For us it's written in the context of the character.'

REFERENCES: As Gale and Evelle clean themselves up in a garage washroom after escaping from jail, the letters 'O.P.E.' and 'P.O.E.' can be seen scrawled on the doors. These are the recall codes from *Dr Strangelove or: How I Learned to Stop Worrying and Love the Bomb* (Stanley Kubrick, 1963) and are possibly included as a reference to *Raising Arizona*'s nuclear paranoia imagery (see **EVER AMERICA**).

This film also contains a self-reference from the Coens, one so obscure that audiences would not understand it for another seven years. Hi's worksuit is emblazoned with the Hudsucker Industries logo in reference to a script they had completed but not filmed, *The Hudsucker Proxy*.

CASTING: The Coens took a little convincing before they took Nicolas Cage, nephew of legendary director Francis Ford Coppola, on as their lead. For his own part the actor had immense enthusiasm for the role. 'The script was incredible, one of the best

I'd ever read,' Cage says. 'I loved Hi, he has a rhythm all his own.' After meeting him, however, the Coens were unconvinced that Cage was right for the part, having seen him play more streetwise, urban characters in films such as *Rumble Fish* (Francis Ford Coppola, 1983) and *Valley Girl* (Martha Coolidge, 1983). Cage pursued the role enthusiastically and convinced Joel and Ethan to let him test for it. They were slightly dubious over Cage's ability to do the Deep South accent, but gave him the part anyway. In the event, Cage mastered the accent fairly easily with the support of a vocal coach. Before heading down to the shoot, he showed the script to 'Uncle Francis', who commented, 'It looks great but where is all this stuff coming from?' This anticipated the uncertain reaction of the critics to the Coens' particular sense of humour (see **CRITICAL RECEPTION**).

As noted, the Coens wrote the part of Ed for Holly Hunter. The Georgia-born actress had found frequent employment on Broadway since starting out in the early 1980s, but had only done occasional movie work. She had a role in the low-budget horror picture *The Burning* (Tony Maylam, 1981) and worked for two months on *Swing Shift* (Jonathan Demme, 1984), only to have most of her material cut from the finished movie. *Raising Arizona* was her first leading role and paved the way for her Oscar-nominated appearance in *Broadcast News* (James L Brooks, 1987). These two films launched a career that has seen her collect both a Best Actress award from Cannes and a Best Actress Oscar for *The Piano* (Andrew McAlpine, 1993). 'There is no pretence to her, you don't get any tortured angst with Holly,' says Joel. 'She doesn't play it safe, she's always pushing.' She later worked with the Coens on *O Brother, Where Art Thou?* Also appearing in *Raising Arizona* was the actress she had recommended for *Blood Simple*, Frances McDormand, in the role of Dot.

The film marked the beginning of the Coens' long working relationship with John Goodman, who was cast as Gale. *Raising Arizona* was one of two breakthrough roles for Goodman, who came to the film directly from *True Stories* (1986), directed by Talking Heads frontman David Byrne. *Raising Arizona* invited comparisons with *True Stories* in terms of its setting and ironic approach and the Goodman connection emphasised this. 'It's a coincidence,' Joel stresses. 'We chose [Goodman] before *True Stories* was shot.' The Coens found that he matched well with William Forsythe, who they cast as Evelle, and when they came to shoot the sequence where the convicts escape from prison, the apposite visual suggestion of a birth was created. 'They both had these faces – they looked like grown-up babies,' says Joel. 'We just decided on the spot to continue the baby theme.' Soon after *Raising Arizona* the theatrically trained Goodman won a regular role in the TV sitcom *Roseanne*, in which he appeared for eight seasons. The Coens have continued to use him and he has delivered two of the best performances seen in any of their movies, namely Charlie Meadows in *Barton Fink* and Walter Sobchak in *The Big Lebowski*: he also appeared in *O Brother, Where Art Thou?* and did voice work under a pseudonym on *The Hudsucker Proxy*. He's balanced this more critically lauded work (which also includes *Storytelling* (Todd Solondz, 2001) and a further turn with Nicolas Cage in *Bringing Out the Dead* (Martin Scorsese, 1999)) with amiable roles in box-office fluff such as *Arachnophobia* (Frank Marshal, 1991) and *The Flintstones* (Brian Levant, 1994).

Trey Wilson was cast in the role of Nathan Arizona. Wilson began his film career acting in such projects as *Vampire Hookers* (Cirio H Santiago, 1979) and he came to *Raising Arizona* from the undistinguished Bryan Brown/Brian Dennehy vehicle *F/X* (Robert Mandel, 1986). *Arizona* did pave the way to more high-profile roles in *Twins* (Ivan Reitman, 1988), *Bull Durham* (Ron Shelton, 1988) and *Married to the Mob* (Jonathan Demme, 1988), but sadly Wilson's career was cut short just as it was taking off (see **Miller's Crossing**).

The casting for the Lone Biker of the Apocalypse was rather more unconventional. 'He's not really an actor,' Joel says of Randall 'Tex' Cobb. 'He's a former boxing champion . . . In the beginning he was more someone who brawled in the streets in Texas, then who tried without real success to make a career in boxing.' The Coens, who above all prefer to work with people whom they trust, didn't feel terribly comfortable with Cobb. 'He's less an actor than a force of nature,' says Joel, noting that he wouldn't be keen to engage Cobb's services on future projects. 'He played his role well in *Raising Arizona*, but he posed problems.' For example, Cobb had difficulties with riding the bike, falling off at one point and skidding along the ground (a take which Joel asked to be printed in case it could be used somewhere).

The major casting hurdle was finding a good-humoured, patient baby to fill the role of Nathan Junior. 'Nathan Junior is supposed to be having the time of his life and he's not the least flustered by anything that goes on,' says Circle Films' James Jacks, who acted as executive producer on *Raising Arizona* (see **PRODUCTION**). 'We wanted a baby who would go through anything and still look happy.' Realising that it was unreasonable to expect a young child to look happy at all times, they set out to find twins who could share the Nathan Junior role. This is normal practice in the movies, because American law says that babies can only be worked for a limited time, then they have to be rested. 'We figured twins would allow us to keep working if one was getting cranky.'

The Coens needed a lot of babies anyway, for the lengthy scene where Hi kidnaps Nathan Junior from his five-berth crib. All in all fifteen were employed, although only thirteen are credited on the finished movie: one of the fifteen was fired for learning to walk during filming. Once he walked he refused to crawl as he was required to do. The Coens had intended to select two from those employed for this sequence but in the event they decided that TJ Kuhn Jr was the best and he played Nathan Junior for the rest of the film. 'It was a risk, but it paid off,' says Jacks. 'TJ just did what he was supposed to do. He appeared to be smarter than any adult in the movie.'

PRODUCTION: 'We learned a lot between our first and second films,' says Joel. 'There's a big jump in your confidence in terms of your craft after you've made your first feature – or at least it was for us.'

Raising Arizona was the first of a three-picture extension to the Coens' deal with Circle Films, the company that had distributed

Blood Simple. Circle were pleased, although a little surprised, that these lauded young filmmakers chose to stick with them. 'There was nothing on paper [after *Blood Simple*],' says Jim Jacks. 'I half expected them to say, "Look, we can make movies for studios now." ' It wasn't as if the Coens hadn't had offers from the major Hollywood studios, but they wanted to retain creative control and they appreciated what Circle had done for them. 'We trusted them,' says Joel simply, 'it was natural to work with them.' The Coens were willing to peg their budgets low, which made their movies affordable to financiers outside of the majors. Circle was willing to back the film to the tune of $3 million and Jacks took an executive producer credit, but they left Joel and Ethan to their own devices. As production commenced, 20th Century Fox put up a further $3 million in exchange for distribution rights, although they too agreed that the Coens could retain complete control over the project.

The film was shot over twelve weeks at and around Carefree Studios in Greater Phoenix, where the *New Dick Van Dyke Show* had been made, and again they saved money with a non-union crew. However, while the actors were rehearsing, the Coens and Barry Sonnenfeld spent almost as much time again – ten weeks – performing test run-throughs of scenes on location. This appears to have been motivated by their experience on *Blood Simple*, where they'd learned that while a location may look good to the naked eye, practical problems can easily arise during shooting. Sonnenfeld shot test footage for a number of sequences with a Super-8 camera, which gave him and the Coens an idea of whether the camera movements were feasible and the settings would accommodate their plans. This proved to be highly beneficial: in the case of the picnic scene, they had hoped to make use of the tallest fountain in the world (with a spout of 250 feet) as a backdrop. However, on reviewing the Super-8 footage they realised that the surrounding lake caused glare on the camera and the fountain didn't show up properly on the film anyway, so the location was reconsidered. At the end of this process, the three filmmakers were able to prepare their storyboards based around the locations, using the same meticulous approach that had served them well on *Blood Simple*.

Nicolas Cage had mixed feelings about the Coens' working methods. On the one hand he found that the shoot went smoothly because everything was planned carefully in advance. They went into shooting satisfied with their script and storyboards and they stuck with them, unlike some other films Cage had worked on where the script had been altered during filming. On the other hand, he found them reluctant to 'accept another artist's vision' and during the shoot described them as 'autocratic', although he acknowledged that this was sometimes the case with relatively inexperienced directors. (For their own part, the Coens didn't seem to detect any problems: 'Nic's a really imaginative actor. He arrives with piles of ideas that we hadn't thought about while writing the script, but his contribution is really in line with the character we'd imagined.') There were occasions when they deviated from the storyboards, such as the scene where Hi, Ed and Nathan Junior take their photograph with the timer function on the camera. 'We shot it static,' says Joel of the original set-up for the shot that sees them waiting for the camera to go off. 'We went back four weeks later and shot it as a tracking shot. It wasn't storyboarded as a tracking shot, it was something we decided to do after we shot the scene.'

The Coens were keen that the camera should be dynamic above all. Naturally, this meant that they again employed 'shakicam' as they had on *Blood Simple*. The most obvious use of the technique can be seen in the lengthy zoom along the streets to the Arizona house, over the front lawn, up to the window and into Florence Arizona's mouth as she screams. 'The shot was done in three pieces, and it's broken up with cuts,' the Coens recall. 'A lot of people remember it as being one long shot [but] there are flash cuts of Nicholas Cage turning his head.' One of the shots was done with the 'shakicam' moving along the streets and up to the ladder to the window, another used a remote camera to run up the ladder and stop at the curtains, and a final shot in the studio used a dolly. This final shot was the trickiest to achieve and had to be done in reverse, because the rushing camera would not have been able to stop at the ideal distance from actor Lynne Dumin Kitei's face. Instead it started close to her mouth, which was illuminated with the aid of fibre-optic lights mounted around the lens, and was rushed away from her by the grips. A set of curtains was then thrown across the camera so that it would match up with the second segment of the sequence. They had planned to finish with a zoom right into Kitei's inner throat, but this had the effect of deflating the dynamism of the rush as well as matching poorly with the first shot of the next scene as Hi wakes up, and so this final part was trimmed.

Also filmed in reverse, for fairly obvious reasons, was the shot where Gale and Evelle return to the convenience store at high speed and brake in front of Nathan Junior with inches to spare. (Now that Joel has a child of his own, he says, 'I don't know if I would have been more nervous [doing those shots], but I wouldn't want to use my baby.') The car's bumper was rocked at the start of the shot to give the impression of braking, then it reversed away from the baby down the road. The camera was under-cranked in order to make the car appear to be moving more quickly, with the section when the car was stationary restored to normal speed. The varying camera speeds all contribute to the look of the film, which the Coens were determined should be 'wacky'. 'Every time I put on a lens,' Sonnenfeld says, 'Joel and Ethan would ask, "Does it look wacky enough?" ' He used a 17 mm lens for much of the film, which has a tendency to distort things so that they look 'like you're shooting them in miniature. Lots of exteriors look like they were shot inside with a cheap blue screen.' The idea was to achieve an 'open' look, as opposed to *Blood Simple*'s claustrophobia.

While the Coens prefer to cover a scene from several angles rather than spend a long time tinkering with the lighting for one angle, they paid particular attention to the lighting on certain sections. The opening montage was intended to look like a storybook as its pages were turned, so they worked to make it 'colourful and beautifully lit'. (Within this sequence was the desert sunset, which was made more dramatic by being hugely speeded up. Stand-ins for Hunter and Cage sat in the sun loungers, motionless, for forty minutes while a regulating device called an intervalometer caused the camera to expose frames at the rate of roughly one every three seconds.) Meanwhile, the Biker was intended to look like a cartoon character, so Sonnenfeld overlit him. This was easy to do in most shots because the Biker is mostly seen only in exterior scenes, but for the scene in Nathan Arizona's office light had to be accommodated by placing a window behind him in the set, so that he could be lit in silhouette.

A great deal of shooting time was taken up by the chase sequence, after Hi steals the pack of Huggies, which was left to the end of the production period. This meant a lot of night shooting, which caused some headaches for Sonnenfeld. The Coens wanted to keep on using wide-angle lenses for these scenes, but 'A major pain of using wide angles is the lighting – there's nowhere to put the lights.' Sonnenfeld used high-speed Kodak 5294 film for these sequences because it does not require as much additional lighting as other film stocks, although neither he nor the Coens were satisfied with the results. 'It's grainy, low-contrast, and has a salmon cast,' he says, and after *Raising Arizona* he and the Coens agreed not to use it again. He did try to combat the problems of 5294 by overexposing the negative as he had during *Blood Simple*. 'The blacks are richer and the grain is reduced. You can bring it back down in the lab.' (This time around, his camera reports to Du Art Labs read, 'Make look nice.')

During the sequences where Hi races through the supermarket, Sonnenfeld told the Coens that he was getting flare off the fluorescent lights and suggested that the camera be raised. However, the Coens ruled this out on the grounds that a higher camera would not be sufficiently wacky. 'The lower a camera, the more dynamic it is,' Sonnenfeld says. 'You get a sense of power from the legs, from the things on the floor.' This also meant that, while the film is narrated by Hi, it often takes the viewpoint of a baby. 'Shakicam' was employed again as Hi ran through the suburban house: the shot was originally attempted with the camera tracking backwards as Cage ran towards it, but with the wide-angle lens it looked like the house was a back-projection. The wide angle also meant that, in the close space, the walls appear to warp, but with Cage focusing the viewer's attention the Coens decided not to worry about it. They wanted a slightly rough look anyway and indeed they re-shot some scenes because they looked too slick. The 'shakicam' was key to this: 'The Coens are control freaks,' says Sonnenfeld. 'With the Steadycam, the camera just floats there out of control.' (The odd look of the material unnerved Fox when they saw the dailies, so much so that they wondered whether they should sell shares in *Raising Arizona* to the public.)

The Coens did exercise some restraint when a shot seemed to them to be a bit *too* weird. For the shot when the Biker throws Hi to the ground, Sonnenfeld devised what he dubbed the 'Barrycam', which involved strapping Sonnenfeld to a board, resting on a pivot. Sonnenfeld had a handheld camera that, when the Barrycam was dropped, simulated Hi's point-of-view as the Biker cast him to the ground. When viewed back later, however, it just didn't look right. While the production generally went smoothly, all involved were aware that the stakes were higher on *Raising Arizona* than they had been on the previous movie and there was less room to mess around. 'The attitude on *Blood Simple* was "Just go for it, 'cause if we screw up, no one will know about it," ' said Sonnenfeld as the production was coming to a close. 'I still take chances, but there's no question we're more scared.'

MUSIC: 'I have very fond recollections of movies like *Raising Arizona*,' says Carter Burwell, 'because it was very definitely the trade-off between imagination and budget.' The composer found his imagination challenged by the constraints, since he needed to base his score around a couple of instruments. This meant honing the score down to a few pertinent sounds that would resonate strongly with the material and compensate for the score's limitations. Because Burwell has an aptitude for popular forms, his scores often reflect the kind of music that the characters might listen to as well as relating to events on-screen. Hence, in *Arizona* the music is mainly played bluegrass-style on an acoustic guitar, although it draws on a wide range of sources (most notably Beethoven's 'Ode to Joy' which accompanies Hi and Ed's wedding).

Ethan also notes that they were keen to 'connect the characters through the music. Holly sings a lullaby in the movie and we asked the composer to introduce it into the musical theme that accompanies the bounty hunter.' The use of a lullaby reflects the Biker's apparent origin in Hi's dream, but it is played on a synthesiser to give it a mechanised, ominous air.

CRITICAL RECEPTION: 'I have a problem with movies where everybody talks as if they were reading out of an old novel about a bunch of would-be colourful characters,' Roger Ebert declared of *Raising Arizona* in the *Chicago Sun-Times* on 20 March 1987. It appears that he didn't warm to the distinctive Coen humour after seeing it for the first time and struggled to describe it. He found it 'arch and artificial' and thought that this inhibited the film's progress while distracting the viewer. 'What we have here is a film shot down by its own forced and mannered style.' Unimpressed, Ebert awarded the film one and a half stars, but his wasn't the harshest comment. 'The amazing thing about *Raising Arizona* is how it can move so fast, be so loud and remain so relentlessly boring at the same time,' wrote Sheila Benson in the *Los Angeles Times*. Benson also began the long-running debate over the Coens' attitude to the ordinary people they portray in their films. 'It comes swathed in a caul of superiority towards its characters, just plain folks.'

Vincent Canby was willing to be a little more generous, describing the Coens as 'talented – up to a point' when reviewing *Raising Arizona* for the 11 March 1987 issue of the *New York Times*: 'Like *Blood Simple* it's full of technical expertise but has no life of its own.' And while he believed that there were many good, funny ideas in the script these were let down by the direction, which was 'without decisive style'. Canby felt the Coens were better scriptwriters than directors, writing that, '*Raising Arizona* may well be a comedy that's more entertaining to read than to see.'

'Quite possibly there has never been another film like *Raising Arizona*,' was *Variety*'s verdict, invoking the aforementioned *True Stories* and also *Repo Man* (Alex Cox, 1984) as its closest relatives. 'Whilst the film is filled with many splendid touches and plenty of yocks, it often doesn't hold together as a coherent story.' This review also provided the most accurate assessment of the film's chances of success: '*Raising Arizona* may not be everybody's cup of tea, but it's fresh enough to find a faithful following with the right handling.' Pauline Kael, writing in the *New Yorker*, was willing to go a little further: 'This broad farce is no big deal, but it has a cornpone-surreal quality and a rambunctious charm.' She rather enjoyed the stylised nature of the visuals and the dialogue. 'The film is storyboarded like a comic strip; it has a galumphing tempo.'

One of the movie's more positive reviews came from Rita Kempley of the *Washington Post*. 'The co-writing Coens are like a couple of big kids who got cameras for Christmas; they're full of raw comic energy, as silly as they are sophisticated,' she wrote in the 20 March 1987 edition. Gratifyingly for Ethan and Joel, she found it to be sympathetic and clever, and admired their technical skill in achieving effective comic irony around Hi's perceptions. She ended by noting that 'The Coens are coming from the New Left-Field with this zany answer to the alarmist milk-carton-kids campaign, a send-up of endearing dolts, desperation and disposable diapers.'

British reviews were similarly mixed. *Sight and Sound*'s review was one of the best: 'More comedy than thriller, *Raising Arizona* at first seems far removed from characteristic Coen territory,' remarked Tom Milne in the Summer 1987 issue, prematurely attempting to define the Coen 'characteristic' after just one film. Nevertheless he soon found the Coens to be adept at humour, regarding the situations of *Raising Arizona* as 'wonderfully funny in their own right' but also admiring its handling of cartoonish figures: 'while its characters do not bleed – the violence, with the biker finally blown into fragments, is pure *Tom and Jerry* – they have a surprisingly touching vulnerability.'

Others weren't so sure. Steve Jenkins of *Monthly Film Bulletin* compared it favourably to *Crimewave* in the July 1987 issue, but even that wasn't saying much. 'Whilst *Raising Arizona* is much more cleverly judged and infinitely funnier, it too is ultimately flawed by a kind of overkill.' Jenkins appreciated the Coens' talent, as well as their attempt to provide an alternative to the prevailing forms of 'blandly designed audience-reflecting fodder' that constituted Hollywood comedy at the time, but felt that their approach wasn't quite right. 'One only wishes that some of its energy had been dissipated in order to leave more space for its characters to breathe.'

BOX OFFICE: *Raising Arizona* was released on 20 March 1987 to an impressive return. The film grossed $22,847,000 on release in America despite competition from the previous week's big success, *Lethal Weapon* (Richard Donner, 1987). Considering *Arizona* was made for just $6 million, that's a healthy figure.

DIALOGUE TO SKIP BACK FOR:

Prison Counsellor: 'Why do you say you feel trapped in a man's body?'

Inmate: (with *very* deep voice) 'Well, sometimes I get the menstrual cramps real hard.'

Reporter: 'Sir, it's been rumoured that your son was abducted by UFOs, would you care to comment?'

Nathan Arizona: 'Don't print that, son. If his momma reads that she's just gonna lose all hope.'

Evelle: 'Balloons. Hey, do these blow up into funny shapes at all?'

Storekeeper: 'Well, no. Unless round is funny.'

ANALYSIS: As most critics identified at the time, *Raising Arizona* deliberately showcases a very different side of the Coens to *Blood Simple*. Where *Blood Simple* was bleak, dark and unsettling, *Raising Arizona* opts to be funnier, lighter and ultimately easier to watch. Indeed, this is probably the easiest Coens film to watch full stop, with its only real contender for that title being *O Brother, Where Art Thou?* In later films they would become more adept at combining these two contrasting sides to great effect, slotting comedy into thrillers and blackness into comedies.

It must be said that *Raising Arizona* paints a more convincing picture of a sexual relationship than *Blood Simple* managed. This is perhaps because, in Hi and Ed, the Coens created two characters whom they found funny and were therefore more interested in. They're a yin-and-yang pairing, something which Hi makes explicit when the couple apply for adoption, hoping that his criminal past and her impressive service record in the police will cancel each other out. Even their problems in having a child are split equally between the two of them: they can't have one naturally because Ed is barren, but they can't adopt because of Hi's criminal record (although one might say that the fault lies more with Hi because his problem falls within his own control and Ed's doesn't).

The fact that there's more humour in *Raising Arizona* does help to make its protagonists more sympathetic. Hi is an everyman struggling to better himself, and although he's not the sharpest tool in the box the audience warms to him because his dopey commentary on events is funny. The audience also sees that he feels guilty about what he does and this leads them to view Hi as weak-willed and unable to resist the temptation to commit crimes. This is an essential part of the groundwork for the film's success because Hi and Ed are about to commit a crime that, if it happened in real life, the viewer would probably find unforgivable (see **GENRE**). Kidnapping was to become a favourite theme of the Coens', being the basis for *Fargo* and *The Big Lebowski* and popping up in minor ways in the likes of *O Brother, Where Art Thou?*

One common Coens theme that was glimpsed in *Blood Simple* and is developed more fully in *Raising Arizona* is that of social inequality. In *Blood Simple* this was limited to the character of Marty, who owns a bar and has a comfortable lifestyle, and the way that he loses his wife to a common bartender. While Marty tries to wield power, however, he isn't very good at it and so the theme is not strongly pronounced. In *Raising Arizona* society is clearly divided into haves and have-nots. Not only does Nathan Arizona have a successful business, a large house and the respect of the community, but he also has more children than he could wish for. (His children are also the result of money, because Florence needed to have expensive fertility treatments in order to conceive.) He's a ubiquitous figure, so much so that Hi presumes that the audience will recognise the name. Note that during the chase sequence his advertisement is on the TV in the living room.

The question that critics frequently raise in relation to this common theme of wealthy, older men wielding power (Sidney J Mussburger from *The Hudsucker Proxy*, Wade Gustafson from *Fargo* and the eponymous Big Lebowski are other examples) is whether it is intended to be a criticism of Western capitalist society. This is in spite of the fact that the Coens have asserted that they aren't interested in tackling such themes, and this is often borne out in the films: in the case of *Raising Arizona* Nathan is shown to be a decent guy at the end. It seems more likely that such characters are included because they are so useful for drama. The Coens are fascinated by losers and their desperate attempts to rise above their station in life, and in order to place conflict into the story it's important that life's winners are also present. When the have-nots want something they try to steal it from those who have. (Indeed, if the Coens were *really* interested in depicting social inequalities their films would probably not show poor people stealing from rich people, but poor people stealing from other poor people. This is what tends to happen in reality, since the rich don't usually come into contact with the poor at all.) As the Coens are fond of reminding us, their films are primarily designed to entertain (see **Barton Fink**).

One of the best things about *Raising Arizona* is that it doesn't beat about the bush in terms of setting up and resolving its situation. The film begins with a lengthy pre-titles sequence that takes the form of a montage with a voice-over from one of the participants, starting with Hi's first meeting with Ed at the mugshot and ending with their decision to abduct one of the Arizona quints. It tells the audience everything they need to know about the story so far, setting them up quickly for the main plot. The title sequence then gives the audience a conscious break to absorb what they've been told, then the film proper begins, in a non-montage format to indicate that the interesting bit has arrived. This starts with Hi in the quints' bedroom, trying to take one of the babies, and ends with him (and Ed) putting Nathan Junior back, as the film comes full circle. This final scene also eschews the wacky camera style of the rest of the film, indicating that the madness that possessed the characters during these events has passed. Having used the montage technique to make the prologue distinct from the rest of the film, the Coens go on to similarly differentiate the epilogue by making it a dream sequence that may, or may not, be true (although Hi's dream of the Lone Biker turns out to be precognitive and Hi believes that the dream may have been responsible for bringing him into the world).

This film also sees the Coens play with standard cinematic devices for the first time. Immediately after the opening credits, a series of captions appear, telling the audience the place, the date and the time. This does serve a purpose to a certain extent, since it acts as a signal that the narrative is moving out of the montage format that has been used to tell the story thus far. However, it seems to be there mainly so that the Coens can pull a little joke by having Nathan Arizona look at his watch just as a caption comes up to tell the audience that it's 8.45 p.m., before Nathan can announce it himself. What's funny about this is that the audience isn't expecting a further caption to come up, having already been told when and where this is taking place. The addition of a more specific caption to give the exact time seems to appear purely for the sake of pre-empting Nathan, and it gives the impression that the film has a life of its own, going over the heads of its characters to speak directly to the audience. This early joke is an effective way of establishing a degree of artifice early on and therefore introduces the viewer to both the overall style of the movie and the Coens' sense of humour.

GENRE: *Raising Arizona* sees the Coens playing it about as straight as they ever do and going for a caper comedy. All of the themes are treated lightly, from armed robbery to child abduction. It joins a particular strain of comedies where the heroes are criminals, which can be tricky to carry off, because while the characters need to be sympathetic the filmmakers need to consider whether they should condone the crime.

A scriptwriter has three options when approaching this problem. The characters can either get away with the crime (which is unusual, hence the enforced unresolved ending of *The Italian Job* (Peter Collinson, 1969)), get caught (which is a bit of a downer) or manage to cover up the deed by returning everything to how it was at the beginning – in other words, reverse their actions. The Coens take the last option, which poses its own problems because it means an overall lack of forward movement. At the end of the movie, Nathan Junior is returned to his rightful parents and Gale and Evelle break back into prison; although these returns to the status quo are neatly and convincingly effected this does make *Raising Arizona* slightly less satisfying in plot terms than other Coen films. The emotional journey of the characters is substantial but nothing really changes, just as the genre demands. In later movies they would embrace the down ending that comes with having the hero get caught (see **The Man Who Wasn't There**) or just dispense with heroes altogether (as in the lengthy sections of *Fargo* which don't feature Marge Gunderson).

The film also wound up fitting into another 'genre', although this happened by accident. It's an odd phenomenon when similar movies arrive at the same time, despite being made independently from each other, and the result can be that a genre emerges overnight and then dies off just as quickly. Similarly, *Raising Arizona* would up being pigeonholed with the 'baby comedies' released close to it, such as *Three Men and a Baby* (Leonard Nimoy, 1987) and *Baby Boom* (Charles Shyer, 1987). It's a much better film than either of those but the association seemed to make the public receptive to it. The late 1980s seemed particularly prone to this: a similar thing happened the next year when 'body-swap comedy' became an accepted genre for a few months, around the releases of *Big* (Penny Marshall, 1988) and *Vice Versa* (Brian Gilbert, 1988). Both of these cases can be related to prevailing trends in America at that time: the 'body-swap' typically involves adults becoming children and/or children becoming men, reflecting nostalgia for more innocent times, while the baby movie reflects the obsession with family (see **EVER AMERICA**).

EVER AMERICA: As with *Blood Simple*, *Raising Arizona* is contemporary (there are direct references to Reagan's presidency, Yoda pyjamas and *Dallas*). This would be their last movie set in the present day until *Intolerable Cruelty*. Again, it's a reflection on the world around it, electing to comment on the Western family unit.

As tends to be the case when the prevailing politics of the time are right wing, in the 1980s family was considered very important and indeed this is what everybody in *Raising Arizona* prizes above all else. It's debatable just how implicitly critical the Coens are being of this attitude. There are two 'proper' family units present in the film, the Arizonas and Glen and Dot's family. While Nathan initially seems like a tyrant and a cynic, barking orders to subordinates and plugging his furniture store when speaking to the press about his kidnapped son, he reveals a far softer side at the end of the movie and advises Hi and Ed to stick together. Glen and Dot's family are clearly utterly awful: Glen is a boorish racist, Dot treats her kids like puppies and the children themselves are unruly and destructive (they are first seen in a superb cutaway shot, pounding Hi's car with sticks). However, it seems more likely that they are intended not as a general comment on the family as an institution but on how much more deserving Hi and Ed are and how unfair it is that they can't have children of their own.

While *Raising Arizona* does reflect a philosophy of the human need to start families, the situation in America is hardly portrayed as ideal. It's the system that prevents Hi and Ed from adopting, a system that Hi has set himself against long ago (and which he blames for all of his problems). Nevertheless, Nathan Junior seems to stir parental longings in every person who sees him, such as Glen and Dot and even Gale and Evelle: both pairs initially plan to hand him over for the reward money but end up deciding that they'd rather keep Nathan Junior for themselves. The two escaped cons form a particularly unorthodox family unit but their concern for the baby is genuine.

What's also very noticeable is that each person who takes charge of Nathan Junior names him after themselves: Glen wants to call him Glen Junior and Gale names him Gale Junior. Hi and Ed's affection for each other is such that Ed refers to him as Hi Junior and Hi calls him Ed Junior (during Glen and Dot's visit), which is laudable in its own mad way but still reflects a desire to mould the child after themselves in a fashion that is ever so slightly sinister. Everybody who gets hold of him tries to make him into a miniature version of themselves rather than a person in his own right, in what seems to be a comment on just *why* people become so keen to have a child of their own. Not unusually, its commentary was taken as endorsement in some quarters. Mike Zink, pastor of Family Life Centers in Seattle, organised a picket against the movie, saying, 'It encourages people to view children as objects and, in that way, encourages child abuse, child neglect and kidnap.'

The choice of location is also apposite, principally because Arizona is dry and barren, like Ed's uterus. (As visual metaphors go, it isn't exactly deeply buried – Hi makes the connection himself in his opening narration – but it's worth noting for the whistling prairie wind that can be heard as Ed receives the news.) However, there's another good reason for setting it in the desert, which is that it provides a suggestive backdrop for the thread of apocalyptic fear that runs through the movie.

Timothy Wright discusses this thread in an essay entitled 'Hope in the Midst of the Nuclear Threat'. By the 1980s the threat of nuclear annihilation was something that ordinary people had been forced to learn to live with, a shadow that most people tried to ignore as far as possible. Hi and Ed are ordinary people trying to build a future for themselves, and in this context it's interesting to consider the role of the Lone Biker of the Apocalypse. Leonard Smalls does possess the menacing air of the nuclear threat, even though this is often done for comic effect. He kills defenceless animals and sets fire to plants without even touching them. Despite his evil appearance he is working on the side of the law by tracking down Gale and Evelle, and he wants to return Nathan Junior to his parents (if only for the reward money). Wright notes that 'His endorsement by the authorities augments his expanded role as an instrument of justice. His prophetic character unites the violent disposition of a Hell's Angel with the biblical horseman of the Apocalypse.' Note that he also appears to spring from Hi's nightmares, from some part of the brain where the things people don't like to think about are stored.

Set against this is Nathan Junior, a symbol of a better future which all the characters covet for different reasons. This sees them all scrabbling for hope in a world where their future seems uncertain. Hi's final defeat of the Lone Biker indicates that these fears can be overcome, while the return of Nathan Junior to his parents and Gale and Evelle's return to prison sees the characters accept that there are no quick-fix routes to improving the future and all they can do is work to improve the present. It's a good theory, although Wright notes that he cannot be sure if this is a conscious or unconscious reflection of 1980s America on the part of the Coens. While Joel and Ethan have repeatedly claimed that they don't plant hidden meanings in their films, those *Dr Strangelove* references on the washroom doors do seem pertinent in this context.

AVAILABILITY: *Raising Arizona* is available on DVD in Britain and America, although both versions come up short on extra features. The Region 1 scores slightly higher than the Region 2, since while they both feature the original trailer, the Region 1 disc also has some TV spots. That said, the TV spots are hardly a massive draw and owners of VHS copies may wish to wait for a special edition of the DVD.

THE COENS' VIEW: 'This movie is about parenting and neither of us is a parent. But we're not really intimately acquainted with murder, either, and we made a movie about killing people.' (Joel in 1987)

VERDICT: 'It's a crazy world . . . Someone oughta sell tickets.' While there is undoubtedly a sense of ironic detachment in the Coens' treatment of their material, *Raising Arizona* is still a cosy viewing experience. Its wacky camera style and the warmth of its colours gives it a thoroughly harmless feel, even though the events it depicts should be fundamentally violent and distressing in nature. The film's unwillingness to take its own situations seriously, however, may make it difficult for some viewers to care about what happens to the characters. In this case its success rests on whether the viewer finds it funny or not.

What *Raising Arizona* undoubtedly achieves is to create an internally consistent world for its story to take place in. The visual style and the language developed for the characters gives the film as a whole an aesthetic that's highly distinctive and quite unlike any other movie. That's a good thing in itself but it doesn't mean that people will like the finished product. Some viewers have reacted badly to the aesthetic, and while a portion of these would have done so because it was unfamiliar to them, others will simply dislike it because it's so stylised. This has been a problem for the Coens throughout their career, particularly with *The Hudsucker Proxy*. Thankfully these problems have lessened with time as audiences have become more au fait with Joel and Ethan's sense of humour and visual approach. Those who do engage with it will appreciate its ability to transport the viewer into a world that seems two steps to the left of reality.

Hence, the film achieves what it sets out to do and can be considered a success on that score. It's supposed to be a comedy and, sure enough, it's often very funny (Cage shows a comic touch here that has been largely underexploited in his subsequent films). It was also, and this shouldn't sound too cynical, a shrewd move to make a light comedy after *Blood Simple* as this demonstrated that they were capable of making a more straightforward audience-pleaser. The financial success of this, their second directorial effort, surely didn't hurt either. ('It's like a real cheap and shameless bid at making a commercial movie,' Ethan deadpanned at the time. 'We decided to sell out and that was the first decision.') However, while one could make a case for pretty much any of the Coens' other movies being their best, it would be a surprise to hear anybody claim that title for *Raising Arizona*.

Miller's Crossing (1990)

(Colour – 115 mins)

Circle Films Presents a Ted and Jim Pedas, Ben Barenholtz, Bill Durkin Production
Directed by Joel Coen
Produced by Ethan Coen
Written by Joel Coen and Ethan Coen
Co-producer: Mark Silverman
Line Producer: Graham Place
Executive Producer: Ben Barenholtz
Director of Photography: Barry Sonnenfeld
Production Designer: Dennis Gassner
Costume Designer: Richard Hornung
Edited by Michael R Miller
Music by Carter Burwell
'Danny Boy' Sung by Frank Patterson
Supervising Sound Editor: Skip Lievsay
Casting by Donna Isaacson CSA and John Lyons CSA

CAST: Gabriel Byrne (*Tom Reagan*), Marcia Gay Harden (*Verna*), John Turturro (*Bernie Bernbaum*), Jon Polito (*Johnny Caspar*), JE Freeman (*Eddie Dane*), Albert Finney (*Leo*), Mike Starr (*Frankie*), Al Mancini (*Tic-Tac*), Richard Woods (*Mayor Dale Levander*), Thomas Toner (*O'Doole*), Steve Buscemi (*Mink*), Mario Todisco (*Clarence 'Drop' Johnson*), Olek Krupa (*Tad*), Michael Jeter (*Adolph*), Lanny Flaherty (*Terry*), Jeanette Kontomitras (*Mrs Caspar*), Louis Charles Mounicou III (*Johnny Caspar Jr*), John McConnell (*Cop – Brian*), Danny Aiello III (*Cop – Delahanty*), Helen Jolly (*Screaming Lady*), Hilda McLean (*Landlady*), Monte Starr, Don Picard (*Gunmen in Leo's House*) Salvatore H Tornabene (*Rug Daniels*), Kevin Dearie (*Street Urchin*), Michael Badalucco (*Caspar's Driver*), Charles Ferrara (*Caspar's Butler*), Esteban Fernández, George Fernandez (*Caspar's Cousins*), Charles Gunning (*Hitman at Verna's*), Dave Drinkx (*Hitman #2*), David Darlow (*Lazarre's Messenger*), Robert LaBrosse, Carl Rooney (*Lazarre's Toughs*), Jack David Harris (*Man with Pipe Bomb*), Jery Hewitt (*Son of Erin*), Sam

Raimi (*Snickering Gunman*), John Schnauder Jr (*Cop with Bullhorn*), Zolly Levin (*Rabbi*), Joey Ancona, Bill Raye (*Boxers*), And Featuring the Remarkable Voice of William Preston Robertson

SUMMARY: An East Coast city in the 1920s, run by Irish gang boss Leo O'Bannion. Another boss, Johnny Caspar, asks permission to kill Jewish bookmaker Bernie Bernbaum, but Leo refuses because he is in love with Bernie's sister Verna. Unbeknown to Leo, his advisor, Tom Reagan, is also sleeping with Verna.

Leo has Verna followed by one of his men, Rug, who then turns up dead. Leo believes that Caspar killed Rug and tries to close Caspar down. Tom has a gambling debt that both Bernie and Caspar offer to settle, but Tom refuses both. Tom concludes that Caspar didn't kill Rug because he's still trying to cut a deal to kill Bernie. Instead, Tom reasons that Verna killed Rug, but she won't admit it. Tom voices his suspicions to Leo, reluctantly offering as evidence that Tom was with Verna on the night Rug died. Leo dismisses Tom from his service. The balance of power is tipping towards Caspar and Tom goes to him to get Leo off his back. Caspar wants Tom to dispose of Bernie personally as a token of good faith. Bernie begs Tom not to, knowing that Tom has never killed anybody before. Unseen, Tom lets Bernie escape and tells him to skip town, but Bernie returns to cause trouble for Tom.

Tom plays all sides off against each other, convincing Caspar that the Dane has been scamming him with a guy called Mink. (Mink has actually been running scams with Bernie.) The Dane tries to prove that Tom didn't kill Bernie, but they find what seems to be Bernie's body at Miller's Crossing. Bernie calls Tom and confirms that the unidentifiable body was actually Mink. The Dane eventually realises this and tries to kill Tom, but Caspar believes Tom's story and kills the Dane. Tom tricks Bernie into killing Caspar for him, then Tom kills Bernie himself to make it look like Caspar got him in the shoot-out. It turns out that Mink killed Rug out of paranoia. Leo realises that Tom was playing Caspar off and asks Tom to work for him again, but Tom turns the offer down.

DEVELOPMENT: Again, the Coens decided to make a film that was consciously different from their last and settled on the idea of doing a gangster movie. Their starting point was an image: 'Big guys in overcoats in the woods – the incongruity of urban gangsters in a forest setting.' The Coens were to spend a long time trying to come up with a title for this film – for a while it was called *The Bighead*, after a nickname they had applied to Tom Reagan – but kept drifting towards the location of that first scene: Miller's Crossing. ('We couldn't think of a better title,' says Ethan. 'Sometimes they come, and sometimes they don't.')

'We weren't thinking so much of gangster pictures, just novels,' Joel says of the influences on *Miller's Crossing*. The prime influence was Dashiell Hammett, whose work Joel says uses the gangster genre as a vehicle to talk about people. 'In Hammett, the plot is like a big jigsaw puzzle that can be seen in the background. It may make some internal sense, but the momentum of the characters is more important.' The production notes for *Miller's Crossing* acknowledge the influence of Hammett's 1929 novel *Red Harvest* (the one that gave *Blood Simple* its title) on the Coens' script. However, there is no mention of another Hammett novel, 1931's *The Glass Key*, whose central character, Ned Beaumont, is the right-hand man of Paul Madvig, the boss of a corrupt city. The senator's son has been murdered and Madvig seems the likely suspect: Ned Beaumont delves into the crime in the hope of preserving the balance of power in the city. The similarities between *The Glass Key* and *Miller's Crossing* have sometimes been overstated: some have suggested that the Hammett estate could have sued for plagiarism. It isn't the same story, but a number of similar characters are present and the relationship between Ned Beaumont and Paul Madvig is very similar to that between Tom and Leo. '[Tom is] the quintessential Hammett guy,' says Joel. 'You're not let in on how much he knows and what exactly he's up to. He tests the other characters to see what they want and uses that to his advantage.' Adds Ethan: 'He's got principles and interest, and I don't think he's a pure man.' It's the nature of people who do bad things that interests Hammett, and clearly it interests the Coens as well.

There's also a character called Bernie Despain in *The Glass Key*, a bookmaker who skips town because he owes money to Ned Beaumont. Hammet describes him as 'a small man, short and stringy, with a head too large for his body' and a face that was 'swarthy, large-featured except for the eyes, and strongly lined across the forehead and down from the nostrils past the mouth.' It seems likely that Joel and Ethan had this character in mind when they created Bernie Bernbaum.

One important element of the Hammett narrative is that it's highly convoluted, and accordingly the Coens started to weave a knotted story from their starting point of a character playing two opposing sides off against each other, but a few months into the process they got completely stuck. Having set numerous problems for Tom in the first half of the script, they found themselves unable to resolve them in the second half. They talked to various colleagues at length and stayed over at friends' homes in an effort to shake themselves out of the block they'd worked themselves into, but nothing seemed to work. In the end they halted work on the gangster script and picked up another idea that was inspired by their difficulties, a story about a screenwriter with writer's block called *Barton Fink*. Three weeks later they returned to *Miller's Crossing* and found their heads clear enough to finish the job. The script was finally completed eight months after they had started, although they wound up doing a rewrite of that second half before production began (see **CASTING**).

REFERENCES: The opening scene, as Caspar explains his problem to Leo in Leo's office, immediately puts the viewer in mind of *The Godfather* (Francis Ford Coppola, 1972).

The name of the Dane recalls the central character of *The Killers* (Robert Siodmak, 1946), a boxer known to all as 'The Swede'.

'Drop' Johnson has a souvenir from one of his boxing matches on his apartment wall, a poster advertising his bout with a man named Lars Thorvald. The name of his opponent is taken from Raymond Burr's character in *Rear Window* (Alfred Hitchcock, 1954).

As with *Raising Arizona* there is also a forward reference to a later Coen film. Tom's apartment block is named the Barton Arms, after the lead character from the script they'd written in the middle of work on *Miller's Crossing*.

CASTING: The role of Tom Reagan was not written with anybody in mind, but from the casting call the Coens chose to engage the services of Irish actor Gabriel Byrne. This had a substantial impact on the movie's development. 'When I read the script out loud to myself,' Byrne recalls, 'I said "My God, this could have been written by somebody from Dublin!" ' This had not been the Coens' intention. 'The part was originally an American part,' Byrne says, but he suggested at the audition that he could read the lines in his own accent. 'We were sceptical,' says Joel, 'but we said, "Fine, go ahead, try it." He did it and we liked the way it sounded.' Byrne notes that 'as Ethan says, they "got mugged by the whole Irish concept".' The essential character, however, remained in place with Byrne in the role. 'When we sat down and talked about it – not very long because they're not into a lot of big discussions about character and stuff – the essential thing was that he *had* to be inscrutable,' Byrne says, noting that he was instructed to play the part deadpan throughout and never give anything away to the audience.

The Coens had written the role of Leo with Trey Wilson, who had played Nathan Arizona in *Raising Arizona*, in mind. Wilson agreed to play the part but sadly died of a stroke just two days before shooting began. The Coens discovered that the esteemed British actor Albert Finney was immediately available and sent him the script. 'It seemed like a comic strip, in a sense, when I first read it,' Finney remembers. 'The casualness of the violence amused me a great deal. But it's extremely rich stuff.' He agreed to take the part and, in the event, production only had to be delayed by ten days, during which the Coens took the opportunity to do a substantial rewrite on the still-troublesome second half of the script. However, they didn't make any changes to Leo's character to accommodate the enforced recasting (Leo barely appears in the second half anyway). 'What's strange is that the part would never have been written without Trey in mind,' Ethan says, 'whereas now it's impossible for us to imagine any other actor than Finney in the Leo role.' As the Coens had already agreed that Byrne would use an Irish accent for his performance, Finney decided to inflect his affected American accent with an Irish brogue as well.

The role of Johnny Caspar, Leo's rival, was also not cast in the way that Joel and Ethan had anticipated. 'I read the script in August,' says Jon Polito, 'and I said, "I only want to play Johnny Caspar." ' The Coens had written the character as being around 55 years of age: Polito was 38. 'They wanted me to read for all the other gangster characters, but I said no.' Polito's work had mostly involved crime drama of various kinds, ranging from *Compromising Positions* (Frank Perry, 1985) to three different roles in *The Equaliser* on TV. After *Miller's Crossing* he was to work with the Coens on *Barton Fink*, *The Hudsucker Proxy*, *The Big Lebowski* and *The Man Who Wasn't There*.

The Coens also took the opportunity to cast John Turturro, whom they had seen doing theatre in New York and wanted to write a part for. (By the time production got moving, they had written not one but two roles for the actor, since they had penned *Barton Fink* with him in mind.) As well as his theatre experience, Turturro had worked with three of the great New York-based directors on *Hannah and her Sisters* (Woody Allen, 1986), *The Color of Money* (Martin Scorsese, 1986) and, most prominently, *Do the Right Thing* (Spike Lee, 1989). As well as *Barton Fink*, the Coens would go on to employ him for *The Big Lebowski* and *O Brother, Where Art Thou?* – with none of his characters being particularly sympathetic. The Coens feel that this is his main strength: 'It's amazing how he allows himself to be humiliated in front of the camera.' Also arriving from the New York stage, in her first major film role, was Marcia Gay Harden.

Two future Coen regulars took small roles. Steve Buscemi, soon to become an icon of indie filmmaking with too many film roles to list, played Mink here and returned for the Coens' next four movies. *Miller's Crossing* provided Michael Badalucco, later to appear in *O Brother, Where Art Thou?* and *The Man Who*

Wasn't There, with one of his earliest film roles. There were also two cameos in the film from Coen colleagues: an uncredited Frances McDormand took the role of Caspar's secretary, while Sam Raimi made a brief appearance as the smirking gunman who dies violently in the siege sequence.

PRODUCTION: After the strong profit margin of *Raising Arizona* the major Hollywood studios had become more interested in the Coens, resulting in Warner Brothers offering them the chance to direct the *Batman* movie that it had been trying to get off the ground since 1979. However, they knew that they wouldn't get complete control over the finished product and decided to stick to their own projects. (In the end, Tim Burton made a great success of *Batman* in 1989.) After getting a substantial advance from Fox for *Raising Arizona*, Circle Films cut a deal with the studio to finance Joel and Ethan's new movie. Fox provisionally agreed to supply the $14 million budget of *Miller's Crossing* on the strength of a two-line pitch, with the option to back out once they had seen the completed script. Fox didn't back out, even though the deal stipulated that they would have no say over any aspect of the film. The finished product would arrive with them ready for duplication and distribution.

The Coens started out production proper on *Miller's Crossing* by writing four pages of description regarding how they envisaged the locations. Along with line producer Graham Place they took these notes to three different cities to see how they matched up. Despite the fact that the movie's setting is an unnamed analogue of Chicago, the closest match turned out to be New Orleans. There was a movement during the 1930s to preserve the city's architecture and the loose soil of the region meant that few tall buildings had ever been constructed there. 'New Orleans is sort of a depressed city; it hasn't been gentrified,' Ethan says. 'There's a lot of architecture that hasn't been touched, storefront windows that haven't been replaced in the past 60 years.' This meant that, in 1989, much of New Orleans still looked as it did in the 1920s. Another factor was that the Coens had decided that they wanted the location work to have an ominous feel, which meant that the shoot was scheduled to take place during the winter of late 1989 and early 1990. However, they didn't want to risk a snowfall in the middle of production and so a southern city seemed more sensible.

The inhabitants of New Orleans were very co-operative during filming: two institutions that had never before permitted a film crew through their doors – the long-established gentlemen's club the International House and the exclusive Louise S McGehee School – changed their minds for *Miller's Crossing*. The House doubled for Leo's club while the School doubled for Caspar's house. Some sequences required sets to be built and these were also done in New Orleans. The Coens hired a large garage from another set of brothers: a firm of local real-estate brokers called Toye Brothers, who held the property on New Orleans's Annunciation Street.

This being a very different kind of story to *Raising Arizona*, the Coens also decided to adopt a distinctly different camera style. '*Raising Arizona* was low and wacky and the camera was a character,' Barry Sonnenfeld says, noting that the wide-angle lenses used on that film meant that the viewer was not guided towards looking at any particular object in the frame. They elected to use long lenses for *Miller's Crossing*. 'With longer lenses, you can really focus the audience's attention, and since this is such a word-driven movie, you want to bring the audience's attention much more to the characters.' The camera work on *Miller's Crossing* is much slower and more reserved, with actors often shot from a slight distance rather than in close-up, reflecting the guarded nature of the characters. It makes use of traditional filmmaking devices such as the over-the-shoulder shot (it used to be accepted practice in Hollywood to shoot a conversation by viewing each actor from a position just over the shoulder of the other). It also eschews the Coens' love of keeping the camera in motion, with little of their usual tracking and drifting in evidence. The film does become more stylised for a brief moment near the end, as Tom comes close to losing control of the situation at Caspar's house. When Caspar kills the Dane there are dolly rushes (zoom-ins achieved by moving the camera forward on a wheeled platform, as opposed to using a zoom lens) on 'Drop' Johnson, Caspar and Tom, as Tom watches the violence unfold around him.

Miller's Crossing is probably the Coens' most deliberately designed film apart from *The Hudsucker Proxy*, and not just in terms of its evocative period setting. Production designer Dennis Gassner (who learned his craft at Francis Ford Coppola's Zoetrope Studios and came on board with the Coens when their previous designer, Jane Musky, proved unavailable) worked with Barry Sonnenfeld to create a continuity of colour throughout the film. 'We wanted this movie to look handsome,' Sonnenfeld says, 'so we made everything very dark. The colours of the sets and costumes were muted, and there were lots of dark greens and browns.' This chimed well with the Coens' initial idea of the incongruity of having gangsters in the woods – even when they aren't in the woods, the colours suggest that they are. Gassner put together a flow-chart of coloured paper that broke down the film's dominant colours on a scene-by-scene basis, a technique that was enthusiastically adopted by the Coens: 'The colours in *Miller's Crossing* are more controlled than anything we've done,' says Joel. This extended as far as switching film stock for the scenes at Miller's Crossing itself: while the rest of the movie was shot with Kodak film, Sonnenfeld advised using Fuji for the green-dominated woodland scenes 'because Fuji greens are much more muted than Kodak.'

Another of Gassner's suggestions that the Coens seized upon was that they make use of columns wherever possible. He mentioned this at their first meeting and remembers that 'Ethan said, "Yeah, right, that's what we need." Because first of all, you have trees in a forest, and architectural columns show strength – it's a manly movie.' Jimmy Otis, who was out in New Orleans scouting locations, remembers a sudden change of instructions at this point. 'The boys phoned me from New York, saying, "Go back and look at such-and-such again" – locations they had rejected. And everything I went back to that they had rejected before had immense columns.'

Gassner was naturally keen that the settings should be authentic, at one point splashing gin around a cotton mill to give it the ambience of a gin mill ('I like to provide as much detail as I can,' he says, 'so that ultimately the actors feel comfortable enough to create the characters'). However, he was equally interested in creating 'the emotional state of Tom's world, as he gravitated toward whoever seemed to have the power at any given moment.' For example, he was instructed to make Tom's apartment resemble the inside of Tom's head. 'Dennis is very low-key and incredibly organised,' Joel says. 'He's also easy to communicate with, probably because he's very script-oriented. He seemed to be coming at the story from the same fundamental level that we were.'

The most memorable sequence in the movie, for the filmmakers and the audience, was the one in which Caspar's men attempt to murder Leo at his home. 'It's about time at that point to shed a little blood,' says Ethan. 'The movie's in danger of becoming tasteful, you know?' Although it is smoothly edited in the completed movie, it was shot at two different houses and a street in an entirely different location – plus some of the interiors were done in studio. The tracking shot that opens this sequence sees impressive use of sound, as the death of Leo's watchman does not have to be enacted and yet it is still communicated successfully, making the shot easier to achieve. However, the next piece of action was somewhat tricky, involving Leo diving under his bed and shooting one of the hoods in the leg and then the head. A squib was planted on the hood's head but it didn't explode properly, something that Joel and Ethan only discovered in the cutting room, so that shot had to be remounted.

The second gunman, shot by Leo from outside the house, was played by two men for his death scene: actor Monte Starr and stunt co-ordinator Jerry Hewitt. The task of holding the heavy Thompson machine gun while it fired off wild rounds, with the squibs planted up and down the actors' backs exploding continually, was not easy. 'You have to sell that body language, taking the bullet hits,' says Ethan. 'What sells the hit is the dance. We always knew we wanted to do that.' The shudder that goes through a person when they're being riddled with machine-gun bullets was christened 'the Thompson jitterbug' by the Coens, who kept adding more elements to the gunman's death as they planned the scene, such as the chandelier, the paintings and his own toes. 'All kinds of fun things,' Joel says. 'It was a lot of fun blowing the toes off. The only regret is that it goes by so fast, you almost kind of miss it. They're a highlight.'

Albert Finney also had to deal with the wild action of the Thompson in the final part of this sequence, as he follows the hoods' car down the street and fires on it. The mischievous Coens placed a bucket behind him and challenged him to land as many spent cartridges in it as possible. Ethan notes that 'he got a very high percentage. Technically, he's a very good actor.' The Coens had become disturbingly fond of the Thompson during the production process, even though it caused a lot of retakes on account of its tendency to jam. 'The gun is incredibly loud, though,' says Joel, 'and it does vibrate. You can see it sort of jingle. The whole thing was a very satisfying experience.' The sequence was completed by the addition of the ballad 'Danny Boy' on the soundtrack (see **MUSIC**).

The final shot was the keynote image of the movie and was, Ethan says, one of the first things that the Coens had come up with, 'without really knowing how it was supposed to fit in'. This was the hat on the woodland floor that blows away in the wind. In the end it ran under the opening credits (although Tom refers to it as a dream he had and later the Dane throws Tom's hat off into the woods as they search for Bernie's body). This shot was achieved by whipping the hat away on a fishing wire: a purpose-made lightweight hat was used and the image was shot at high speed to make it appear to have been caught on the wind. In addition to this one, five identical versions of the hat were made for Gabriel Byrne to wear. 'The hat really becomes a big symbol in the film,' Ron Neter, the unit manager, says. 'Every time Tom gets knocked down, the hat falls off, and people are always handing it back to him.'

The hat was the subject of much controversy while the Coens were promoting the film, as many journalists seemed obsessed with what it was supposed to mean. Gabriel Byrne had long since given up searching for hidden depths to the hat, having asked the

Coens what it meant during production. 'Joel said, "Ethan, come here, Gabe needs to know what the significance of the hat is," ' Byrne says. 'And Ethan said, "Hmm, yeah. It *is* significant." And then walked away.' Ultimately, Byrne's conclusion is that 'you don't *have* to know, you don't have to know, that's the point. It's like an abstract painting; you don't *have* to know what it's about, it produces a feeling and that's enough.'

DELETED SCENES: One scene that appears to have been dropped from the final draft before shooting would have slotted in just before Tom meets Mink on his way to see Leo. As Tom enters the club, the coat-check girl (named Beryl) slaps him. It transpires, as she launches a torrent of invective at him, that Tom told Beryl that he would pick her up from work the night before and did not keep his promise.

Photos exist from another cut scene, indicating that it was shot but not used. This takes place in a speakeasy as Tom asks two of Caspar's guys (Bert and Rooster) about the state of play of the war with Leo. This is a lengthy sequence, also involving the police arguing whether a man they've just killed worked for Leo or Caspar, and it fits just after the Dane sees Verna leaving the gym. It seems designed to give a flavour of the war-torn city but its omission gave the film – and Tom himself – greater focus.

A final cut scene was supposed to fit between the penultimate and final scenes of the film, with Tom telling Verna that he didn't kill Bernie. It appears that this was never shot. Since the overall effect is that she still doesn't believe that he's being straight with her (his claim that he passed out in a bar and returned to his apartment to find Caspar and Bernie dead outside is improbable and she slaps him at the end of this exchange), the scene is dispensable. Her cold shoulder to Tom at Bernie's funeral says it all.

MUSIC: With the Irish flavour of the film becoming stronger as a result of Gabriel Byrne's contribution, it began to seem an appropriate starting point for the score. 'When we were finishing the movie we started listening to a lot of Irish music,' says Ethan.

'Gabriel gave us a whole list of stuff. The tone and feeling of the music seemed really appropriate.' Joel adds, 'The song on which Carter Burwell based the main theme is an old ballad suggested by Gabriel.' The song in question is called 'Come Back to Erin Carter'. All of the songs were old enough to be in the public domain, so Burwell was free to plunder them as he saw fit. The composer was also required to take his craft into new territory. 'In *Miller's Crossing*, we all agreed that it should be an orchestral score,' Burwell says, 'but we also knew that I knew nothing about orchestral music! That didn't faze [Joel and Ethan] at all.' Pragmatically, Burwell learned how to write for an orchestra and took the job.

The Coens had decided to use 'Danny Boy' for the attempt on Leo's life even before Byrne made his suggestions. Since the music is diagetic (i.e. it can be heard by the characters and is therefore part of the fiction of the film) most filmmakers would probably have tracked down a contemporary version of the song, a recording that people would really have listened to in the 1920s. However, the Coens decided to make a new recording of the song and enlisted the Irish tenor and actor Frank Patterson to sing it (hence his prominent credit on the movie). This is the key to why it works so well in context. The new version was paced to fit the finished scene as a part of the score, rather than added in as a piece of stock music, and Patterson was able to watch the action and match the rhythm of his vocal to the unfolding violence.

'Because it's emotional and overwrought, it worked as a counterpoint to other aspects of the movie,' Joel says of the *Miller's Crossing* score. 'Our thinking sort of evolved on that and turned 180 degrees around as we started listening to different things.'

CRITICAL RECEPTION: One can see the standard critical line on the Coens beginning to harden in Roger Ebert's review of *Miller's Crossing*, although he was kinder to it than he was to *Raising Arizona*. 'The pleasures of the film are largely technical,' he wrote in the *Chicago Sun-Times* on 5 October 1990. 'It is likely to be most appreciated by movie lovers who will enjoy its resonance with films of the past,' he continued, but he believed that the narrative was not strong enough to involve the viewer. He further complained that, 'This doesn't look like a gangster movie, it looks like a commercial intended to look like a gangster movie.' Not only were the sets and costumes overdesigned in Ebert's eyes, so were the plot and the dialogue.

The film didn't appeal to Vincent Canby either, another reviewer who had been unmoved by *Raising Arizona*. '*Miller's Crossing* wants to be both fun for the uninitiated and for those who are hip to the conventions of the genre that is being recalled,' he wrote in the *New York Times* on 21 September 1990. 'The real world impinges on the movie only by accident.' Canby was one of those viewers for whom the film's Irishness posed some problems, noting that he found the movie difficult to follow despite its simple plot, and a major factor in this was that Byrne's dialogue was not always comprehensible to him. His overall impression was one of 'so what?'

Gary Giddins of the *Village Voice* went even further, regarding the film as actively distasteful. 'Joel and Ethan Coen may represent the apotheosis of classroom cinema,' he wrote on 25 September 1990. '*Miller's Crossing* is so clever about its sources, which are categorical but unacknowledged, that it has little life of its own.' He went on to complain that the film had gratuitously made its less appealing characters either gay, Jewish or both, noting that 'the film has nothing to say about the nature of sexual outlawry in the '20s: it merely sets up [Bernie, Mink and the Dane] as objects of ridicule and underscores the ridicule by making them queer.' Bernie was deemed the most offensive character, although Giddins did not mention that the Coens themselves are Jewish.

By contrast, *Variety* was optimistic about the film's chances of success, predicting that it would be better-remembered than the similarly themed and higher-profile *Dick Tracy* (Warren Beatty, 1990). The reason? 'Substance – the missing ingredient in so many of the year's flashy filmic exercises – is here in spades.' All aspects of the film came in for praise, except the title that was felt to be 'rather bland'. In particular, the reviewer felt that, unlike many other recent films, the violence of *Miller's Crossing* was justified by the narrative, and they appeared to find a heart to *Miller's*

Crossing that others did not. 'Classic-quality outing surely will put Fox square at the box-office if the studio's marketers can mount a campaign as good as this film.' Unfortunately they didn't.

On its arrival in Britain, *Empire* called *Miller's Crossing* 'a very clever, stylish story of friendship, loyalty and betrayal', singling out the visuals for particular praise: 'It looks great, although almost too audaciously at times.' The attempt on Leo's life was particularly noteworthy in the reviewer's opinion, although the reviewer encouraged the Coens to put aside their influences with their next film and create something that stood free of references and allusions. *Time Out*'s Geoff Andrew, however, found plenty of depth in *Miller's Crossing*. '[The Coens'] latest operates both on the surface, as a genre film, and on a deeper level, as an ironic commentary on that genre which, though witty, never lapses into simple parody,' he wrote in the 13 February 1991 issue. Andrew was highly impressed with the film's structuring in all departments and rated it as the Coens' best yet.

Steve Jenkins, while restrained in his praise, thought *Miller's Crossing* an improvement over *Raising Arizona*. 'The film's particular strength derives from a sense that the film-makers have tapped a kind of essence of Hammett, outside any specific theme or plot,' he wrote in the February 1991 issue of *Monthly Film Bulletin*, 'and worked outwards from this, basing their own highly expressive visual and rhythmic style on solid generic foundations.' Jenkins was particularly impressed at the manner in which the Coens frequently subverted the genre in which they had chosen to work, and he also commended the film's pacing, where a period of calm would be punctuated by sudden violence. He had previously criticised *Raising Arizona* for being a little *too* frenetic, with the characters not given space to breathe: evidently he found the style of *Miller's Crossing* more satisfying.

Geoff Brown of *The Times* agreed, noting that the film could not be described as an action movie in spite of its graphic violence. 'Words dominate,' he wrote on 14 February 1991, describing the script as 'a masterful piece of Hardboiled Baroque'. However, he did complain that the central characters were not sufficiently engaging. 'With its cipher of a hero and precise, brooding visuals, *Miller's Crossing* becomes almost an abstract distillation of the gangster genre,' Brown said, noting a sense of self-consciousness permeating the whole and resulting in 'a film hemmed in by quotation marks'.

BOX OFFICE: In a quite astonishing piece of poor timing, the Coens' period gangster movie *Miller's Crossing* was released on 22 September 1990, just three days after Warner Brothers' period gangster movie *GoodFellas* (Martin Scorsese, 1990). While they are very different movies ('I love it,' Joel said of *GoodFellas*, 'but the story and style are completely different, like day and night'), they were obviously gunning for similar markets and *GoodFellas* completely swamped the Coens' movie at the box office. *Miller's Crossing* grossed just $4,693,759 on its American release while *GoodFellas* managed almost exactly ten times as much ($46,743,809). 'It's difficult to analyse why it failed,' says Joel, 'but it was still a disappointment to us.'

The Hudsucker Proxy is often quoted as being the Coens' only true commercial failure because the others cost so little that it must have been easy to make the money back. However, as *Miller's Crossing* cost $14 million to make, even when overseas box office, video sales and TV screenings are taken into account, it may not have gone into profit, even now.

AWARDS: *Miller's Crossing* only managed to grab one award, for Best Director at the 1990 San Sebastian Film Festival. However, it was also selected to open the New York Film Festival of that year.

DIALOGUE TO SKIP BACK FOR:

Verna: 'Leo has got the right idea. I like him. He's honest and he has a heart.'

Tom: 'Then it's true what they say. Opposites attract.'

Caspar: (sending his son out of the office) 'Take the kid and wait in the car. Give him a penny, boys!'

Frankie: 'I ain't got a penny, boss.'
Caspar: 'That's a penny you owe him.'

Dane: 'Where's Leo?'
Mobster: 'If I tell ya, how do I know you won't kill me?'
Dane: 'Because if you told me and I killed ya and you were lyin' I wouldn't get to kill ya then.'

ANALYSIS: *Miller's Crossing* is all about being in control, and the fact that it is often necessary to maintain a façade if you wish to do so. As Tom tells Leo, in a town where feudalism rules, the town is run by whoever can convince the population that they are in charge. If a person doesn't maintain the correct appearance it can bring them down. Tom's ability to anticipate (and, to an extent, control) the reactions of others keeps him in control of the situation for most of the film, only slipping because he's not as ruthless as he seems. Although he frequently says that people can never completely know each other, the audience can see that he knows most of the other players in this drama very well indeed.

What sets Tom apart from the other characters is that he doesn't make decisions based on personal attachments. He is permanently neutral: as Verna says, he doesn't like or hate anybody. In fact, you can tell that his bonhomie when he meets with Caspar for the second time is an act because he never usually smiles. He seems to like Leo but isn't afraid to lose him as a friend, and he's willing to sell out the likes of Bernie and Verna for the sake of keeping the peace. Meanwhile, Leo is loyal to Verna and Verna is loyal to Bernie, while the Dane is loyal to Mink and Mink, too, is loyal to Bernie. Tom even manages to win the trust of Caspar and turn him against the Dane. Because of this, Tom's biggest problem is Bernie, who is equally willing to sacrifice everybody else – although Bernie's reasons are more selfish than Tom's. Bernie has embraced being disliked and mistrusted as a way of life, perhaps as a way of dealing with the disadvantages of being Jewish.

Note that none of the film's numerous racial slurs against Jews and Italians come from Tom – as somebody who never takes anything for granted, he doesn't hold prejudices. He dislikes Bernie not because Bernie is Jewish but because he threatens the status quo. Tom doesn't particularly like having to sacrifice somebody but he is aware that more people will die if the war is not averted and he's comfortable with that trade-off. It isn't just that Tom doesn't want to kill people; he seems to dislike violence full stop. While Bernie accuses him of being unwilling to dirty his own hands, his reaction to violent acts is clear distaste. There are two examples of this in the scene where the Dane tries to kill him, as he flinches when Caspar kills the Dane and stops him from beating 'Drop' Johnson around the head. He is constantly being beaten up and rarely fights back: when he resorts to beating Caspar's thug with the chair, his attacker is amazed. It seems that Tom's aversion to violence is well known, as is the fact that he has never killed anybody. The one time when it would be more prudent for him to do so, out in the woods with Bernie, he can't bring himself to do it.

This is later shown to be a big mistake, as with Bernie out of the way Tom's task would have been a good deal easier. Bernie doesn't respect Tom's mercy, returning to Tom's apartment to compromise his position with Caspar (and this time he sits in the opposite chair, suggesting the shift of power in their relationship). Even then, however, Bernie finds it hard to get the upper hand, becoming slightly upset when Tom plays it cool and demanding that Tom stop making smart-mouthed comments. He is, however, possessed of a misplaced arrogance, casually stating that if Tom had caught him, he'd have just cried again like he did at Miller's Crossing. He holds Tom's mercy in contempt and it's little surprise that Tom kills him at the end, even though this does break his moral code. He isn't about to make the same mistake again.

As the relationships between the characters unfold the viewer sometimes gets the sense that something is being left unsaid, which points the way towards a homosexual love triangle between Bernie, Mink and the Dane, although it's off-screen and mostly coded so as not to scare away the less enlightened portions of the audience. The first hint of this is during Mink's only on-screen appearance (a scene-stealing performance from Buscemi). Mink's already nervous disposition becomes more nervous still when Tom asks just what Mink is doing hanging around with Bernie and Mink stresses that he and Bernie are only friends. Things become more explicit when more is revealed about Eddie Dane: Mink is described as 'Eddie Dane's boy' by Caspar and others, suggesting that the relationship is common knowledge but not spoken of. The Dane's attitude towards women is demonstrated when he meets Verna and she escapes his clutches, as he appears to believe that all women are 'whores' and his attitude towards them borders on the psychotic. This is indicative of a certain 'macho' homosexuality that can grow from an idealisation of masculinity combined with a complete antipathy towards women. Take into account the Dane's rage when he believes that Tom has killed Mink, and a mirror of the film's heterosexual love triangle (Tom, Verna and Leo) emerges. (Oh, and it's worth noting that, when Mink is revealed as Rug's killer, Tom has already told us that Rug was killed with a woman's gun – which, in a piece of genius plotting, throws Tom off and leads him to suspect Verna instead.)

Before anybody tries levelling an accusation of homophobia at the Coens for making the gay characters in *Miller's Crossing* the least likeable ones (namely the Dane and Bernie), it's worth considering that there is a possible gay subtext in the dynamic between Tom and Leo, a reading which has become popular with many Coen commentators. Leo is the only person to whom Tom has any loyalty, and even when he 'betrays' Leo it's for his own good (sometimes you have to hurt the one you love . . .). This might also account for the passionless nature of Tom's relationship with Verna (he sleeps with her because it's the closest he can get to Leo) and his unwillingness to work for Leo again when Leo and Verna get engaged. Verna suggests that Tom is jealous of her relationship with Leo: Tom's reaction is unreadable and it's noticeable that Verna fails to specify who he's supposed to be jealous *of*, although she clearly believes that he wants her to himself. Note also that the Coens do not employ a voice-over like Hi's in *Raising Arizona*, despite the fact that *Miller's Crossing* has a more complex plot and is arguably in greater need of one. It is also in keeping with the hard-boiled school of crime fiction (and the films based on such fiction) to provide a commentary from the central character. The fact that Tom has no such narrative voice suggests that the Coens wish his motives to remain ambiguous. (The audience does get a small insight into his mind in the title sequence, which seems to be the dream that he later explains to Verna and which, like Hi's, seems to be precognitive. The hat didn't change into something else because this is not a fantastical dream, but a vision of something that will happen to Tom later on.)

There is the question of the portrayal of Verna as the film's only female character and how sympathetic it is, since she takes the role of crime fiction's *femme fatale*. The role is traditional but paints a rather negative view of women as manipulating their sexuality to get what they want. Verna certainly fits the bill in that one of the male characters goes with her wishes against his better judgement, and she is openly using him for her own ends. However, this is balanced by the fact that she uses Leo for unselfish ends. At best the *femme fatale* is usually trying to get material wealth from the man she seduces, and at worst she manipulates him to get him to kill somebody else, but Verna sticks to Leo in order to get protection for her brother. (Not that Bernie seems to appreciate it that much, painting a negative picture of his sister to Tom and even suggesting that she was interested in incestuous sex with him.)

GENRE: Again, because the Coens have taken 'inspiration' from one of the classic American crime writers and applied their own idiosyncratic visual style to it, *Miller's Crossing* has the style of a noir. However, it's worth noting that Dashiell Hammett's books were never embraced by the noir school in the way that fellow Coen touchstones Raymond Chandler and James M Cain were. The most famous film to be based on a Hammett novel, *The Maltese Falcon* (John Huston, 1941) is often credited with kick-starting the noir movement, but although it set a trend for detective stories it is fairly conventional in terms of style and does not visually resemble noir. There are a number of movies from the year or so prior to *The Maltese Falcon* which show the noir hallmarks more strongly (the visual influence of European expressionist cinema along with flashback narrative can be seen in films like Boris Ingster's 1940 movie *Stranger on the Third Floor*). Thematically *Miller's Crossing* owes as much to the 1930s school of gangster movies, such as *The Public Enemy* (William Wellman, 1931) and *Angels With Dirty Faces* (Michael Curtiz, 1938).

The most noir-ish element of the film is its plot, which is deliberately confusing so as to disorientate the viewer. The world of noir is a nightmarish, claustrophobic one in which the characters (and viewer) become trapped, unable to relax and desperately trying to keep up with events. From the very first scene of *Miller's Crossing* the audience hears characters talking about other characters whom they haven't yet met, giving vital information about those characters that the audience will probably have forgotten by the time the characters actually appear. For most people the film will need a minimum of two viewings to be fully understood. There's also a curious contrast between the pace at which the plot develops, which is very fast, and the pace at which each individual scene moves, which is usually very slow (aided by the largely static camera). This is the inverse of *Raising Arizona*, where the characters (and camera) move very fast but ultimately get nowhere.

In a complex crime drama every event ends up having some significance because there's no time for distractions and often it's the tiny details which cause people's downfalls. The characters in *Miller's Crossing* act as if they are aware of this and look for the significance in every event, which is why the Coens throw in a red herring when Rug is killed. Rug's death, the trigger cause of events, is a farcical event in itself: Mink had no reason to believe that Rug had been assigned to follow him by the Dane and shot Rug out of pure hysteria. Comically, nobody ever manages to work out why the killer took his hair, and there's a good reason for that: it was taken by a child who found the body and ran off. (The boy also has a cute dog with him, which was probably Joel's idea: when asked how their approaches to filmmaking differ, the

Coens' standard answer is that Joel likes movies about dogs and Ethan doesn't.) Even Tom keeps trying to work this point out, asking Bernie why Mink took the wig. As with *Blood Simple*, the Coens often enjoy letting the audience in on things that the characters don't know. In this case it's an effective way of making Tom more likeable: with the plot of *Miller's Crossing* being so complex, there's a danger that the audience would become alienated from Tom because he's thinking ahead of them. Because there's this one piece of information that the viewer knows and Tom never finds out, the viewer feels that they have something over him.

While the Coens clearly enjoy writing the hard-boiled dialogue, especially when those lines are spoken in JE Freeman's growling monotone, there are a number of touches that are pure Coen and unobtrusively subvert the seriousness of the genre. Their delight in having characters use words that don't seem to suit them is apparent ('Jesus, Tom, I was just speculatin' about a hypothesis'), as is their love of repetition. Just about every speaking character says 'Jesus, Tom!' at some point, including the superb scene where one of Caspar's minions is advancing on him and Tom hits him with a chair (his shocked, almost upset reaction makes this the funniest scene in the film, especially when the camera cuts back to Tom, still holding the chair and unsure what to do).

EVER AMERICA: The Coens' first period piece draws heavily on Hammett, not only for its story and its characters, but also its view of the period in question. Peter Korte and Georg Seesslen identify in *Joel & Ethan Coen* that most crime fiction and gangster movies of this period feature characters who are on the side of the law: the cop who won't be corrupted, the politician who wants to clean up the town and so on. Even the detectives of Chandler and Spillane work against evildoers, if only for the money. However, in Hammett's stories there are no good guys. Given the conventions of the genre it's surprising to see that in *The Glass Key* (and in *Miller's Crossing*), not only does the head of organised crime have the Mayor in his pocket, but he himself is also a political figure. The two are indistinguishable, since he who operates crime operates the city, and therefore crime has become so normal that it is practically legitimate. The audience expects to be given a character who is more or less on the side of right, but in this world everybody is corrupt, everybody is searching for the angle and, if possible, playing it. Everybody in the film is part of the corruption in some way.

It is this situation that Tom is working to maintain in *Miller's Crossing*: it may be corrupt but it works, it is better than having a war, and he is well placed to live comfortably within that system. It doesn't look like a desirable way of life, since Tom is required to stay alert in order to maintain his position within this Darwinian system, but within the world of *Miller's Crossing* an alternative is unthinkable. Like the city in *The Glass Key* it is never named (although it operates like Chicago), and the film goes one step further than Hammett's novel by never venturing outside (some of *The Glass Key* takes place in New York). There may as well not be a world outside for all these characters care: Bernie goes back on his promise to skip town, and when Verna suggests that she, Tom and Bernie leave together Tom sarcastically suggests that they could all go to Niagara Falls. The audience tends to side with Tom simply because the narrative follows him for the majority of the film, but on a number of occasions people point out that, despite his commendable avoidance of violence, he often gets others to do his dirty work for him. The distinction between having somebody killed and doing the deed yourself is perhaps not as clear as Tom would like to believe.

Hammett's world was undoubtedly stylised and in pastiching it the Coens have accentuated this, but he did have something to say about America during the Depression and prohibition: what the Coens offer here is effectively a commentary on his commentary.

AVAILABILITY: A selection of special features have been prepared for a DVD of *Miller's Crossing*, although the release has not been scheduled at the time of writing. It will feature interviews with Barry Sonnenfeld, Gabriel Byrne, Marcia Gay Harden and John Turturro.

THE COENS' VIEW: 'The hat in *Miller's Crossing* was really there from the beginning. In some weird way in our own heads, the obsession with the hat was kind of central to the whole idea of the movie.' (Joel in 2000)

VERDICT: 'You take a page outta this guy's book. A little less you talk and a little more you think.' In retrospect, *Miller's Crossing* is an atypical Coen production. It's more traditionally shot than their other work and, although it drew complaints of overstylisation, the design is chiefly to evoke both Hammett and the 1920s, rather than to play with the viewer in the way that, say, *Barton Fink* does. If it had been a straight adaptation of a Hammett novel, rather than an original story that mimicked his style, its approach would probably have been commended.

Most notably, it's a Coen brothers film where none of the main characters are losers and all are, in one way or another, adept to their situation. They all have ways of exercising power – Tom is highly astute, Bernie is ruthless, Caspar is determined, Verna is alluring, Leo is authoritative – but all can be brought down by human weaknesses. All of these people are the real deal. In purely dramatic terms, therefore, it functions more smoothly than most of the Coens' films, because everybody is capable of fulfilling the plot function that they are required to fulfil. This does make its characters slightly more difficult to identify with, although Tom Reagan remains a classically cool anti-hero (the scene in which he returns home, sits down, throws his hat onto his foot, picks up the ringing telephone *in his own time* and deals with the call before finally greeting the hitherto unseen Bernie, is a marvellously laconic performance from Byrne).

Despite all of this, it contains more than enough typically Coen touches (most notably, deriving humour from generic conventions) for it to fit comfortably into their canon, while also suggesting how versatile they can be. The resolution of its twisted plot is highly satisfying, assuming you've been able to follow it, and it's one of the Coens' best-looking films. Solidly brilliant.

Barton Fink (1991)

(Colour – 116 mins)

Circle Films Presents a Ted and Jim Pedas, Bill Durkin, Ben Barenholtz Production
Directed by Joel Coen
Produced by Ethan Coen
Written by Ethan Coen and Joel Coen
Co-producer: Graham Place
Executive Producers: Ben Barenholtz, Ted Pedas, Jim Pedas, Bill Durkin
Director of Photography: Roger Deakins
Production Designer: Dennis Gassner
Costume Designer: Richard Hornung
Music Composed by Carter Burwell
Edited by Roderick Jaynes
Associate Editor: Michael Berenbaum
Supervising Sound Editor: Skip Lievsay
Dialogue Supervisor: Philip Stockton
Casting by Donna Isaacson CSA & John Lyons CSA

CAST: John Turturro (*Barton Fink*), John Goodman (*Charlie Meadows/Karl 'Madman' Mundt*), Judy Davis (*Audrey Taylor*), Michael Lerner (*Jack Lipnick*), John Mahoney (*WP Mayhew*), Tony Shalhoub (*Ben Geisler*), Jon Polito (*Lou Breeze*), Steve Buscemi (*Chet*), David Warrilow (*Garland Stanford*), Richard Portnow (*Detective Mastrionotti*), Christopher Murney (*Detective Deutsch*), IM Hobson (*Derek*), Meagen Fay (*Poppy Carnaham*), Lance Davis (*Richard St Claire*), Harry Bugin (*Pete*), Anthony Gordon (*Maitre d'*), Jack Denbo (*Stagehand*), Max Grodénchik (*Clapper Boy*), Robert Beecher (*Referee*), Darwyn Swalve (*Wrestler*), Gayle Vance (*Geisler's Secretary*), Johnny Judkins (*Sailor*), Jana Marie Hupp (*USO Girl*), Isabelle Townsend (*Beauty*), And Featuring the Golden Throat of William Preston Robertson

TAGLINE: 'Between heaven and hell, there's always Hollywood!' Also: 'There's only one thing stranger than what's going on inside his head. What's going on outside.'

SUMMARY: New York 1941, and young playwright Barton Fink is the rising star of Broadway. The movie studio Capitol Pictures offers him a lucrative screenwriting contract that he reluctantly accepts (he feels that he may be selling out). He moves to Hollywood and checks into the Hotel Earle. Barton meets with studio head Jack Lipnick, who assigns him to write a wrestling movie. He isn't sure how to go about this and puts off his writing duties by talking to Charlie Meadows, an insurance salesman who lives in the room next door at the Earle. Barton looks for advice on his script, but meetings with producer Ben Geisler and fellow writer WP Mayhew don't help. An impatient Geisler tells Barton to have a script treatment ready to explain to Lipnick the next morning. Barton panics and calls Mayhew's secretary, Audrey, for help. She comes to the Earle and they have sex.

Barton awakes to find that Audrey has been murdered next to him. Charlie tells him not to call the police and helps him to dispose of the body. Barton bluffs his way through the meeting with Lipnick. Charlie heads off to New York, leaving a parcel with Barton for safekeeping. Later, Barton is questioned by two LAPD detectives, who tell him that Charlie's real name is Karl 'Madman' Mundt, a wanted felon who has decapitated several people. Barton returns to his room and examines Charlie's parcel. It's the right size and shape to contain a severed head. His writer's block clears at last and he completes the script in a single sitting. The detectives return and arrest Barton, suspecting that he is in cahoots with Charlie, but then Charlie arrives, kills them and frees Barton. Charlie explains to Barton that he was trying to help. Barton leaves the Earle with just his script and Charlie's parcel. Barton delivers his script, but Lipnick hates it and tells him that he won't produce the picture. Barton must honour his contract by staying around and writing for Capitol but Lipnick says that the studio will not produce one of Barton's scripts until he writes a better one. Barton goes to sit on the beach – where he meets a girl who exactly resembles the one in a picture that hung in his hotel room . . .

DEVELOPMENT: The Coens famously wrote *Barton Fink*, a movie about a man with writer's block, after getting bogged down midway through writing the convoluted *Miller's Crossing*. 'It was just going really slowly,' says Ethan. 'It took us a really long time. I guess because the plot was so involved, we just got sick of it at a certain point.' Joel concurs: 'It's not exactly writer's block, but sometimes you hit a wall in terms of thinking about the plot or something . . . it just becomes easier, when we'd get together to write, to think about something else.'

Even before they decided that the protagonist would be a struggling Hollywood scriptwriter, the brothers began *Barton Fink* with the concept of the sinister, rundown Hotel Earle. (This idea, says Joel, had been 'rattling around for a time'.) They had also decided that they wanted to write a character for John Turturro, and when they decided to incorporate their problems with *Miller's Crossing* into the script, he became a screenwriter. The Coens found that, just as they'd hoped, their work rate increased immediately. 'It actually got written very quickly, in about three weeks,' says Joel. 'I don't know what that means.'

It certainly helped that the Coens, with their keen interest in movie history, knew the subject matter fairly well. 'We didn't do any research, actually, at all,' says Ethan. 'Maybe one of the things that contributed to the writing of the script was that we'd previously read some stuff.' Joel notes that a book called *City of Nets* by Otto Friedrich, about 1940s German expatriates working in Los Angeles, was useful background. Both Coens had already read it when they came to write *Barton Fink*. 'It was one of the things that started us thinking about Hollywood as a setting. But we didn't go out and do research beyond it.'

One part that is *not* historically accurate, nor was it ever supposed to be, is the idea that the wrestling movie was ever a popular genre. 'We thought it was like a joke,' Ethan says. 'It kind of goes past people: "Oh yeah, wrestling picture." ' (This author must admit to being unsure, on first viewing, whether this was some archaic, long-forgotten genre or a very funny gag.) Unfortunately, while making the film they discovered that the historically real Wallace Beery, who is to star in Barton's movie, made a picture called *Flesh* (John Ford, 1932) in which he played a German wrestler in love with a homeless girl. 'We were sort of disappointed that there actually was such a thing. It makes it a little more pedestrian that it really exists.' Still, the idea that it was an accepted genre like the western or the musical remains funny, as does the formula that Audrey outlines for it, and Ethan later added a new entry to it (see **The Naked Man**).

In *Barton Fink* Beery works for the fictional Capitol Pictures, but in reality, he was under contract to MGM in 1941. This points towards the inspiration for the character of Jack Lipnick: MGM's legendary co-founder and production head Louis B Mayer. There are also elements of Jack Warner, head of Warner Brothers, in the character (the part where Lipnick wears a military uniform from the costume stores is something that Warner actually did during the Second World War), as well as former Columbia Pictures boss Harry Cohn (see **CASTING**).

Similarly, WP Mayhew and Barton himself are based loosely on real people. Mayhew partly derives from the novelist William Faulkner. '[John Mahoney] really does resemble Faulkner, physically,' Joel says. 'Although the character in *Barton Fink*, obviously – outside of the physical resemblance and the fact that he's an alcoholic – [Mayhew] really doesn't resemble Faulkner very much in any other respect.' There are other similarities: Faulkner was also from the southern states (Mississippi), went to Hollywood and had an affair with a secretary (not his own but Howard Hawks's). In the 1940s all his novels dropped out of print and he had to beg Warner Brothers for a job, which he was given but only received a junior writer's pay (then $300 per week). Most interestingly, MGM wanted Faulkner to write the aforementioned *Flesh*, and screened Beery's *The Champ* (King Vidor, 1931) for him. Faulkner walked off the lot in disgust. There is certainly enough of a character resemblance for *Halliwell's Who's Who in the Movies* to note *Barton Fink* under its entry for Faulkner.

Clifford Odets, who was associated with the left-wing Group Theatre and who wrote the plays *Awake and Sing!* and *Waiting for Lefty*, was in part the model for the main character. 'Barton *is* based on Clifford Odets from the point of view of his background,' says Joel, 'but it's not really supposed to be [him]

. . . Odets had a much more successful career in Hollywood than Barton.' Many critics and viewers did make too strong a connection between the characters and their inspiration: Roger Ebert, for example, drew the comparison that Odets 'did go to Hollywood in the late 1930s and write a boxing picture, *Golden Boy* [Rouben Mamoulian, 1939], which did not drip with political commitment.' In fact, Odets only wrote the play on which *Golden Boy* was based: the scriptwriters who adapted it removed much of his social commentary, so the parallel is far from direct. However, Odets was equally ambivalent about the film industry: 'Hollywood, like Midas,' he once remarked, 'kills everything it touches.'

While the Hollywood connections added colour, the element of the movie that the Coens were most interested in remained the dynamic between Barton and Charlie, and the script moved towards that in its final act, as it was always intended to. 'When Barton awoke and discovered the corpse near him, we wanted it to be a surprise without clashing with what had gone before,' says Joel. For this reason, they were always aware that the material building up to the violent twist should have a surreal quality. 'We were conscious that the demarcation line was very tight,' says Ethan. 'We needed to astonish the audience without alienating them from the movie.' The movie had to be slightly off-centre throughout and this was how the portrait of Hollywood as a contradictory, illogical world came about, rather than as a deliberate satire. 'The world he has to deal with during the day, this surreal Hollywood, when he goes out to find some sort of anchor, is even more disorientating than the hotel room,' says Joel. 'The starting point wasn't that we were going to do a Hollywood story and I hope it doesn't feel like that.'

REFERENCES: When Barton goes to Mayhew's bungalow, the title of the movie Mayhew is working on is displayed as 'Slave Ship'. The 1937 movie *Slave Ship*, directed by Tay Garnett (who also directed the 1946 version of *The Postman Always Rings Twice*), was based on a story by William Faulkner and starred Wallace Beery.

As an in-joke, Ben Geisler has a poster on the wall of his office that depicts one of the cut scenes from *Miller's Crossing*.

CASTING: The two lead roles of *Barton Fink* were cast in Ethan and Joel's minds before they even started work on the script. As the Coens got to know more actors and found people they worked well with, they started to write parts with those actors in mind, and so it was with this project. Most of the inspiration for the script had come, Joel says, from 'the idea of a big seedy hotel with John Turturro and John Goodman', and the two actors in question were immediately engaged for the roles when *Barton Fink* started to move ahead.

'When we first talked,' says Turturro, 'they said, "It's really a responding character – you've played more initiating characters," and I said, "It sounds interesting".' It seems highly likely that if Turturro hadn't taken the part, *Barton Fink* would not have happened. Fortunately the Coens rarely encounter actors who don't want to work with them. 'This was specifically something we wanted John to play, and it's also specifically not like the things he usually does,' says Joel, 'so what exactly we were going to get, we didn't really know.' Turturro became highly committed to the role, spending a couple of months out in Los Angeles with the Coens prior to the start of shooting, 'just to be in touch with them, because they understand the character so well. I think it's close to them in some ways: they've been through it; they're writers.' He also read *Jews Without Money*, Michael Gold's account of the origins of the socially conscious writers of the 1930s, and he learned how to type, although, playing a character with writer's block, he would rarely be called upon to do so for the cameras.

Unlike Turturro, John Goodman had already worked with the Coens before they wrote the *Barton Fink* script, having appeared in *Raising Arizona* (*Miller's Crossing*, of course, had yet to be filmed). Again, Ethan notes that the part was written for the actor, 'but it's also not like the stuff he usually plays. It's related to what people are used to seeing him in, but at the same time totally different – it subverts all that.' It was certainly a contrast to his previous movie, *King Ralph* (David S Ward, 1991); work on both this and *Roseanne* meant that he only had a small window in which to fit *Barton Fink*, but the role was made feasible by the fact that all of his scenes were set in either Barton's room or the hotel corridor. However, he was keen to work with the Coens again and particularly enjoyed the ambiguities of the script and his character in particular: 'It's really good writing. It leaves you a lot of leeway.'

In addition to Turturro, two further members of the small cast came to the film from *Miller's Crossing*. Jon Polito took a slightly smaller role than he had done in the previous film, playing Lou Breeze, while Steve Buscemi, who only appeared in one scene of *Miller's Crossing* as Mink, came on board as the bell-hop, Chet. Two others were to work with the Coens again on later films: Tony Shalhoub, who played Ben Geisler, would return for *The Man Who Wasn't There*, while John Mahoney would come back for *The Hudsucker Proxy*. The British-born Mahoney had done a great deal of stage work before moving to Hollywood, and his resemblance to Faulkner made him an ideal choice for WP Mayhew. Since *Hudsucker* in 1994 he has become better known for playing Martin Crane in the TV sitcom *Frasier*. Shalhoub came to the film from roles in *Quick Change* (Howard Franklin, Bill Murray, 1990) and *Longtime Companion* (Norman Rene, 1990).

The other significant roles in the production were taken by Michael Lerner and Judy Davis. Lerner was a well-known character actor who was familiar to the public from regular roles in a number of TV series, including *Starsky and Hutch* and *Hart to Hart*. What may well have suggested him for the role of Lipnick in *Barton Fink* was that he had previously played Harry Cohn in the TV biopic *Rita Hayworth: The Love Goddess*. Davis, an Australian, had turned from singing to acting in her twenties and came to *Barton Fink* from Woody Allen's *Alice* (1990).

PRODUCTION: The Coens' fourth and final picture for Circle Films was again funded by a large advance from 20th Century Fox. The *Barton Fink* script indicated a more low-key production than *Miller's Crossing* and accordingly it required a smaller budget. Of the $9 million required, the vast majority came from

Fox in exchange for domestic distribution rights, despite the commercial failure of *Miller's Crossing*. After all, a few million dollars is not a vast amount of money to a company of Fox's size, and with those losses they were buying a degree of prestige.

The Coens' usual cinematographer, Barry Sonnenfeld, was unavailable to work on *Barton Fink* as he was making his directorial debut, *The Addams Family*. (Sonnenfeld's film did very well at the box office and he continues to make technically impressive popular hits, such as 1997's *Men in Black* and 1999's *Wild Wild West*. As a result, he has not collaborated with the Coens since *Miller's Crossing*.) Joel and Ethan looked around for a replacement and settled on British cameraman Roger Deakins, whose work they had seen on such films as *Sid and Nancy* (Alex Cox, 1986) and *Stormy Monday* (Mike Figgis, 1987). They sent Deakins the script and, although his agent advised him against accepting the job, Joel and Ethan flew to London to meet Deakins and he decided in their favour. He has worked on all of the Coens' subsequent films and has found himself increasingly in demand as a result, winning an Oscar in 2002 for his work on *A Beautiful Mind* (Ron Howard, 2001).

Due to the Coens being New York-based and the independent nature of their productions, none of their first three movies had involved any work in Hollywood, but the setting of *Barton Fink* made it necessary to head for the heart of America's entertainment industry. They hired a small office near the beach and decamped to Los Angeles, where *Barton Fink* commenced shooting on 27 June 1990. 'Shooting in LA was a real departure for Joel and Ethan,' comments Ron Neter, the film's unit manager, 'but I think they had a good time out here.' Even those segments supposedly set in New York were shot in LA: the Orpheum Theatre, where the first day's filming took place, stood in for the Broadway venue where Barton's play is being performed (while Barton silently mouths the dialogue, the voice of the actor on the stage, unseen by the camera, is also that of Turturro). The other New York scenes, in which Barton goes to a restaurant and bar to receive praise for his work, were filmed in Long Beach, on the dry-docked ship *Queen Mary*.

As in *Miller's Crossing*, set designer Dennis Gassner worked with costume designer Richard Hornung to create a continuity of colour through the film, with the main change coinciding with Barton's move from New York to Los Angeles. 'New York is black and white, black dresses with little bits of jewellery and hair up, very controlled,' explained Hornung. He used more colours and patterns in the scene where Barton lunches with Geisler and introduced still more from that point on, culminating in 'the chaos of the USO dance near the end of the picture, with all these funny patterns, dots and jazzy plaids, skirts and blouses, real high shoes, anklets and big plastic jewellery'.

In keeping with the claustrophobic atmosphere of the film, very little material was shot out of doors. The meeting by Lipnick's pool, which was filmed at a private house in Beverly Hills, was one such scene; another was the exterior of Mayhew's bungalow on the Capitol Pictures lot, which was in reality a part of the Columbia Pictures lot previously owned by MGM. Apart from the scene in which Barton, Mayhew and Audrey have lunch, the only other substantial exterior material was the film's ending, as Barton stumbles along the beach. This was done at LA's Zuma Beach and gives a sense of release after the oppressiveness of what has gone before.

Ironically, two real hotels were used to stand in for entirely different places while none of the material in the Hotel Earle was shot in one. The closed-down Ambassador's Hotel doubled for the interior of Mayhew's bungalow as well as the commissary where Geisler and Barton have lunch, although the mural of the New York skyline was supplied by Dennis Gassner. (Gassner reproduced this from one he had seen in a photo of a restaurant in Paris.) Meanwhile, the Park Plaza Hotel was used for the men's washroom at Capitol, as well as the venue for the USO gathering near the end of the film. There was a minor problem during shooting for the latter scene, as the fire sprinklers went off over the orchestra and soaked them through, but fortunately the crew had already covered all the angles from which the orchestra could be seen and could carry on without them.

The various parts of the Hotel Earle (the slogan for which, 'A Day or a Lifetime', was taken from a hotel at which the Coens stayed during the production of *Blood Simple*) were located in three places. The lobby was in fact the lobby of the Wiltern Theater. Gassner had developed a concept for the design of *Barton Fink* which he called 'distressed Deco', and although the owners of the theatre balked at his suggestion that the newly laid carpets could do with a little 'distressing', he was permitted to dress the location by placing half-withered banana trees around it. 'We wanted an art-deco style and a place that was falling to pieces, having known better days,' says Joel. The idea was that the hotel reflected the character of Charlie at all times, with the wallpaper paste dripping down as Charlie sweats. 'At the end, when Goodman says he's a prisoner of his own mental state, that it's like a hell, the hotel has already taken on that infernal appearance.' The banana-tree motif was carried over to the design of the wallpaper that covers the Earle's corridors, which has a pattern of rotting brown banana leaves. 'We wanted the whole thing to feel organic and decayed,' the Coens say. 'We used a lot of green and yellow to suggest a feeling of putrefaction.'

Two versions of the corridor outside Barton's room were built in an old seaplane hangar near Long Beach, one for ordinary filming work and a specially rigged version for the infernal scene at the end. The final part of the Earle seen in the film, Barton's room, was constructed on a soundstage at Culver Studios, as was Lipnick's office. Barton's room features the same ambience of decay, with its rattling pipes and mosquito infestation. 'We got a letter from the ASPCA [American Society for the Prevention of Cruelty to Animals] on this movie,' notes Joel. 'They'd gotten a hold of a copy of the script and wanted to know how we were going to treat the mosquitoes. I'm not kidding.' It was on this set that Roger Deakins was called upon to pull off the movie's most audacious shot, in which the camera pans off Barton and Audrey as they are about to have sex, goes into the bathroom, over the sink and down the plug-hole. 'The shot was a lot of fun and we had a great time working on it,' says Joel, although it's not clear whether Deakins found it quite so enjoyable: 'After that, every time we asked Roger to do something difficult, he would raise an eyebrow and say, "Don't be having me track down any plug-holes now." '

The shot is, however, entirely consistent with the film's overall camera style, which harks back to the roving camera of *Blood Simple* but is slightly less obtrusive. 'In *Barton Fink*, the camera is very much a character within the room, moving independently of the actors,' Deakins explains. However, the camera stays close to Barton at all times, never granting us a view of anything that happens when he's not there. (The plug-hole shot is the only time it decisively moves away from him, preserving his modesty by merely showing us a blatant sexual metaphor instead.) The camera is fascinated by the curious figure of Barton while always remaining detached, never putting itself in a sympathetic position with him (a number of shots appear to be directly from Barton's point of view, only for him to step around the camera and into the frame). This slight distance makes a substantial contribution towards the ideological ambiguity of *Barton Fink*.

Production wrapped on 10 August 1990 after a 45-day shoot. However, *Miller's Crossing* was about to be released and the Coens were required for promotional duties almost immediately. Upon returning to the film and editing it, the Coens found that they had very little surplus material: 'Nearly everything was used. I remember some shots of studio life in Hollywood we decided not to keep: they were pretty banal,' says Joel. The introduction of Los Angeles with a wave hitting a rock, noted as a sublime moment by many critics, was also the result of some cutting down: 'We filmed other shots to create a more conventional transition [between New York and LA], but we decided not to use them.' By May 1991 the film existed as a complete print, but not a final one (the colour gradings still needed to be adjusted). The Coens decided that it was worth the risk to take the unfinished movie to Cannes and screen it for the panel's consideration on 20 May. The gambit more than paid off (see **AWARDS**).

MUSIC: Coming between his sweeping orchestral scores for *Miller's Crossing* and *The Hudsucker Proxy*, Carter Burwell's score for *Barton Fink* is much sparser and less melody-driven. A large number of scenes feature no score at all, opting instead for tense silence, and nearly all of the scenes that do are in the hotel, usually when Barton is on his own. At these moments, the audience usually hears a halting piano figure, followed by an ominous swell from the strings as Barton's distraction from his work increases. Whatever music there is tends to disappear before it ever gets going, reflecting Barton's blocked existence.

CRITICAL RECEPTION: With *Barton Fink*, the Coens won over a number of critics who had been previously resistant to their charms. 'To someone who has not been a consistent admirer of the Coens' earlier work, *Barton Fink* is a most happy surprise,' wrote Vincent Canby in his Cannes report for the 20 May 1991 issue of the *New York Times*. 'For once [the] movie-buff associations add to the fun of the film.' If anything, his opinion improved when he came to review the film on 18 August for its US release. 'It was said by some at Cannes that *Barton Fink* is a movie for people who don't like the Coen brothers' films.' Canby disagreed, suggesting that it was actually 'for those who were not sure that the Coens knew what they wanted to do or had the authority to pull off a significant work'. For Canby, the Coens' fourth film marked a watershed. 'It's an exhilarating original.'

'*Barton Fink* is one of the most eccentric films to come out of, or take place in, Hollywood in many a moon,' declared *Variety* on 27 March 1991, describing the film as 'accomplished on every artistic level'. Goodman was deemed 'marvellous' and Deakins' photography 'brilliant' and, while the film was thought likely to remain 'elusive to a wider public', every scene 'is filled with a ferocious strength and humour'. The reviewer also noted that, 'It could plausibly be argued that the Meadows character actually doesn't exist, that he is simply a physical manifestation of extreme writer's block.' Everybody had their pet theory about *Barton Fink*. Roger Ebert had an interesting one about the dynamic between Barton and Charlie. 'The Coens mean this aspect of the film, I think, to be read as an emblem of the rise of Nazism,' he wrote in the *Chicago Sun-Times* on 23 August 1991. 'They paint Fink as an ineffectual and impotent left-wing intellectual, who . . . does not understand that, for many common men, fascism had a seductive appeal.' In any case Ebert enjoyed the film, describing it as 'an assured piece of comic filmmaking' and giving it three and a half stars out of four.

While reviewers found *Barton Fink* tough to pigeonhole, many seemed clear on what its message was. 'Whatever this oddball odyssey . . . might be – drama or comedy, satire or statement, heartfelt or just pretentiously overwrought – it's really one hell of an effective chronicle of writer's block,' wrote Edmond Grant in *Films in Review*. While he felt that the movie's themes emerged well early on, 'Those ideas get murkier and murkier as the film goes on, with the second half of the proceedings being a symbolically charged explosion of events that can only be experienced, and not understood.' While others enjoyed this aspect, Grant found it disappointing, feeling that the Coens' desire for spectacle obscured the plot and message. 'That message, clearly enough, is about the commercial trap that Hollywood presented to Faulkner, Fitzgerald, Odets, James M Cain and the like.' Is it? A lot of critics read the film this way and, like Grant, were perplexed at why Barton was so unlikeable as they felt that this damaged the film's point (see **EVER AMERICA**).

Other critics eschewed the idea of *Barton Fink* as a satire on Hollywood. In this light, perhaps the sharpest review came from no less an authority than the playwright Arthur Miller, author of *The Crucible* and *Death of a Salesman*. (The latter is a possible influence on *Barton Fink*'s Hotel Earle: Joel has commented that 'You can imagine it peopled with travelling salesmen who've had no success, with their sad sex lives, crying alone in their rooms.') 'I'm not sure there is a problem with *Barton Fink*,' Miller wrote in the US *Premiere* in October 1991. 'It may be perfect. Maybe I'm not supposed to be sure.' He identified that the film was not supposed to satirise Clifford Odets (with whom Miller was at one time acquainted), or indeed any person or institution, because it was not supposed to be *about* anything. Miller viewed the film as closer to the work of David Lynch – 'Artistically, it belongs to a genre of mere chaos' – and asked whether the film was simply incompetently plotted or whether it demanded of its audience 'a higher irony that will permit us to enjoy it as only superficially awkward while actually, in a profounder sense, it is right on the nose'. However, he encouraged audiences to engage with it. 'It cannot be easily dismissed, since it might reflect the stage at which we have truly arrived – whether in our rise or our decline.'

By the time the film had reached Britain it had been preceded by nine months of hype, from Cannes and from the US reception. 'So is *Barton Fink*, which one American critic breathes of in the same breath as *Citizen Kane*, that good?' asked Shaun Usher in the *Daily Mail* on 14 February 1992. 'Er, yes and no . . . *Barton Fink* is a house of in-joke trump cards which [the Coens] balance with deftness and style before putting a match to the flimsy palace and strolling off, leaving us to sift through its ashes for message or moral.' Usher tended to focus on the Hollywood aspects – 'Some people will be baffled by a period piece which takes it for granted that onlookers can decode the humour' – but for his own part he enjoyed it immensely. 'For those liking it at all, here's a film of the decade, never mind the year.'

Steve Jenkins broadly agreed with Arthur Miller that the piece was more existential than satirical. 'Despite its setting, *Barton Fink* actually shows little concern with notions of classic Hollywood or what kind of culture it represents,' he commented in *Sight and Sound*. 'Barton's problem could be reduced to the fact that he doesn't listen . . . But the film itself works out from rather than towards this conclusion.' The film's ambiguities continued to frustrate some, however. 'Logical plotting and character development fly out of the window as soon as Fink learns that Charlie is dangerous,' complained Christopher Tookey in the *Sunday Telegraph* on 16 February 1992. 'Critics may find such a dénouement intriguing: audiences are more likely to find it infuriating and pretentious.'

One critic who wasn't so intrigued was Angie Errigo, although she felt it worth four stars nevertheless. Her review in the March 1992 issue of *Empire* deemed the twist revelation of Charlie's true nature 'almost as baffling as it is unsatisfying'. Broadly, the review could be applied to any of the Coens' films, as she declared *Fink* to be 'hugely enjoyable for the cinema buff – style, wit and in-jokes abound'. She concluded that, 'The result is, unsurprisingly for these boys, visually enthralling – just don't ask what it all means,' adding a warning: 'those of you who were left cold by *Miller's Crossing* would definitely *detest* this.' However, there were still a few who gave the film an unequivocal thumbs-up. 'The more perversely weird the Coen brothers' films get, the better,' wrote Geoff Andrew in the 12 February 1992 issue of *Time Out*. 'All of the usual preoccupations are present and correct, but even less constrained by traditional genre considerations than before; the result works on numerous levels, thrilling the mind, ears and eyes, and racking the nerves.'

BOX OFFICE: *Barton Fink* was released in the US on 21 August 1991, at the tail end of a summer that had been dominated by the $200 million-grossing *Terminator 2: Judgment Day* (James Cameron, 1991). *Fink* managed $5,726,463 gross which, while a slight improvement on *Miller's Crossing*, was still some way off the movie's $9 million budget. The success at Cannes meant that it made the rest back from the European box office, although Fox only got the domestic rights in exchange for putting up most of the cash, so whether they saw a return on their investment is doubtful.

AWARDS: *Barton Fink*'s haul of awards at the 1991 Cannes Film Festival was nothing short of remarkable. Not only did the film take the Palme d'Or, but also the prizes for Best Director and Best Actor for John Turturro's performance. No film had ever received three prizes at the festival before. The head of the jury was director Roman Polanski, which Ethan described as 'kind of ironic' considering *Barton Fink*'s acknowledged debt to Polanski (particularly his film *The Tenant* (1976)). Not everybody was impressed: Spike Lee, who had entered *Do the Right Thing* in 1989 and lost out to Steven Soderbergh's *Sex, Lies and Videotape*, was furious at missing the prize again. 'It's no coincidence,' he declared. 'If they have a choice between me and Steven Soderbergh or the Coen brothers, they'll go for the golden white boys every time.' It probably didn't help matters that Lee's entry in the 1991 festival, *Jungle Fever*, also starred John Turturro.

At the Oscars, however, *Fink* picked up just three nominations – Art Direction, Costume Design and Supporting Actor (for

Michael Lerner) – and no awards. However, it did score Best Cinematography at a number of other ceremonies, including the National Society of Film Critics Awards, the Los Angeles Film Critics Awards and the New York Film Critics Awards. It also earned acting awards at Los Angeles (Supporting Actor for Lerner) and New York (Supporting Actress for Judy Davis).

DIALOGUE TO SKIP BACK FOR:

Geisler: (on writers) 'You throw a rock in here, you'll hit one. And do me a favour, Fink – throw it hard.'

Barton: (on Charlie) 'He liked Jack Oakie pictures.'
Mastronotti: 'Ordinarily we say anything you might remember could be helpful. But I'll be honest with you, Fink: that is not helpful.'
Deutsch: 'You notice I was not writing it down?'

ANALYSIS: While the character of Barton Fink is not supposed to represent directly Joel and Ethan Coen, it is noticeable that none of the films made before this is so strongly based around one character. *Blood Simple* is split between four protagonists; *Raising Arizona* has a number of scenes that don't feature Hi, focusing sometimes on Nathan Arizona or Gale and Evelle instead; and even *Miller's Crossing* occasionally moves away from Tom. However, Barton features in every single scene of *Barton Fink*. This is *his* story and the Coens want to show us his experience. Writers often avoid writing about writers because they fear the work becoming too self-indulgent. Here, the Coens avoid this by making Barton ridiculous.

Barton is implicitly wrong in everything he says, an effect that is achieved partly by the detached camera style, but also because the comic tone of the film contrasts with Barton's earnestness. Frustrated by their slow progress on *Miller's Crossing*, it seems important to the Coens that they don't take the writing of *Barton Fink* too seriously and so they spend a lot of time poking fun at how seriously Barton takes himself. Take the scene where Garland assures Barton that he won't be abandoning the 'common man' if he goes to write movies: Barton doesn't realise that Garland is joking with him.

When Barton explains his attitude towards writing to Mayhew and Audrey he talks about the writer's need to draw on pain in order to produce something worthwhile. This contrasts sharply with Mayhew's outlook, which initially seems more laid back, even frivolous: the act of invention seems to delight him. However, it quickly becomes apparent that he creates these fictional worlds to escape a real world that he finds increasingly difficult to cope with. Barton romanticises the pain of the writer but he doesn't fully appreciate the attendant problems. Mayhew's depression may drive him to write, but it has also driven him to drink and the drink is steadily eroding his ability to write, despite his belief that the drink is protecting him from everything he fears.

Barton does not see what he does as entertainment and fails to understand the difference between the limited, middle-class audience of New York theatre (who will, among other things, swallow his rather patronising depiction of the working class) and the mass audience of a Hollywood movie. This attitude will ultimately lead to Lipnick's dismissal of his script but Barton sees it as potentially revolutionary, dreaming of a new school of theatre whose subject is the 'common man'. He talks an awful lot about the 'common man', his 'fellow man', the 'working man' and so on, but this is not based on any real knowledge or experience. He also talks about living 'the life of the mind' and the movie is littered with references to heads and minds (keeping your head, peace of mind, decapitation and so on). Indeed, the only place that Barton lives is in his own mind, writing about an idea of the 'common man' without bothering to find out what such people are really like. He doesn't seem to be able to find inspiration from outside himself and when he looks in the Bible he sees only the words of his own script. He is so obsessed with his work that he doesn't really live, explaining to Charlie that he doesn't have a girlfriend because he wouldn't be able to give her sufficient attention. What this actually says about Barton is that he is too absorbed with himself to let other people in: because he doesn't connect with the world, his work is really only about himself, and his obsession with work is really an obsession with himself.

At their first meeting, Barton gives Charlie his spiel about the 'common man' as an explanation of what he writes about and notes that the insurance salesman is a perfect example. Despite this he does not make any use of Charlie: several times Charlie says 'I could tell you some stories,' and while Barton enthusiastically agrees that everybody has stories, he fails to ask Charlie to tell any. He even cuts Charlie off in the middle of one that sounds particularly interesting, regarding a female client whose payments were overdue and whose husband was away on business.

Even worse, despite the fact that Barton has been assigned to write a film about wrestlers, a subject he knows nothing about, he fails to ask Charlie's advice. It's an amazing stroke of luck that he has an ex-wrestler living next door but he doesn't make any use of this, noting that he has little interest in writing about it as a sport. His finished draft of the film is criticised for featuring too little action: Lipnick may be a philistine (and hasn't even read the script, see **EVER AMERICA**) but he has a point when he tells Barton that the act of wrestling contains poetry of its own. (We've also seen how wrestling reflects the life of the 'common man', during the brawl at the USO dance.) Barton has his own agenda, and it's one that seems to have less to do with standing up for the 'common man' and more to do with imposing himself on the dramatic medium. Revealingly, at one point Barton puts his feet into the shoes of the 'common man', only to discover that he's too small for them.

It's very telling that, when called upon to give the police any information about Charlie, all he can recall is that he was an insurance salesman and admired the movies of vaudeville star Jack Oakie. This is because, as Charlie points out, Barton doesn't listen. Charlie has, in his skewed way, been trying to teach Barton something, although the nature of the lesson is not clear (which is hardly unusual in this movie). Charlie genuinely does empathise with the 'common man' and wants to help him out, which in his tortured psyche equates to committing murder. When he screams

'I'll show you the life of the mind!' over and over, flames tearing along the corridor beside him as he guns down the cops, he's showing us the life of *his* mind. (Whether the hotel is actually on fire is a moot point, as the fire always follows Charlie. It could be purely a reflection of him: see **GENRE**.) Ultimately, though, Charlie sums up Barton's situation with great clarity, describing Barton as 'a tourist with a typewriter'.

It's debatable whether Barton actually learns anything from this experience. The trigger for the loosening of his writer's block seems to be the revelation of Charlie's true nature, but in the end the script that he comes up with seems remarkably similar to his play (the final line is almost identical in each). Whether he still has the capacity to learn is also left open. Some critics suggest that Barton is right when he ponders whether he only ever had one play in him, that he has no real talent, but Lipnick's suggestion that Barton simply needs to grow up rings truer (it is reinforced by Audrey when she notes that one version of the wrestling narrative sees the wrestler looking after an 'idiot man-child': if this film casts Charlie as the wrestler, that makes Barton the idiot man-child). 'We're certainly hard on Barton,' says Joel. 'The whole movie is a kind of conspiracy of abuse heaped on him. But basically I think he's a little misguided and naïve.'

As noted in the *Raising Arizona* chapter, many critics have attempted pseudo-Marxist readings of the Coens' films, seeing them as critiques of the social inequalities inherent in the capitalist system. Yet in *Barton Fink* the viewer is shown a man from a comfortable background with a creative vocation who believes that he is speaking up for the 'common man', and his endeavours are made to seem ridiculous at every turn. The fact that the Coens have given him a similar background to themselves – north-eastern, Jewish, intellectual – is partly because this background is common to a lot of Marxist intellectuals and revolutionaries, but it may also be that he embodies certain things that they want to avoid in their own work.

More than a few critics have pointed out *Barton Fink*'s thematic resemblance to *Sullivan's Travels* (Preston Sturges, 1941). Sturges was in many ways a model for the Coens: he was

Hollywood's first successful writer-director, opening the door for the likes of Welles, Wilder and Huston, and above all he is admired for his natural, fluent, witty dialogue. (Like Barton, he was a playwright before moving to Hollywood.) In *Sullivan's Travels*, a director of popular Hollywood comedies decides that he wants to tackle more serious issues. He tries to experience life as a hobo so that he can make a film about human suffering called *O Brother, Where Art Thou?*, but in the end discovers just how valuable laughter is to people who have nothing else. 'Somewhere in a book, I think by Brander Matthews, I read that it was the playwright's job to show conditions but to let the audience draw conclusions,' Sturges said of his film. While many critics, speaking for and against *Sullivan's Travels*, claimed Sturges was arguing that movies should ignore social problems, Sturges himself disagreed. The idea that comedies are important after all 'was Sullivan's conclusion,' Sturges noted, 'not mine. I don't believe that now is the time for comedies or tragedies or spy pictures or pictures without spies or historical dramas or musicals or pictures without music.' Sturges believed that there was room in Hollywood for all of these, noting that art was at its most effective when used to communicate emotions, rather than messages.

What Sturges seems to have been arguing against was didacticism in moviemaking and the idea that a character's story represents an instruction. Sullivan's story is his own: it does not represent anything but himself. The Coens echo this: 'That question about a larger purpose always stops us; there's no larger purpose outside of the story itself.' Above all they value the viewer's right to take what they want away from the film, something which is particularly relevant in this most ambiguous of Coen movies (see also **EVER AMERICA**). Hence, you can read the Coens' movies as critical of Western capitalism, and while of course you can argue that what the creator intended and what comes through in their work are not always the same, it still probably says more about your own view of the world than the Coens'. The Coens are happy to write about working-class characters and often do, but they never claim to *speak* for the working class because they are all too aware that it is not their place to do so. And at the end of the day, they believe that, as Joel puts it: 'If somebody goes out to make a movie that isn't designed primarily to entertain people, then I don't know what the fuck they're doing.'

GENRE: *Barton Fink* is more noir-ish than any of the Coens' previous three pictures. Not only is it set in Los Angeles (the traditional home of the genre) and in the year that noir began to emerge (*The Maltese Falcon* and *Citizen Kane*, two key pictures in the development of the genre, were released in 1941), but the Hotel Earle is a ideal location for such a film.

Aesthetically, if not always thematically, noir has much in common with gothic. The aim of gothic fiction is frequently to create a sense of claustrophobia and disorientation and the same is true of noir. The noir aesthetic partly emerged because extreme lighting and camera angles filtered through from European Expressionism and partly because non-linear storytelling became more acceptable, but it was also because the Second World War meant that restrictions were placed on the materials available for film sets. Sets therefore became smaller and sparser, a factor which also contributed to the tendency of filmmakers to select losers and criminals as their subject matter as opulence and spectacle became more difficult to achieve. Desperate people holed up in small, threatening spaces – a frequently used gothic motif – therefore became more common.

The Hotel Earle is a perfect example of such a location, reminiscent of the Overlook Hotel in *The Shining* (Stanley Kubrick, 1980), which also played host to a man with writer's block. Barton seems satisfied to be there at first because he's afraid of becoming tainted by Hollywood's glamour, but it's a very strange, alienating place, emphasising the isolation that writers often feel when they're working. Roger Ebert suggests that 'There is apparently only one other tenant,' and certainly the audience only ever sees Barton and Charlie, but if this is the case then who do all those pairs of shoes in the hallway belong to? It's possible that the shoes never go inside the rooms, and that they're merely cleaned on a daily basis by Chet. Both are sinister ideas, suggesting that the shoes are there either to make the hotel seem inhabited or that the guests never leave their rooms. (Some commentators note that another guest places a pair of shoes in the hallway during Barton's marathon writing session, but this is Barton himself. The figure is only partly seen, but in the script it specifies that the typing should stop just before the shoes go out and start again just after.)

Apart from the sexual activity in the adjacent room, which Barton and Charlie both hear, there is no evidence that anybody else is staying at the Earle. The suggestion of life behind those closed doors, the oppressive atmosphere of the narrow corridors, the mosquitoes that shouldn't be there, the peeling wallpaper and the rattling pipes, make the hotel seem like a character in itself, contributing to Barton's predicament. Eventually it turns out to be a place where you can go to sleep next to somebody and wake up to find them brutally murdered, a scenario which taps into a common nightmare as gothic narratives often do. Plus, it's always dark as hell in there. The Earle has to act like a character because it is a reflection of Charlie, an impression that is confirmed when it bursts into flames around his rage.

The film also fits into another kind of genre: that of movies about Hollywood, which includes *Day of the Locust* (John Schlesinger, 1974), *The Last Tycoon* (Elia Kazan, 1976) and *The Player* (Robert Altman, 1992). Given the noir connection and the fact that its central character is a writer, its most obvious relative is *Sunset Boulevard* (Billy Wilder, 1950), although its concerns are very different.

EVER AMERICA: Nineteen-forties Hollywood as seen in *Barton Fink* is a hermetically sealed world, operating by different rules to, and showing little awareness of, the world outside it. This is a world of self-delusion, heavy drinking and deceit.

Barton is thrown into this situation with no knowledge of how to go about writing a script for a formula movie. Lipnick gives him very little help, talking quickly and giving him no opportunity to ask questions. Geisler becomes exasperated with Barton when he tries to find out what he's supposed to be doing. Mayhew says he'll help but is always too drunk. Industries that are concentrated in one place have a tendency to be like this, being small enough that everybody can pretty much know everybody yet large enough that the people inside it never have to move outside. Movie people only know other movie people and they have trouble relating to newcomers and outsiders. The attitude of the two cops who come to question Barton shows us the other side of this: when Barton tells them that he's a screenwriter they instantly become sarcastic and hostile. They assume that people in the movie business have an inflated sense of their own importance, and to be honest, most of the people in the Hollywood of *Barton Fink* do. Ego is a major theme in this film. Everybody seems to hate everybody unless it suits their purposes to do otherwise, with writers often at the bottom of the pile (as Lipnick eventually demonstrates, in spite of his previous bluster).

Just as the audience is always aware that Barton's concerns are foolish, they are equally aware that Lipnick isn't genuine because he comes on so strongly. When Barton tells him that he's staying at the Earle, Lipnick suggests moving him to a better hotel and finally suggests that Barton come and stay at his house. He keeps talking about how much he likes Barton but his opinions are only based on things other people have told him. When Geisler tells Barton that Lipnick can't read, it's difficult to tell whether or not he's exaggerating Lipnick's unwillingness to read scripts. It may be literally true.

It's when he's really put under pressure that Barton finally starts to play the game, bluffing his way through the meeting with Lipnick after an early morning whisky to calm his shattered nerves. He comes up with a lengthy artistic justification for his professed unwillingness to talk about a piece of work in progress, to which Lou gives the sensible response, demanding that Barton repay the studio's confidence by telling them what they can expect from Barton's script. However, Lipnick remains on Barton's side and fires Lou, who has been with the company most of his life. The falseness of the gesture is revealed when Lou turns up in the penultimate scene, still doing his job as though nothing had happened.

Lipnick turning sour on Barton is inevitable from the beginning, but the reasons for it may be simple office politics rather than because of anything Barton does. Lipnick mentions towards the end that Lou read Barton's script on his behalf: it's because of Barton that Lou got fired and it would come as no surprise if Lou had rubbished Barton's script because Lipnick's interest in Barton was threatening him. Whatever the qualities of Barton's script (and the viewer is led to suspect that it isn't very good), Hollywood does not operate on merit, but on who has decided to like you on any given day.

That said, the Coens have noted that *Barton Fink* is not intended to represent their experience of Hollywood. While mainstream Hollywood has never really understood the Coens this has hardly impeded their career, and indeed they have been invited into the mainstream before and politely declined (they could have accepted the offer to make *Batman*, for example). They work just outside the system because they like it there and they get the major studios to co-operate when necessary while maintaining final cut. Some critics have suggested that Barton's experience is supposed to show that Hollywood steamrollers the creativity of the individual, but this reading presupposes that Barton is a sympathetic character, which he isn't, really. Having seen how misplaced Barton's aims are, it would seem wrong if he ultimately succeeded, because failure might teach him something valuable. It isn't unusual to find critics who have a love–hate relationship with Hollywood, consuming its product while condemning it as an institution, and many seized upon *Barton Fink* as an attack on the industry.

Michael Dunne addressed the many attempts to pin down the 'meaning' of the film in an article entitled '*Barton Fink*, Intertextuality, and the (Almost) Unbearable Richness of Viewing' for *Literature/Film Quarterly*. 'By trying to reduce the film's meaning to a single clear statement, each interpretation just as clearly turns out to be, as Bakhtin would say, too monological.' Dunne notes that while the film may contain satire on Hollywood, it also pastiches Hollywood product, has a great deal to say about the nature of creativity and satirises certain brands of left-wing politics, among other things. Taking a non-reductive approach, therefore, permits the film to be richer. While there is a degree of satire in the way that Hollywood is depicted in the film, the effect is that it seems surreal, self-important and contradictory rather than actively evil, and much of the satire grows from the fact that it was necessary to make the place seem strange if the movie was to work (see **DEVELOPMENT**).

A rather churlish criticism came from Richard T Jameson of *Film Comment*. 'One of the things the Coens get wrong is the movies themselves – their history and lore, and the accidental/inevitable conjunction of art and zeitgeist.' Jameson picks holes in the movie's depiction of Hollywood, suggesting that it betrays ignorance and disrespect on the Coens' part: its fictional Capitol Pictures 'would make sense as a version of Cohn's Columbia in the early thirties' but 'bears no resemblance to Columbia or MGM or any other studio that could have had Wallace Beery under contract in 1941'. He also complains about the 'careless melange of Faulkner-bio minutiae and libellous distortion' that makes up the character of Mayhew and cites similar problems with Barton as a version of Odets. All of this ignores the fact, however, that *Barton Fink* is not a documentary. It does not purport to be an accurate representation of Hollywood in 1941: the Coens simply took the details that they wanted from the general period, according to whether or not they fitted into the story they wanted to tell. While Faulkner and Odets were the inspiration for Mayhew and Barton they are not supposed to be the same. It is true that in 1941 the Group Theatre was already an established success and Barton's story more properly belongs in the 1930s. However, setting the film in 1941 brings other advantages, such as the sense of distant tension that comes from the impending war (reflected in the names of Mastronotti and Deutsch), although the Coens have claimed that their chief motivation was that they wanted to incorporate the stories about Jack Warner's uniform.

AVAILABILITY: At the time of writing, *Barton Fink* has not been made available on DVD in Britain or America and the VHS is increasingly hard to find. A DVD with limited extras is available in France. Apparently the Coens do plan to prepare bonus materials for a special edition DVD release in the near future.

THE COENS' VIEW: 'We are conscious of the expectations bred by what happens in the early part of the movie . . . and a way to keep the story interesting is to keep the audience a little off balance.' (The Coens in 1992)

VERDICT: 'We all need understanding, Barton. Even you.' It isn't easy to put into words just what makes *Barton Fink* so good, and that's one of the reasons *why* it's so good. It remains consistently fascinating because it poses intriguing questions, usually implicitly rather than explicitly, but refuses to provide any answers. You can think about it and think about it but it will never completely resolve itself. Instead, it lurks in your brain, becoming a better film in retrospect as its subtleties unfold. Its startling images – the body, the beach, the burning corridor – resurface again and again, and continue to mesmerise on subsequent viewings. It may well be the Coens' best film; it may well be one of the best films ever to come out of America.

It comes as no surprise to learn that *Barton Fink* was written very quickly. There's a beautiful emotional continuity to the whole piece that bridges the film's ambiguities, permitting those ambiguities to exist and thereby creating a space for the viewer to bring whatever they want to the film. Without that continuity the ambiguities of character might seem like vagueness, the ambiguities of plot might just be unsatisfying narrative jumps and the detached camera style might seem cold and perhaps even slightly cowardly. It seems likely that the Coens found *Barton Fink* relatively easy to write partly because they were on familiar ground, exploring the nature of a creative vocation, but mainly because it *makes sense* on a fundamental level.

Because of this, *Barton Fink* does not need to give you the answers; it does not need to tell you who is right and wrong. For some commentators this constitutes a frustrating lack of commitment from the Coens, signalling the brothers' unwillingness to make any kind of judgement on the situation they have created. However, for others it is this, rather than the Hollywood in-jokery, that is the film's true pleasure. It is a pluralist's dream, allowing the viewer space to consider the situation from many different viewpoints. There's always the risk that you'll get lost in the middle but it's such a great place to get lost.

The Hudsucker Proxy (1994)

(Colour – 111 mins)

Warner Brothers Presents
In Association with PolyGram Filmed Entertainment
A Silver Pictures Production
In Association with Working Title Films
Directed by Joel Coen
Produced by Ethan Coen
Written by Joel Coen, Ethan Coen & Sam Raimi
Co-producer: Graham Place
Executive Producers: Eric Fellner and Tim Bevan
Director of Photography: Roger Deakins BSC
Production Designer: Dennis Gassner
Film Editor: Thom Noble
Costume Designer: Richard Hornung
Music by Carter Burwell
Visual Effects Produced and Supervised by Michael J McAlister
Mechanical Effects by Peter M Chesney
Supervising Sound Editor: Skip Lievsay
Casting: Donna Isaacson CSA, John Lyons CSA

CAST: Tim Robbins (*Norville Barnes*), Jennifer Jason Leigh (*Amy Archer*), Paul Newman (*Sidney J Mussburger*), Charles Durning (*Waring Hudsucker*), John Mahoney (*Chief*), Jim True (*Buzz*), Bill Cobbs (*Moses*), Bruce Campbell (*Smitty*), Harry Bugin (*Aloysius*), John Seitz (*Benny*), Joe Grifasi (*Lou*), Roy Brocksmith, John Wylie, IM Hobson, Gary Allen, John Scanlan, Richard Woods, Jerome Dempsey, Peter McPherson (*Board Members*), David Byrd

(*Dr Hugo Bronfenbrenner*), Christopher Darga (*Mailroom Orienter*), Patrick Cranshaw (*Ancient Sorter*), Robert Weil (*Mailroom Boss*), Mary Lou Rosato (*Mussburger's Secretary*), Ernie Sarracino (*Luigi the Tailor*), Eleanor Glockner (*Mrs Mussburger*), Kathleen Perkins (*Mrs Braithwaite*), Joseph Marcus (*Sears Braithwaite of Bullard*), Peter Gallagher (*Vic Tenetta*), Noble Willingham (*Zebulon Cardoza*), Barbara Ann Grimes (*Mrs Cardoza*), Thom Noble (*Thorstenson Finlandson*), Steve Buscemi (*Beatnik Barman*), William Duff-Griffin (*Newsreel Scientist*), Anna Nicole Smith (*Za-Za*), Pamela Everett (*Dream Dancer*), Arthur Bridges (*The Hula-Hoop Kid*), Sam Raimi, John Cameron (*Hudsucker Brainstormers*), Skipper Duke (*Mr Grier*), Jay Kapner (*Mr Levin*), Jon Polito (*Mr Bumstead*), Richard Whiting (*Ancient Puzzler*), Linda McCoy (*Coffee Shop Waitress*), Stan Adams (*Emcee*), Karl Mundt (*Newsreel Announcer*), Joanne Pankow (*Newsreel Secretary*), Mario Todisco (*Norville's Goon*), Colin Fickes (*Newsboy*), Dick Sasso (*Drunk in Alley*), Jesse Brewer, Philip Loch, Stan Lichtenstein, Todd Alcott, Ace O'Connell, Richard Schiff, Frank Jeffries, Lou Criscuolo, Michael Earl Reid (*Mailroom Screamers*), Mike Starr, David Hagar, Willie Reale, Harvey Meyer, Tom Toner, David Fawcett, Jeff Still, David Gould, Gil Pearson, Marc Garber, David Massie, Mark Miller, Peter Siragusa, Nelson George, Michael Houlihan, Ed Lillard (*Newsreel Reporters*), Wantland Sandel, James Deuter, Rick Peeples, Cynthia Baker (*New Year's Mob*)

TAGLINE: 'A comedy of invention.'

SUMMARY: The movie opens over New York on New Year's Eve 1958, and the President of Hudsucker Industries, Norville Barnes, is considering leaping from the top of the Hudsucker Building. There is a flashback to one month ago as Norville, fresh from business school, takes a job in Hudsucker's mailroom. Current president Waring Hudsucker commits suicide, leaving no will and no living relatives. His controlling share of the company will be sold to the public in one month. The other board members cannot afford to buy Waring's stock, but they plan to install a new, uninspiring chairman, thereby depressing the price until they *can* afford it.

Norville takes a Blue Letter up to Vice President Sidney J Mussburger. Norville shows Mussburger the invention that he believes will make his fortune – a circle drawn on a piece of paper – and Mussburger installs Norville as chairman. Hudsucker stock plummets in value. Amy Archer of *The Manhattan Argus* determines to investigate Norville and gets a job as his secretary. She runs an exposé stating that Norville is an imbecile, but then she discovers the board's plan to manipulate the stock. Norville shows the board his invention, which is dubbed the Hula-Hoop. Mussburger believes it will finally make Hudsucker into a joke, but instead it builds into an enormous craze and the stock is more valuable than ever. The lift operator, Buzz, shows an increasingly arrogant Norville that he too has an invention: the bendable straw. Norville fires Buzz but plans to keep the invention for himself. Mussburger reveals to Norville that Amy is a journalist and tells Norville to take the fall for this security leak. Meanwhile the *Argus* is about to print the story about Norville stealing Buzz's idea, which prompts Amy to resign in support of Norville.

Mussburger gets a psychiatrist to declare that the depressed Norville is insane and must be removed. Norville goes to his office, puts on his postroom overalls, and climbs out onto the ledge. He falls, then he suddenly stops. The clock-keeper, Moses, has wedged his broom in the workings of the clock and time itself has stopped. Waring Hudsucker, now an angel, appears and tells Norville to read the Blue Letter that he never delivered to Mussburger. It contains Waring's last wishes and bequeaths his stock to whomever Mussburger chooses as the next president. Since Mussburger chose Norville, Norville controls the company. He makes it to the ground safely and reconciles with Amy, then he invents the Frisbee.

DEVELOPMENT: Shortly after the release of *Blood Simple* the Coens were asked how they would approach a comedy, and Ethan noted that they already had a comedy script sitting in the drawer. 'Our comedy begins with a suicide,' he said, 'but it's a very fun suicide. It won't upset anybody.' References to this mysterious project would pop up in interviews for the next few years. When promoting *Raising Arizona* they were asked if they had ever considered setting a movie in the north-west, and referred to an old script 'that does take place in New York . . . the late 1950s. It takes place in a skyscraper and is about big business. The characters talk fast and wear sharp suits.'

This script was *The Hudsucker Proxy*, a film that Joel and Ethan had written while trying to secure distribution for *Blood Simple*. Sam Raimi had moved out to Los Angeles after the success of *The Evil Dead* and so the Coens used his apartment as a base from which to hawk their own debut feature around Hollywood. Their attempts to sell *Blood Simple* met with failure but they did get an opportunity to write a second script in collaboration with Raimi. (Raimi was about to take their first co-written effort, *Crimewave*, into production, and it seems that the trio were always in agreement that the Coens would get to do *Hudsucker*.) The new script bore some similarities to *Crimewave*, with influences from classic Hollywood, a cartoon-like comic style and a man falling from a tall building. 'From there it was a short step to having others jumping, trying to jump, falling, or being dangled, from this high building. It would seem that such a movie would have to be a comedy.'

'We were having fun,' Ethan remembers. 'The script, which contains a lot of traditional genre elements, was marked by a kind of heartwarming fantasy element out of Frank Capra.' The quick-fire dialogue style of comedy typified by Preston Sturges and Howard Hawks was also highly influential. 'But it was bigger and broader, with physical comedy sequences and a lot of oddball action.' When the film eventually got made it was Capra who was mentioned the most in reviews, although Joel stresses this was not the main influence on the script. 'There is Capra in the film, but there's more Sturges . . . Sturges had more of a satirical undertow . . . His relationship to business and society is much more sympathetic to our view than Capra is.' Joel also notes that their primary aim was not to critique capitalism but create a modern-day fairy tale 'with certain common mythical elements –

the good king who dies at the beginning, the evil regent, the callow youth who comes in and supplants the big king.'

What really tied the film together was the addition of the Hula-Hoop. 'We had to come up with something that this guy was going to invent that on the face of it was ridiculous,' says Joel. 'Something that would seem, by any sort of rational measure, to be doomed.' The audience, however, would know that the Hula-Hoop would be a massive success, and the Coens liked the way those two aspects would play off against each other. This in turn inspired much of the film's look and structure, 'the design element that drives the movie, the tension between lines and circles; you have these tall buildings, and then these circles everywhere which are echoed in the plot.' (Spinning objects often supply a keynote image in Coen movies: there's the hat in *Miller's Crossing*, the tumbleweed and bowling balls in *The Big Lebowski* and the hubcap/flying saucer in *The Man Who Wasn't There*.)

The period associations of the Hula-Hoop offered many possibilities: it was the sweeping craze of the 1950s and a watershed in product marketing. In reality the toy had no inventor as such, but the men who made it a success were Richard Knerr and Arthur Melin, who founded and ran the Wham-O toy company. The pair were informed in 1957 by a visiting Australian that children back home would spin hoops of bamboo around their waists. The hoop had been a common children's toy for centuries but it had never been marketed: Knerr and Melin saw an opportunity. They designed a lightweight version made of a plastic called Marlex and named it 'Hula-Hoop' after the Hawaiian dance that users seemed to be emulating as they played. While the Hula-Hoop's popularity didn't spread as impossibly quickly as depicted in *The Hudsucker Proxy* it wasn't far off: Wham-O sold 25 million hoops in just two months. This was fortunate for the company as it couldn't claim to have invented the toy and was unable to patent it: the sheer speed of sales meant that Wham-O was able to make a huge profit before its rivals were able to market their own versions. By the end of 1958, with the craze dying down, Wham-O had made $45 million in profits from the Hula-Hoop. One element of *Hudsucker* that is entirely accurate is that the man responsible for the Hula-Hoop also discovered the Frisbee: Knerr followed up his original brainwave by mass-producing and marketing the flying disc. (There's a disclaimer at the end of the film that acknowledges the fictionality of the Coens' version of this 'true American success story'.)

Joel admits that, while the Hula-Hoop and Frisbee were included in the plot as emblems of the 1950s, they have no idea who invented the bendable straw or when. Indeed, if you search for this information on the Internet you will probably get a bunch of references to 'the person who invented the bendy straw' as shorthand for an inspired genius, with nobody able to supply the inventor's identity. As the script was already made up from a melange of mid-twentieth century motifs, however, any anachronisms could be said to be wholly unimportant (see **EVER AMERICA**).

On completing the script, the Coens and Raimi realised that *The Hudsucker Proxy* was not a feasible project at that stage in their careers. 'The scale of *Hudsucker* was bigger than anything we had ever done before,' says Joel. 'It became clear that it was going to be a really expensive movie to make . . . although it continued to interest us, we put it aside and completed other projects. But we always hoped to go back to it some day . . . There are certain movies that just won't die.'

REFERENCES: The name 'Hudsucker' recalls JJ Hunsecker, the newspaper columnist played by Burt Lancaster in *The Sweet Smell of Success* (Alexander Mackendrick, 1957). (The script for that, incidentally, was co-written by Clifford Odets: see **Barton Fink**.)

The sequence in which Moses battles with Aloysius in the workings of the Hudsucker clock again recalls *Sullivan's Travels* (Preston Sturges, 1941). At the beginning of Sturges's film, the film director John L Sullivan shows the studio bosses the ending of his latest picture, in which two men fight atop a train and both fall to their deaths. Sullivan explains that they are intended to represent Labour and Capital destroying each other. Moses's victory over Aloysius sees conservatism defeated by progress, although their battle is rather more literal as they are fighting for Norville's survival.

CASTING: For the first time the Coens found themselves putting bona fide movie stars in their new project. However, their reputation was growing and securing their desired cast posed no problems. 'We talked over our ideas with Joel [Silver],' says Joel, 'and the first good sign was that we all agreed on who would be perfect for the film. The great thing is that we got everybody we wanted.'

First up was Tim Robbins, who might not have seemed an obvious choice for the naïve Norville given his recent roles in the Hollywood satire *The Player* (Robert Altman, 1992) and the political satire *Bob Roberts* (1992), the latter of which he also wrote and directed. However, the actor was up for a change. 'I jumped at the chance to do a guy who isn't an evil sonofabitch, a guy who had a heart,' he says. 'And Norville's not dumb – he's just ill-equipped to get by in a fiercely competitive world.' Until *Hudsucker* the Coens had largely worked with actors they already knew, but on casting their net further for *Hudsucker* they found that an increasing number of stars were keen to appear in their projects. 'When I finished *The Player* I said what I wanted to do next was to work with the Coen brothers. It's great that it happened.'

Also coming to *Hudsucker* from working on a Robert Altman movie was Jennifer Jason Leigh, who had just taken a role in the ensemble piece *Short Cuts* (1993). Leigh first came to prominence in early teen movie *Fast Times at Ridgemont High* (Amy Heckerling, 1982) and had done acclaimed work on *Last Exit to Brooklyn* (Uli Edel, 1989) and *Single White Female* (Barbet Schroeder, 1992). Since appearing in *Hudsucker* as Amy Archer, Leigh has continued to associate with the Coens, doing dialogue overdubs during post-production on a number of their subsequent films.

The Coens ventured beyond mere 'star' territory when they employed a genuine movie legend to play Mussburger. Paul Newman's career stretches back to the mid-1950s, with credits including *The Hustler* (Robert Rossen, 1961), *Cool Hand Luke* (Stuart Rosenberg, 1967), *Butch Cassidy and the Sundance Kid* (George Roy Hill, 1969), *The Life and Times of Judge Roy Bean* (John Huston, 1972) and *The Sting* (George Roy Hill, 1973). The

Coens note that he was one of their first choices for the role of Mussburger. 'And when we met him, Paul asked what it was that had suggested him to us for the part, but we couldn't think of anything! Which is kinda why we wanted him!' Nevertheless, Newman enjoyed the script and took the role on, seeing Mussburger as 'a road company Machiavelli – and who would turn down a chance to play Machiavelli?' He very much enjoyed working on *The Hudsucker Proxy*, claiming that he hadn't had so much fun on a movie since the hockey drama *Slap Shot* (George Roy Hill, 1977). 'I'm not a comic actor by instinct, but I came to relish every moment of it . . . I had a ball.'

However, when it came to the smaller roles the Coens continued to rely on trusted colleagues. Bruce Campbell, whom the Coens knew via Raimi and who had previously appeared in *Crimewave*, took the part of Smitty, while *Barton Fink*'s Faulkner-a-like John Mahoney was engaged to play the editor of *The Manhattan Argus*. There were one-scene roles for Steve Buscemi and Jon Polito, both of whom had appeared in *Miller's Crossing* and *Barton Fink*: they portrayed the beatnik bartender and Mr Bumstead respectively. John Goodman also made a contribution, providing the exuberant newsreel voice-over, although he was credited under the name of his *Barton Fink* character Karl Mundt.

A further, curious, casting note: the Texan oil heiress and former stripper Anna Nicole Smith appears briefly in a couple of scenes as 'high-fashion model, Za-Za'.

PRODUCTION: Following the critical success of *Barton Fink*, and with their four-picture deal with Circle Films fulfilled, Joel and Ethan felt that now might be the time to try and raise the large budget that they would need to get *The Hudsucker Proxy* off the ground. Their agent Jim Berkus sent the script to his friend Joel Silver, one of Hollywood's most profitable producers (he was behind the *Die Hard* series, the *Lethal Weapon* series and the two *Predator* movies). Silver had long been an admirer of the Coens' work and saw that, with *Hudsucker*, they were trying to put together something with more mainstream appeal. 'The script was the most accessible I had ever seen the Coen brothers attempt,' he says, 'and I wanted to help them make it a reality.'

With his background in 'big, glass-shattering action movies' (Joel Coen's words), Silver might seem an odd choice for the Coens to work with. At first, they thought so too. 'When we heard he was interested, we were kind of suspicious,' says Joel, 'but he said he just wanted us to make it the way we wanted to, and that turned out to be the case . . . You hear all this stuff about him, but from our point of view he did exactly what he said he was going to do.' Silver demonstrated his industry savvy by getting a number of parties to chip into the production. He partly financed the film through his own production company, Silver Pictures, and the rest came from a deal with Tim Bevan and Eric Fellner of the British company Working Title Films. Bevan and Fellner took on executive producer roles and stuck with the Coens for later films (Working Title co-produced *Fargo* and were sole producers of *The Big Lebowski*, *O Brother, Where Art Thou?* and *The Man Who Wasn't There*). Silver also sold the domestic distribution rights to Warner Brothers and the international rights to PolyGram. This secured the $25 million budget required for *The Hudsucker Proxy* and, after passing the money on to the Coens, Silver did not attempt to influence the film's development any further. He didn't even take a production credit.

There have been stories that Silver's working relationship with the Coens was difficult and that their differing backgrounds in filmmaking caused disagreements. The majority of these stories originate from another of the Coens' practical jokes. Having employed their fictional editor, Roderick Jaynes, to write the introduction to the *Miller's Crossing* and *Barton Fink* screenplays, for *The Hudsucker Proxy* they fabricated an interview with Silver and credited it to Professor Dennis Jacobson of the University of Iowa. In this Silver seems to be heavily critical of the Coens' attitude, playing up to the perception of them as anti-commercial filmmakers, claiming that they didn't want a star of Paul Newman's size and noting that, on set, they tended to sulk behind their storyboards. None of this was true, and in fact Silver was sympathetic to the Coens' aims: 'They like being quirky, artistic filmmakers, but they want to have their movie perform as well. It's kind of hard when you make a picture and no-one really sees it.' The Coens' experience of shooting a big-budget picture was, in fact, comfortable and they continue to speak highly of Silver. 'He's a real enthusiast. Once he gets wound up about a project, he just goes for it, which proved to be the case with *The Hudsucker Proxy*.'

Most of the shooting on the Coens' previous films had been done around real locations, but in the case of *Hudsucker* a different approach was required. 'The ambition . . . was to create a fairy tale that would be self-consciously artificial,' says Joel. 'That dictated the decision to do everything on stage sets and to push them beyond reality in terms of scale and design.' While there was some location work done in Chicago, the majority of the film was shot on five sound stages at Carolco Studios and an industrial site, both located in Wilmington, North Carolina. The sound stages were largely required to accommodate the five gigantic rooms envisaged by designer Dennis Gassner. 'You see, we wanted things to be big,' Gassner says, noting that the 1950s-inspired table in the boardroom 'is so long that it had to be constructed in five sections and then assembled on the soundstage'. The size of the sets was intended to create an oppressive feel: Gassner likens the atmosphere of Mussburger's office to that of Mussolini's, and there's a pseudo-fascist look to many of the designs. 'We also transformed a huge empty space that contained a 275-foot-long hallway into a mailroom that looks as if it might have been designed by Albert Speer.' The mailroom was fitted out with 95 mail sorters that were salvaged from scrap and in excess of 350,000 pieces of mail were created to flow around the huge set. The whole was then painted military grey, to serve as a contrast for the more tasteful decor of the upper floors. This wasn't the only notable colour contrast in *Hudsucker*: Gassner and Deakins aimed to make the colours 'muted' up to the point where Norville presents his invention to the board. Thereafter the colours were brighter, with a lot more red used.

The art deco movement and the work of Frank Lloyd Wright were equally important. 'Ethan and Joel wanted an urban look that reflected architectural design that predominated in the 1950s,' Gassner continues. 'The style of the Hudsucker Industries building, both inside and out, derives from several sites in New York.' Gassner also notes that certain buildings in Chicago provided inspiration, such as the Merchandise Mart and the Standard Oil Building. Ultimately this gave the architecture a 1920s look, an anachronism that extended into other areas of the film. The late Richard Hornung, who returned as costume designer, commented that strict historical accuracy was not necessary in order to evoke the period of *Hudsucker*: 'The men's clothes reflect the 30s and the 40s. It all has to do with what looks right for the story.' (See **EVER AMERICA**.)

Hudsucker also required the use of far more visual effects than the Coens' previous movies, and for this they engaged Stetson Visual Services, a company founded by Mark Stetson and Robert Spurlock. Gassner had worked with Spurlock at Zoetrope Studios and recommended him to the Coens when they needed to create *Barton Fink*'s flaming corridor. Before *Barton Fink* wrapped they asked him to return for *Hudsucker*. Overall, the effects were supervised by Michael J McAlister.

Firstly, a model of the fantasy 1950s New York was required for the opening scene. McAlister says that the Coens didn't want a realistic reproduction of the skyline of 1950s New York, 'but rather a stylised version of what might have been there in the 1950s. So it became obvious that the only way to get that specific look was to build and shoot a miniature city.' Gassner defined the look of the cityscape with reference to a book entitled *New York in the Forties*, including the Chanin Building, the French Building and the Bank of New York. 'We took all our favourite buildings in New York from where they actually stood and sort of put them into one neighbourhood, a fantasy vision of New York, which adds to the atmosphere and flavour.' Most of the buildings only needed two faces as they would only be seen from the front and the side, and some background buildings only needed one, although the Hudsucker building was fully three-dimensional. The miniature set, created at a scale of 24:1, took the 27-member crew three months to build, with the footage of it taking a further three months to complete.

The crew also created a model of the Hudsucker clock at a scale of 6:1 for closer shots, including the long zoom on Norville at the beginning. This shot moved seamlessly from the wide shot of the clock to Norville on the ledge, an effect achieved by creating a full-size set of the area around Tim Robbins and nesting this inside the shot of the model clock. 'Marrying a live-action image with a painted or miniature element was, of course, nothing new,' McAlister says. However, in the case of the zoom-in on Robbins from such a distance, keeping the full-size set locked in with the model building, '*that* was state-of-the-art and the only way to do it was with computers.' The work at Computer Film Company in Los Angeles also included creating computer-generated snow and creating the composites of the falling sequences.

To create the two falls, the miniature New York set was hung sideways to allow full movement along the heights of the buildings. McAlister calculated that such a drop would take seven seconds, but for dramatic purposes it was extended to around thirty. Problems occurred when the Coens and Deakins decided that these shots would be more effective with a wider-angle lens. 'The buildings had been designed for an 18 mm lens, but as we tried a 14 mm lens and then a 10 mm, we liked the shots more and more.' However, the wider field of vision meant that the edges of the frame went beyond the fringes of the model city, leaving empty spaces with no buildings. In the end, extra buildings were created from putting the one-sided buildings together and placing them at the edges. Charles Durning's fall was shot conventionally, but because Tim Robbins had to stop abruptly at the camera, his was shot in reverse and he was pulled away from the camera. Over at Computer Film Company, the image was manipulated to make the actor look like he was moving more quickly (his apparent speed increased from 10mph to 100mph).

The biggest problem that the Coens encountered through working on this larger-scale production was that they were physically unable to oversee all of it themselves, something which the detail-obsessed brothers found hard to accept. For the first time in their careers they needed a second unit. Fortunately the only man whom they had ever entrusted to direct their material in the past, Sam Raimi, was between projects and available to take charge of the second-unit material. 'I got to shoot all the fun stuff,' Raimi says. 'Drop a camera 240 feet. A Hula-Hoop rolling through the streets. A guy crashing through a window.' (Raimi also made another acting appearance, as he had in *Miller's Crossing*: he and assistant director John Cameron played two of the men who are seen in silhouette, brainstorming the Hula-Hoop name.) As their co-writer, Raimi had a greater understanding of the script than anybody else they could have employed and had more invested in it being properly realised. It's hard to imagine them being happy to let anybody else oversee their work. In addition, Roger Deakins was spread thinly as he was required to work on no less than four sets – the main unit, the second unit, the model shots and the effects shots. None of the Coens' films since *Hudsucker* has been of a sufficient scale to require a second unit and it seems likely that they will continue to avoid this on all future films.

The scale of the production also meant that the Coens' work was more widely reported on than it had been before. Ominous rumours about the production circulated in *Variety* when the paper picked up on the fact that the Coens had gone back to shoot more material in the middle of post-production. These were reported as reshoots and taken as an indication that *Hudsucker* was in trouble, which Joel had to dispute when promoting the film. 'They weren't reshoots. They were a little bit of additional footage. We wanted to shoot a fight scene [between Moses and Aloysius].' Joel also noted that they had shot additional footage on all of their previous films. 'It was the product of something we discovered editing the movie, not previewing it.' *Variety*'s review of the film also overquoted the budget by more than 50 per cent, and since theirs was the earliest review it seems likely that the subsequent misquotes took their information from there (see **CRITICAL RECEPTION**).

Many people saw *Hudsucker* as the Coens trying to step up into the big league, but the brothers have always regarded their films in isolation rather than as stages in a progression and *Hudsucker* was no exception. 'We're really unambitious, to be honest, in terms of the industry,' Joel said shortly after the film's release. 'It happened with *Hudsucker* that we needed a larger budget than we were used to working with, but only because it was this story.' He noted that they wouldn't have minded making another of their smaller-scale projects if the money hadn't been there for *Hudsucker*, although of course, he could just have been saying that after seeing how little money *Hudsucker* made (see **BOX OFFICE**).

MUSIC: The score for *The Hudsucker Proxy* sees Carter Burwell again extrapolating from the work of others, in this case the Armenian composer Aram Khachaturian (1903–1978). Pieces from Khachaturian's *Gayene* suite (which was first recorded by the composer in 1955) form the basis of both the main opening theme and the music that runs under the Hula-Hoop montage sequence, and another section from it is used by Burwell for the scene in which Norville and Amy meet for the first time. Performed with a full orchestra, Khachaturian's pieces lend the score an appropriate Old Hollywood feel without resorting to Old Hollywood pastiche. Burwell builds the rest of the music around these pieces and the result is one of his best scores (Norville's theme is a particularly charming piece and was, rather oddly, later used in Britain on a Sainsbury's advertisement).

The popular music of the period is also reflected in the character of Vic Tenetta, played by Peter Gallagher, who sings 'Memories are Made of This'. The character is modelled on Dean Martin, the legendary crooner and icon of cool, who released the definitive version of the song in the early 1950s. ('Memories . . .' doesn't feature on the soundtrack album, but Martin's recording is available on *The Very Best of Dean Martin: The Capitol and Reprise Years*.)

CRITICAL RECEPTION: Roger Ebert's review in the *Chicago Sun-Times* of 25 May 1994 encapsulates the general critical reaction to *The Hudsucker Proxy*. On the one hand he declared that 'This is the best-looking movie I've seen in years, a feast for the eyes and the imagination,' but on the other . . . 'it's all surface and no substance. Not even the slightest attempt is made to suggest that the film takes its own story seriously. Everything is style.' Ebert just couldn't decide whether to admire or condemn the film, and on his four-star scale he chose the middle position of two. Most critics had the same misgivings, although they varied massively in their opinion on whether they posed a serious barrier to enjoying the film.

Todd McCarthy, reviewing for *Variety*, was as ambivalent as Ebert. '*The Hudsucker Proxy* is no doubt one of the most inspired and technically stunning pastiches of old Hollywood pictures ever to come out of the New Hollywood,' he wrote on 31 January 1994, but went on to complain that it was nothing more than a pastiche, lacking in 'emotion and humanity'. McCarthy grossly overestimated the film's cost, quoting it at 'somewhere in the vicinity of $40 million'. Such erroneous statements later made the film seem like an even bigger flop than it was. However, McCarthy did praise the Coens for making 'entire jaw-dropping sequences out of incidents that other directors would slide right by'. Georgia Brown of the *Village Voice* came down harder on the film. '*Hudsucker*, for all its ultrasavvy referencing, has none of its sources' simplicity or charm,' she wrote on 22 March 1994. 'More parody than homage, *Hudsucker* is replete with attitude, atmosphere, and decor.' She praised Leigh's performance, but 'Robbins is so goofy, I could barely watch.'

The British reaction to the movie was similarly wary, and some were actively hostile. 'Why do I think *The Hudsucker Proxy* one of the worst movies of this, or any, year?' asked Christopher Tookey in the *Daily Mail* on 2 September 1994. 'First, it is woefully unfunny . . . The slapstick is desperately unamusing and shot in a gloomy, over-emphatic manner. Second, the movie completely lacks charm.' Like those who assumed *Barton Fink* to be a satire on Hollywood then criticised it for not being satirical enough, Tookey seemed to read *Hudsucker* as a fumbled critique of capitalism. 'For it to be so, they needed to have created a more comprehensible company than the fairy palace they have constructed here.' Tookey's comments, along with other poor *Hudsucker* reviews, exude the sense that because the Coens had spent more money this time around, they were no longer being cut any slack. Many critics obsessed over the budget, which in reality was slightly less than the Hollywood average (at that time, around $28 million), and Tookey declared that 'A multi-million dollar budget has been wasted on film-school thinking.' Despite the Coens' belief that they were making a more accessible movie, the finished product was viewed as aloof and elitist, with the usual caveat of 'one for the film buffs', familiar from reviews of previous Coen films, stressed even more strongly. 'A few critics will doubtless congratulate themselves on picking out the numerous cinematic references,' Tookey sniffed before adding, without any apparent irony, 'which range from *Once in a Lifetime* [Russell Mack, 1933] to *Will Success Spoil Rock Hunter?* [Frank Tashlin, 1957].'

Also highly critical was John Lyttle, writing in the *Independent*. '*The Hudsucker Proxy* is one of those films that you go along and watch – stare at, actually – and then stagger out knowing that you couldn't possibly have seen the same film as the reviewers.' Lyttle was working from the assumption that the critics (a) loved *Hudsucker* and (b) couldn't understand why it had been a commercial failure in America, neither of which is true of the vast majority of reviews, so it is unclear who he was railing against. Nevertheless, he supplied a response. 'It takes the mechanism of old movies and high-style genres . . . but leaves out the engine (the heart, if you please) that ran those mechanisms.' Again, the budget was overquoted and used as a stick with which to beat the Coens, suggesting that more money carried with it a responsibility to make a movie that appealed to more people (although this, surely, is the concern of the companies that invested in the film, not the critics). 'They make movies for film buffs. You can hear them when they spot a lift from *My Girl Friday* [sic] or *It's a Wonderful Life* [Frank Capra, 1945] – they make an amused sound.'

The more positive reviews merely accepted the movie's style for what it was and appreciated the pleasures it offered elsewhere. 'As usual, the Coen brothers have created a brilliant film about archetypes and movie ghosts,' Geoff Brown wrote in *The Times* on 1 September 1994. 'For something with heart and a cast of humans, you must go elsewhere . . . Sometimes the Coens' exuberance stops your breath. Elsewhere, the strain of sustaining the artifice shows.' Derek Malcolm, reviewing for the *Guardian*, did not feel that the budget had been misused. 'No one could say that the new $25 million film is less stylish than the others,' he wrote in the 1 September 1994 edition. 'Certain sequences, in fact, are as good or even transcend anything that the brothers have done before.' Nevertheless, he suggested that at this stage in their career the Coens should be stretching themselves a little more: 'We are, however, starting to expect more from the Coen brothers.'

One critic who did enjoy the movie was Kim Newman, who described it as 'An archetypally populist story [told] in an arcane style that won't disappoint their fans but may be hard to take for many.' His review in the October 1994 issue of *Empire* called the Coens 'the most exciting contemporary filmmakers never to have had a crossover hit', implying a degree of regret that *Hudsucker* would not provide that crossover. Newman also disagreed with the suggestion that the film had no heart, noting that while the arch nature of the characters and story meant that some viewers would find them uninvolving, 'human warmth is imported by the sheer joy of the directorial flourishes'. Overall he awarded the film four stars out of five, saying that 'Whilst not to everyone's taste, this is without a doubt one of the most exhilarating films of 1994.' Newman also reviewed *Hudsucker* for *Sight and Sound*, which went some way towards compensating for its lack of advocates. 'While the earlier Coen films went beyond pastiche, this wholly delightful urban parable is content simply to juggle much-loved elements and present them with a cinematic verve that easily equals the originals,' he wrote in September 1994.

Probably the least critical review came from Alexander Walker, writing in the *Evening Standard*. Walker spoke of being saddened by the film's commercial failure, seeing this as an indication that audiences had forgotten how to engage with the values that had made such great cinema in the age of classic Hollywood. 'The sad thing about this is that it takes bravado to make such a film today – and the bravado hasn't been rewarded at the box office . . . The public's indifference may eventually be the public's loss.'

BOX OFFICE: The disparity between how much this movie made and how much it cost is almost physically painful. *The Hudsucker Proxy* was released in America on 11 March 1994. This is traditionally a lean period for movies, with few major releases coming out between the New Year and Easter, but on the plus side it does mean that small releases and curios don't get swamped. Yet again, however, the Coens were badly hit by the success of another recently released film. This time it was down to bad luck rather than bad planning, as the British romantic comedy *Four Weddings and a Funeral* (Mike Newell, 1994) proved a surprise hit and ultimately grossed over $50 million in America (ironically, like *Hudsucker*, it was co-produced by Working Title).

Even taking this into account, the performance of *The Hudsucker Proxy* was disastrous, with a final gross of just $2,816,518 from American box office. To save you working it out, with a budget of $25 million that means a loss of more than $22 million. Ouch. The movie will have made some further cash on worldwide release and video sales, but when a movie has made so little on initial release there's no rescuing it. The Coens have stated that they would be happy to work with Silver again, but after losing this much money on *Hudsucker* it comes as little surprise that he hasn't taken them up on it.

DIALOGUE TO SKIP BACK FOR:

Board member: (on Waring Hudsucker) 'Every step he took was a step up. Except, of course, this last one.'

Mussburger: 'Norville, let me shepherd you through some of the introductions here. Try not to talk too much. Some of our biggest stockholders . . . no, scratch that. Say whatever you like.'

Norville: 'Failure should not lead to despair, for despair looks only to the past, in business and in love . . . the future is now.'

ANALYSIS: So why didn't people take to *The Hudsucker Proxy*? The answer is that it's a very, very strange film. Even the films that it mines for inspiration are exaggerated and twisted out of shape. It is by far the Coens' most stylised film and it's understandable that critics and audience alike were slightly taken aback. That doesn't, however, mean that the many criticisms that have been levelled at it are necessarily valid.

What *Hudsucker* does is take the idea of stylising a movie scenario and push it to the limit. Audiences are used to seeing movies that take place either in something that is recognisable as the real world (either today or at some point in history) or in a fantasy world (such as the Earth in the future, another world or a magical past). If something is set in a fantasy world then you can get away with just about anything, because the audience doesn't expect realism. It's also possible to set something in the 'real' world and get away with stylising it if there are distinct fantasy elements. Tim Burton managed to sell a skewed version of the contemporary world in *Batman* (1989) and *Batman Returns* (1992) because the presence of Batman meant that people didn't expect realism (indeed, *Hudsucker* gives us some clues as to what the Coens' version of *Batman* would have been like). However, to tell a fairly conventional story of a young man's attempts to make it in the world of big business with so little heed to realism is a difficult thing to do.

The fact is that 'realism' is not the same as reality. Realism is an aesthetic like any other, a style in which you shoot your film to achieve a certain effect, and it's often used to disguise some contrivance in the plot. Take James Bond movies, for example: everybody knows how silly and contrived the plots of most of them are, but they have usually been designed, constructed and shot realistically. In *You Only Live Twice* (Lewis Gilbert, 1967) Blofeld has constructed a secret volcano base from which he is launching his own spacecraft to hijack other spacecraft. While this idea is by no means impossible it is fairly ludicrous, and the audience finds it easier to accept because they are provided with a realistic context for it. It's a kind of unspoken agreement between the filmmakers and the audience to play by a certain set of rules, an agreement broken by the Coens in *The Hudsucker Proxy*. Instead, they crank the contrivance up as far as they can.

Firstly, there's the timescale of the film. It all takes place over the course of a month, during which time Norville Barnes rises, falls, rises, falls and rises again. Events move astonishingly quickly: no sooner is Norville hired than he is made president of the company. You couldn't get a new product developed, produced and shipped inside the entire timescale of *Hudsucker*, yet Norville achieves that with the Hula-Hoop inside about a week: not only that, but the product has time to be branded a failure before subsequently becoming a resounding success. There's even time for a backlash against Norville as he is branded a one-trick pony. And at some point here Christmas is supposed to fall! Most companies find it impossible to get anything done at all in December, never mind produce the toy sensation of the decade.

But then, Hudsucker Industries is an idea of what a company is like rather than an actual company. Until Norville presents his Hula-Hoop idea the audience has no idea what the company does, although the 'Industries' part suggests that it makes things. Possibly. The fact is, it doesn't matter. This vague impression reflects the way that most employees in a big company only get a partial view of what's happening at any one time and don't see the big decisions. More significantly, Hudsucker is not *an* industry, it *is* industry. The important thing is Hudsucker's sheer size and its monolithic, dominant nature, not just as a building on the New York skyline but as a component of the American economy. It's a place where people can come to make their fortunes, so Norville signs up, despite the foreboding line in the job ad: 'Low pay and long hours. NO EXPERIENCE NECESSARY.'

Speaking of working long hours, notice how Norville never goes home? Notice how nobody is ever seen at home, and they are very rarely seen doing anything outside of work? That's because they've been pared down to their most basic elements, the elements necessary to tell the story, and their home and social lives aren't part of that. The closest the film ever gets to depicting an outside life is when Amy is twice seen reading a newspaper on the train, presumably commuting, and even then she's working while she does it by keeping up-to-date on the news. The result is that all of the characters in *The Hudsucker Proxy* are defined by their jobs. They *are* their jobs, in fact and, aside from a couple of diners, the beatnik bar and surrounding streets, the action takes place exclusively in the Hudsucker Building and the offices of *The Manhattan Argus* – in other words, the workplaces of the main characters, Norville and Amy. Even on New Year's Eve the Chief and Smitty are still at the office, the Hudsucker board is sitting around the table (in party hats) and Moses is still watching over his clock.

The Hudsucker Building itself is a very strange place, too, a retro-futurist art deco fantasy with little regard for logic. Although the script was written prior to the release of *Brazil* (Terry Gilliam, 1985) the visuals of the finished product certainly show its influence on the Coens, particularly in the mailroom sequences. *Brazil* and *Hudsucker* both endeavour to make their workplaces look huge and complex, while the employees are made to appear very small. As with the Hotel Earle in *Barton Fink*, the company is made into a silent character in itself, not least because once Waring (its father) dies, nobody manages to take control of it until Norville's discovery at the end. It also operates with a surreal and oppressive logic, like the way that Max Kloppitt Jr's pigeonhole is small because he's junior. Norville is barely given a chance to learn his job before he is thrust into it, being warned several times that if he makes a mistake his pay will be docked. The best expression of this is the announcement of Waring Hudsucker's death, which is flat but oddly poetic and concludes with the statement that the moment's silence will be deducted from the workers' pay.

Also mentioned here is the concept of 'Hudsucker Time', which seems like a joke at this early stage in the film but turns out to be real. The giant clock on the front of the building actually dictates the passage of time around the Hudsucker Building, and when Moses rams his broom into the cogs, time just stops. It is at this point that any sense of consistent reality breaks down, as Moses turns to the camera and asks the audience if they've got any better ideas on how to rescue the situation. Then, an angel appears and the audience has suddenly been plunged into fantasy territory, but it may be too late for many of them to adjust. The Coens (and Raimi) cheat completely here because there is no logic to how the time-stoppage works other than that which is needed to progress the plot satisfactorily. Mussburger is completely frozen in time but Norville has merely stopped falling: he can still talk and move. The snow continues to fall, which could be because even Hudsucker Industries can't influence the heavens but is more likely because it looks good. Norville is incredibly lucky not to hit the ground when he is saved by the false teeth. Everything else goes on as before when the clock starts again but Norville doesn't carry through the velocity from his fall (he hits the ground gently when time restarts for the second time). It's a purely fantastical resolution.

For all of its references to and derivations from other movies, *The Hudsucker Proxy* resembles nothing so much as a living cartoon. Mussburger's perpetual-motion desk toy stops click-clacking when he commands everything to wait, reflecting the way that cartoons often inject life into inanimate objects. When Byron throws himself at the plexiglass window he doesn't bounce off it – he sticks to it and slowly slides down because it's funnier. Indeed, if this had been an animated feature nobody would have batted an eyelid at the stylised aspects of plot and design – *The Simpsons* gets away with very similar things on a weekly basis. *Hudsucker*'s two elaborate lightning flashbacks as Mussburger hangs from the window supported by his trousers, flashbacks which then cancel each other out for comedy effect, is a technique that could have come straight from *The Simpsons*.

Many people complained that *The Hudsucker Proxy* has no 'heart', that it's a technical exercise that the viewer can admire but not become involved in. However, this is ultimately a comedy (it says so in the tagline) and should be judged on those terms. People didn't make the same complaint about the highly stylised Zucker/Zucker/Abrams comedies *Airplane* (1980) and *The Naked Gun* (1988), both of which did very well at the box office. The main difference is that Zucker/Zucker/Abrams tend to bombard the viewer with jokes and favour surrealism over subtlety, where Coen/Coen/Raimi weave their gags into the narrative and tend not to go for the cheaper ones. It's also true that *Airplane*'s parodying of disaster movies and *The Naked Gun*'s lampooning of cop-show clichés are more accessible to a mass audience than *Hudsucker*'s resurrection of Frank Capra and Howard Hawks (see **GENRE**). An appreciation of those films is not essential in order to enjoy *Hudsucker*, but it does provide a way in to the film. And that, in the end, seems to be why audiences reacted poorly to the film: they couldn't find a way in.

There's one other problem that is worth taking note of in retrospect, which is that all of the publicity for *The Hudsucker Proxy* focused around a keynote image of Tim Robbins holding a Hula-Hoop. This seems strange given the Coens' keenness on maintaining control over all aspects of their films. Could they not get control over publicity as well? If they did have control then they should have vetoed the poster because the presence of a Hula-Hoop negates a lot of their good work in constructing the plot. The film is obviously designed so as to lead the audience to believe that Norville really is a buffoon. He says he's invented something that will make his fortune but it's just a circle drawn on a piece of paper (he proudly notes that he designed it himself). The viewer is given no clues as to what his invention is supposed to be until . . . halfway through the film, he shows a working model to the board and the camera pans down, revealing that it's a Hula-Hoop, the toy phenomenon of the 1950s. The audience recognises it but the board does not, because in the fictional 1958 of *The Hudsucker Proxy* Hula-Hoops have not yet been invented and Norville is the visionary who came up with the idea. This signals an abrupt change in the audience's attitude towards Norville – or at least it would if the audience hadn't gone into the film with Hula-Hoops in mind. The second the viewer sees Norville's circle on the piece of paper and hears him say, 'You know, for kids!' they can guess what his invention is. The carefully constructed build-up is rendered instantly pointless by having a Hula-Hoop on the adverts. It's like writing 'BY THE WAY, ILSE GETS ON THE PLANE WITH VICTOR AT THE END' in large letters on the poster for *Casablanca* (Michael Curtiz, 1942).

GENRE: Unlike the Coens' other films, Joel says, '*Hudsucker* truly is a comment on the genres it draws from.' Those genres are,

Above M Emmet Walsh suffers during the gruesome climax of *Blood Simple*

Left Reed Birney prays for reprieve in *Crimewave*

Above Nicolas Cage as the feckless Hi in *Raising Arizona*

Below Gabriel Byrne and Albert Finney take care of business in *Miller's Crossing*

Above 'I'll show you the life of the mind!' John Goodman in *Barton Fink*

Right A comedy of invention: Tim Robbins, Paul Newman and Jennifer Jason Leigh in *The Hudsucker Proxy*

Above Frances McDormand and John Carroll Lynch in *Fargo*

Left 'You're darned tootin'!' William H Macy as the hapless car salesman in *Fargo*

Top right 'F*** it, Dude, let's go bowling.' Jeff Bridges, John Goodman and Steve Buscemi in *The Big Lebowski*

Bottom right Michael Rapaport and Rachael Leigh Cook contemplate revenge in *The Naked Man*

Above 'Damn! We're in a tight spot.' John Turturro, Tim Blake Nelson and George Clooney in *O Brother, Where Art Thou?*

Left Billy Bob Thornton as the laconic barber in *The Man Who Wasn't There*

Top right Tony Shalhoub and Frances McDormand in *The Man Who Wasn't There*

Bottom right George Clooney and Catherine Zeta-Jones as the scheming lovers of *Intolerable Cruelty*

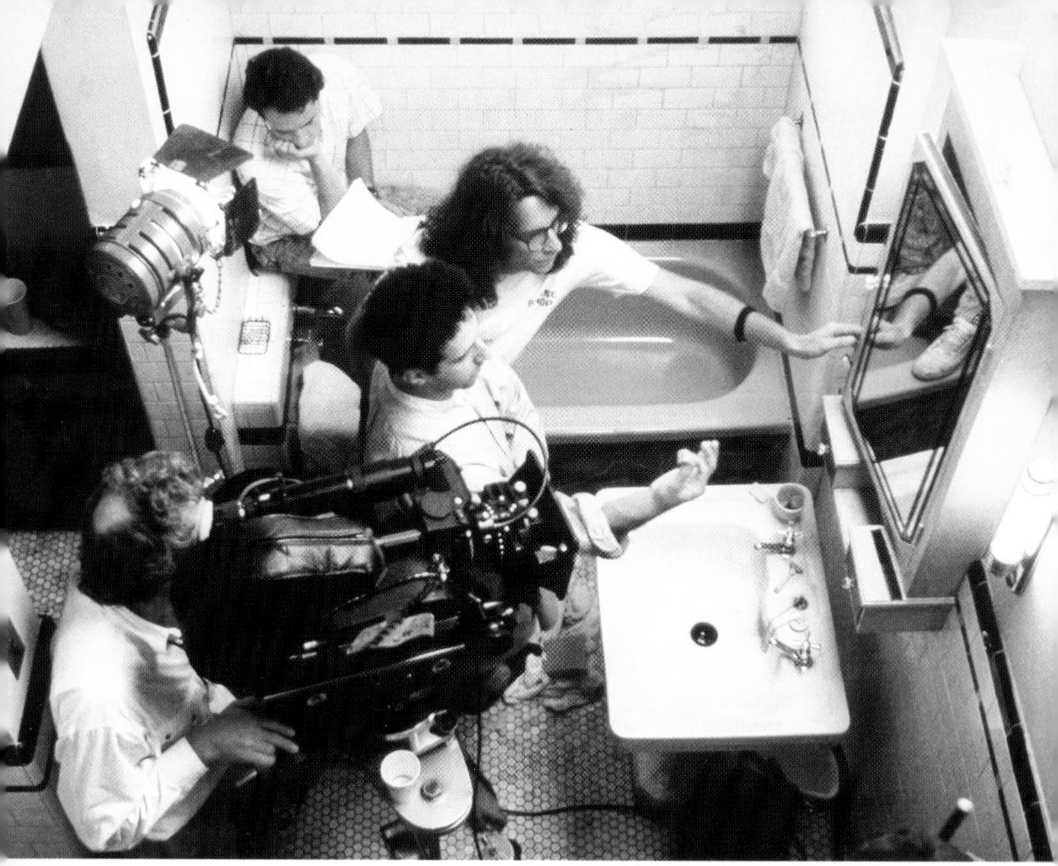

Above On the set of *Barton Fink*

Below Joel (*left*) and Ethan Coen contemplate *The Man Who Wasn't There*

principally, the screwball comedy and the modern parables exemplified by Frank Capra.

Hudsucker is not directly based on any Capra movie, but it does use his common themes, devices and motifs to construct a film like Capra would have made. For example, elements drawn from *It's a Wonderful Life* (1945) include beginning the film with a man on the brink of suicide and then skipping back to show us how he got there, the evocative Christmas setting (although Norville's jump happens on New Year's Eve rather than Christmas Eve) and the fact that his outlook changes due to the intervention of an angel. There's also the policeman and the cabby who run a self-reflexive commentary on Norville and Amy's first meeting, like the ones who spruce up George and Mary Bailey's home on their wedding night, and the image of the ruined Norville being ridiculed in the street recalls a couple of scenes from *It's a Wonderful Life*. The character of Norville is very much the naïve hero whom Capra takes as his subject in films such as *Mr Smith Goes to Washington* (1939), in which an ambitious, wide-eyed young politician makes his way to the big city. Sinister older figures try to manipulate him but he comes out on top in the end: it's a victory for the little man. *Hudsucker* unfolds in a completely different way but the themes are roughly the same. (It wasn't the only Capra-styled comedy of 1994: across town, Andrew Bergman was shooting *It Could Happen To You*, starring Nicolas Cage.)

The most obviously derivative character in *The Hudsucker Proxy* is Amy Archer. Anybody who has seen *His Girl Friday* (Howard Hawks, 1940) will find it impossible to watch *Hudsucker* without thinking of Rosalind Russell's performance. Norville's description of Amy could equally apply to Russell's character, Hildy Johnson: 'She's probably one of these fast talkin' career gals, thinks she's one of the boys.' A woman operating in a man's world, Hildy works twice as hard to prove that she deserves it. She's a little more modest about her achievements than the Pulitzer-flaunting Amy but they're both acknowledged by their colleagues to be the best they have. Amy and Smitty's bantering is very much like that of Hildy and her editor, Walter. (Amy's editor, however, is more like Perry White from the *Superman* comics, which is probably Raimi's influence.) Many critics complained about Jennifer Jason Leigh's rather mannered performance, which is perhaps understandable if you don't realise that she's doing an impression of somebody else (not only Russell but also Katherine Hepburn).

His Girl Friday is often described as the fastest-talking comedy in Hollywood history, an award which the Coens seem to be trying to contest in *The Hudsucker Proxy*. In addition to Leigh there's another rapid-fire performance from Jim True as Buzz the lift operator. In his first appearance he has already come up with a series of tasteless jokes about Waring Hudsucker's death, and he operates the lift in a series of rhymes linking everyone's name with their destination. When Mr Levin complains that he doesn't work on floor 37, Buzz tells him to walk down. Maintaining the flow is more important to Buzz than doing his job properly. This speech pattern is common to all of the characters in *Hudsucker*, who speak with a surreal rhythm. It's like the dialogue you hear in musicals, where the fact that the characters often break into choreographed song and dance means that notions of 'realistic' speech patterns are often set aside in the regular dialogue. This allows for such things as a spontaneous, unified declaration of allegiance to the Hud, as well as the montage sequence in which Norville is installed as president while the board members roar with laughter around him. The Coens push this so far in *Hudsucker* that the result can be unsettling.

Oddly, critics have often complained that they don't make movies like those old Hollywood comedies any more (in 1975 *The New Yorker* described *His Girl Friday* as 'The kind of terrific verbal slam-bang that has vanished from current film-making'), but when *Hudsucker* came along and tried to replicate that style the verdict was that it didn't work and was only of enjoyment to people who still watched and enjoyed those old movies. Maybe the smaller-scale, more theatrical aesthetic of early talkies was the only style in which a script like this would work, but enough people have watched and enjoyed *The Hudsucker Proxy* to suggest otherwise.

EVER AMERICA: Of all the Coens' movies, this is the one with the strongest sense of 'Ever America': a fantasy America rooted in nostalgia for a more optimistic, outgoing age. This is because it draws from a number of different eras and fuses them into an exaggerated ideal. 'It's not anachronistic as much as free, partly because of that fairy tale feel, that "once-upon-a-time" thing,' says Ethan. 'We almost had to arbitrarily pick a date and say, "OK, it's 1958", but the period is indeterminate.' The same is true of the place. 'Nominally, it's New York – but when you see the shots of the buildings, it's more generally Metropolis.' Like David Lynch, whose *Blue Velvet* (1986) did similar things in a small-town setting, the Coens push this vision so far, making it so bright and sanitised, that it becomes sinister. Lynch uses it because it's a great backdrop for the disturbing events that unfold behind closed doors in his films, but the Coens use it because it fits the story of a young man who has nothing but is determined to rise to the top. It's the American Dream, so central to Capra's movies, retold with a degree of irony.

Hudsucker's world-view is not based on any real idea of what 1958 was like, but on the world-view depicted in its source movies. John Harkness identified this as the film's major problem in an article for *Sight and Sound*, since its situation derived from Capra while its hero came from Sturges. 'The world created in [Sturges's] films is benign and harmless. His heroes do battle with their own limitations, rather than with the malevolent forces of darkness that range themselves against Capra's heroes.' Harkness maintains that the two are incompatible, because Norville should not be able to survive in this hostile environment. 'There isn't enough weird logic in the universe to save Norville Barnes from Sidney Mussburger, so the film's ending turns out to be more improbable than anything in Sturges or Capra.' It's a very interesting theory (as is his suggestion that the machine-gun dialogue only works in a more confined setting), but what saves Norville from Mussburger is not the 'weird logic' stopping of the Hudsucker clock – this merely provides an exciting context for the big twist. It's the rediscovery of the Blue Letter that turns things Norville's way, and this is all planted in an entirely logical fashion earlier on in the film. It would have been equally possible for Norville to find the letter before he'd fallen, but it would be less dramatic. It may be an odd fusion but the Sturges-type eccentric inventor *can* work in Capra's world, especially if he has been invested with the naïve courage that sees Capra's heroes win through.

That this discussion of *Hudsucker*'s time and place has mutated into yet another analysis of how it draws upon Hollywood's past is an apt indication of just what kind of film it is.

AVAILABILITY: *The Hudsucker Proxy* is available in America on Region 1 DVD, although there are no extra features. The only version available in Britain is a panned-and-scanned VHS. Both versions use the film poster on the cover with Robbins bearing the Hula-Hoop, thereby continuing to spoil this important plot point for a whole new generation of viewers (see **ANALYSIS**).

THE COENS' VIEW: 'There was a lot of press [about how] if you weren't familiar with all these [earlier] movies you'd be missing something, you wouldn't "get" the movie in some sense, which is definitely not the case.' (Ethan in 1994)

VERDICT: 'You told me you were gonna bring a smile to the hips of everyone in America, regardless of race, creed or colour. Finally there'd be a thingamajig that would bring everyone together! Even if it kept them apart, spatially.' It's important when looking at *The Hudsucker Proxy* to avoid getting hung up on how much it cost. The budget is really not the issue here. *Hudsucker* may have cost more than the Coens' other movies, but to its credit you can see exactly where all that money has gone when you're watching it. A glance at sets like the mailroom and Mussburger's office demonstrates this: it's very big, very bold and designed to the hilt. I've talked about the Coens creating coherent fictional worlds within their films and, while this normally comes from the characters and the camera style making a real place look slightly surreal, in *Hudsucker* they've literally constructed a fully conceptualised environment for their story to take place in. It is – and few people have ever seen fit to deny this – beautiful to look at. The budget has clearly been put to good use, and any arguments about the Coens having 'sold out' by making a more expensive movie are nonsense. Any problems *Hudsucker* has originate not from the money, but from the script and the Coens' approach to filming it.

The question everybody asks is where the film's 'heart' is. It's true that *Hudsucker* is *extremely* arch. The entire film seems to be in quotation marks, nothing represents anything real, and some people find that off-putting. But this is cinema: it's fabricated by nature. Who says it has to pretend to be real? Who says you have to believe in the characters in order to have a good time? As noted before (in **ANALYSIS**), realism is an aesthetic like any other and it is used to achieve certain effects. A somewhat different aesthetic has been used in *The Hudsucker Proxy* and it's one that had been out of common usage for decades. Just because audiences didn't have an adequate frame of reference for this style, does this mean that trying to resurrect it is a bad idea? *Hudsucker* has frequently been viewed as mere homage, pastiche even, probably because everything the Coens do comes with a layer of irony. This leads to the suggestion that only those with an equal love of the source material will understand, never mind appreciate, the film. However, there is a genuine attempt here to recycle and remodel those old movies in a way that would be viable for a 1994 audience. Joel Silver, whose populist nose has rarely failed him, certainly thought so. Unfortunately it didn't come off.

It is true that the choices made by the Coens in *Hudsucker* mean that it is not a particularly accessible film, but this does not, by any means, make it a bad one. It's a beautiful, strange, but comprehensively conceptualised piece of work.

Fargo (1996)

(Colour – 98 mins)

PolyGram Filmed Entertainment Presents
In Association with Working Title Films

Directed by Joel Coen
Written by Ethan Coen, Joel Coen
Produced by Ethan Coen
Executive Producers: Tim Bevan, Eric Fellner
Line Producer: John Cameron
Director of Photography: Roger Deakins ASC
Production Designer: Rick Heinrichs
Costume Designer: Mary Zophres
Music by Carter Burwell
Film Editor: Roderick Jaynes
Assistant Editor: Tricia Cooke
Supervising Sound Editor: Skip Lievsay
Casting by John Lyons CSA

CAST: Frances McDormand (*Marge Gunderson*), William H Macy (*Jerry Lundegaard*), Steve Buscemi (*Carl Showalter*), Peter Stormare (*Gaear Grimsrud*), Kristin Rudrüd (*Jean Lundegaard*), Harve Presnell (*Wade Gustafson*), Tony Denman (*Scotty Lundegaard*), Gary Houston (*Irate Customer*), Sally Wingert (*Irate Customer's Wife*), Kurt Schweickhardt (*Car Salesman*), Larissa Kokernot (*Hooker #1*), Melissa Peterman (*Hooker #2*), Steven Reevis (*Shep Proudfoot*), Warren Keith (*Reilly Diefenbach*), Steve Edelman (*Morning Show Host*), Sharon Anderson (*Morning Show Hostess*), Larry Brandenburg (*Stan Grossman*), James Gaulke (*State Trooper*), J Todd Anderson (*Victim in the Field*), Michelle Suzanne LeDoux (*Victim in Car*), John Carroll Lynch (*Norm Gunderson*), Bruce Bohne (*Lou*), Petra Boden (*Cashier*), Steve Park (*Mike Yanagita*), Wayne Evenson (*Customer*), Cliff Rakerd (*Officer Olson*), Jessica Shepherd (*Hotel Clerk*), Peter Schmitz (*Airport Lot Attendant*), Steven I Schafer (*Mechanic*), Michelle Hutchinson (*Escort*), David Lomax (*Man in Hallway*), José Feliciano (*Himself*), Bix Skahill (*Night Parking Attendant*), Bain Boehlke (*Mr Mohra*), Rose Stockton (*Valerie*), Robert Ozasky (*Bismarck Cop #1*), John Bandemer (*Bismarck Cop #2*), Don Wescott (*Bark Beetle Narrator*)

TAGLINE: 'A homespun murder story.' Also: 'Small town . . . big crime . . . dead cold.'

SUMMARY: 1987. Minneapolis car salesman Jerry Lundegaard is in financial trouble and knows that his wealthy father-in-law won't help him willingly. He hires two criminal lowlifes, Carl Showalter and Gaear Grimsrud, to kidnap his wife, Jean. He intends that Jean's father Wade will put up the ransom for his daughter, then Jerry will deliver it to Carl and Gaear but take half for himself. Gaear and Carl will also receive a brand-new car.

Carl and Gaear stop at a motel in the town of Brainerd and pick up two prostitutes, then proceed to Minnesota and kidnap Jean. Passing through Brainerd again, they are pulled over by a police officer. Gaear kills him and two other witnesses, abandoning their bodies on the side of the road. When the bodies are found, Brainerd's police chief, Marge Gunderson, ascertains that the murders were committed by somebody from out of town, driving a car recently taken from a dealer's lot, and her investigation leads her to Minneapolis. Carl and Gaear hole up in a cabin near Brainerd and Carl phones Jerry to demand the full ransom. However, while Jerry has told Carl and Gaear that the ransom is $80,000, he has told Wade that it's $1 million, intending to take the other $920,000 for himself.

Jerry finds Marge at the showroom speaking to Shep Proudfoot, the man who put Jerry in touch with Gaear. Jerry acts suspiciously when questioned about the car, which Marge believes may have been taken from his showroom. Shep, angry that the police have traced Carl and Gaear's crimes to him, finds Carl and beats him up, motivating Carl to call Jerry and set up a handover. Wade insists on going in Jerry's place, but Carl shoots Wade and escapes with the money. Carl returns to the cabin, burying the $920,000 on the way so that he can hide it from Gaear. When Carl arrives he finds that Gaear has killed Jean, and when Carl demands to be allowed to take the car, Gaear kills him too. Marge speaks to Jerry again: he panics and runs. On her way back, Marge spots the car parked outside the cabin. Behind the cabin, she finds Gaear feeding Carl's body into a wood chipper and takes him into custody. Meanwhile, Jerry is located in North Dakota and is likewise arrested.

DEVELOPMENT: 'Everything we have done before has been entirely fictional, [with] plots and characters that were self-consciously artificial,' Joel said while promoting the movie. '*Fargo*, on the other hand, was a conscious effort to explore the spectrum of a series of non-fictional events.' The style of the film was also intended to be more realistic in keeping with the story. At the time, the brothers talked a great deal about how they had worked with the material. Ethan noted that as he and Joel looked into the facts, 'the characters of Jerry and Marge were the ones that intrigued us most. They both sounded like very ordinary people with ordinary sensibilities that became involved in a scenario that was anything but ordinary.' Joel added that it is not uncommon for movies based on true stories to adapt the characters and the narrative to make them work more efficiently. 'In this case, however, we just left the characters . . . to play their parts. There was no need or desire on our part to tidy this one up – the characters very clearly speak for themselves.'

As is now well known, all of this was lies, a confidence trick played on the audience (see **GENRE**). The Coens had tried to avoid being rumbled too quickly by claiming that they had altered the location slightly and acknowledging that the conversations and relationships between the characters were based on guesswork. When asked where the murders *really* took place, Ethan said, 'I could tell you, but then I'd have to kill you.' However, the more questions people asked about the story, the more difficult it became for the Coens to cover up and they eventually admitted that they'd made most of it up, although it was true that a man had his own wife kidnapped and a series of deaths ensued. 'We heard about it through a friend who lived near to where the drama took place in Minnesota,' says Ethan. 'Generally speaking the movie is based on a real event,' adds Joel, 'but the details of the story and the characters are invented.' They didn't do any further research into the story and merely used what they'd heard from their friend. 'But, by telling the public that we took our inspiration from reality, we knew they wouldn't see the movie as just an ordinary thriller.'

As well as altering the audience's perception of their movie, the device imposed a different style on the Coens. 'We wanted to do something that was unlike the movies we had done in the past,' Joel says, 'which were all sort of self-consciously artificial.' In terms of story, the movie is no more based on a real crime than *The Hudsucker Proxy* is based on the story of the Hula-Hoop, but the treatment of the material, in terms of both scripting and direction, is far more 'realistic' and that's the major difference between *Fargo* and the Coens' other movies. 'The impetus was the previous movie, which was the most stylised of all,' says Joel, although he acknowledges that 'realism' is, in its own way, just as contrived. 'By starting from real events, we've arrived at another form of "stylisation". The results are maybe not as different as we'd envisaged.'

Although it was useful for the Coens to make a cheaper movie after flopping with *Hudsucker* (see **PRODUCTION**), it's likely that they would have followed up with *Fargo* whether *Hudsucker* had been a success or not. 'We began it before shooting *The Hudsucker Proxy*, then returned to it; so it's difficult to evaluate the time it took us,' says Ethan. 'What's certain is that the writing was easy and relatively quick.' Until then, the Coens had been resistant to shooting in their home state: Ethan remembers that, during the early part of the Coens' career, 'my whole association with Minnesota, where we grew up, was very dull.' *Blood Simple*, he recalls, 'had to be shot anywhere but in Minnesota.' More than a decade later, having gained some emotional and geographic distance from the place, they started to feel differently. Having decided to retain the location of the real-life kidnapping they started to incorporate other ideas that were specific to the area, ideas they'd never been able to use before. Joel recalls that they drew upon their experiences of raising the budget for *Blood Simple*. 'I remember having meetings with these hardened businessmen who would hang out in the local coffee shop and then put their parkas and galoshes on and slog out into this Siberian landscape.' The accents also contributed a great deal, although this element would later draw criticism to the Coens. 'Sometimes the way we approach writing something is through the dialogue and the rhythm of the speech,' Ethan says. 'That flat, Midwestern effect was what was interesting to us about this script.'

Ethan describes the scene where Jerry tries to sell a customer the TruCoat as 'almost a verbatim transcript of my experience [of buying a car]. We were interested in the psychology of a person who constructs those pyramid financial schemes but can't project themselves a minute into the future or imagine the consequences.' Like all the characters, Jerry was designed to appear convincingly ordinary. 'Marge and Jerry are both very banal, like the interiors and landscape,' says Joel. 'But she is banal in a good way, a good person where he is evil . . . Being pregnant: you can't get more ordinary.' This was also the motivation behind the rather incongruous scene in which she meets her old school friend, Mike Yanagita. 'We wanted to give another point of view of Frances' character without it being related to the police enquiry,' says Joel. 'That's also what happens in the scenes with her husband.' Ethan adds that, 'Our intention was to show the story had a relationship to life rather than to fiction, setting us free to create a scene that had no relationship to the plot.' Paradoxically, this is one of the things that makes it seem *less* like a true-crime story, since it seems unlikely that such a minor incident would have made it into any record of the events.

Although nearly all of the action happens in Brainerd and Minneapolis, the film was named after the place where it opens. When asked why they chose *Fargo* over *Brainerd*, the Coens replied that it was just a better title. 'It's literally the sound of the word that we liked,' says Ethan. 'There's no hidden meaning.' It wasn't the first movie to be given that title: a 1964 road movie directed by Brian G Hutton took its name from the North Dakota town.

REFERENCES: There's an obvious visual reference to *Psycho* (Alfred Hitchcock, 1960) in the sequence where Gaear discovers Jean hiding in the bathroom. She falls, pulling the shower curtain down, and the brief shot of the curtain popping off the rings recalls the murder of Janet Leigh.

In the scene with Carl at the Celebrity Rooms, Carl's escort asks him if he's from Minnesota, and he replies that he's 'Just in town on business. Just in and out. Just a little of the old in and out.' 'The old in-out' is the slang euphemism for sex in *A Clockwork Orange* (Stanley Kubrick, 1971). This is Carl's idea of a joke, but his date isn't impressed.

CASTING: Having cast bigger names in the central roles for *Hudsucker*, the Coens retreated back into their repertory company for two of *Fargo*'s main characters. While Frances McDormand's career had steadily blossomed since her movie debut in *Blood Simple*, the last time the Coens had employed her was for a small, uncredited role in *Miller's Crossing*. Joel claims that Frances, whom he had married in 1985, cajoled him into writing another part for her to play ('I don't get that from John Turturro, you know, I don't get that from him at home,' he complains). Hence, when writing *Fargo*, he and Ethan created the character of Marge with her in mind. McDormand says that earlier on in her career, she didn't want people to think that she was getting movie roles just because she was married to a Coen. 'Now it doesn't matter,' she says. 'If people want to say I slept with him for thirteen years to get the part in *Fargo*, let them!'

The other Coen regular to return was Steve Buscemi, who had appeared in their previous three movies, all in fairly small parts (he only has one scene in *Miller's Crossing* and *The Hudsucker Proxy*, and a few as Chet in *Barton Fink*). 'We are aware of his [psychotic] persona in other movies and wanted to push that in a specific direction,' Joel says. 'We wanted to write something substantial because he is so good.' Having first cast him in a quick-speaking role in *Miller's Crossing*, the Coens gave him another hugely verbal character to play in *Fargo*. Gaear, Carl's partner in crime, was also cast in the Coens' minds during the writing process: Peter Stormare, who had worked extensively in Swedish theatre, not only as an actor but also as a director and playwright. By the time of *Fargo* he had moved to America, where his acting roles included *Awakenings* (Penny Marshall, 1990).

'Peter's an old friend of ours,' says Ethan, 'and it seemed interesting, given his Swedish origins, to give him this part.'

Of the main roles, the only one not written with the actor in mind was Jerry. 'We imagined him a sloven, uncomfortable in his body, a little overweight,' says Joel. In the event the role went to William H Macy, a highly versatile actor usually cast in supporting roles and character parts. His work includes *Radio Days* (Woody Allen, 1987) and *Benny and Joon* (Jeremiah Chechik, 1993), but at the time of *Fargo* he was best known from his role as Dr Morgenstern in the hit medical drama *ER*. 'Casting Bill we went in the other direction [from our conception],' Joel continues. 'He is neat and tidy, not as we envisioned him . . . He is very put together, but tight and repressed.' Ethan also notes Macy's thorough conceptualisation of the character: 'Bill refused to do a single scene without this inane pin on his suit, in token of five years' service to car dealership.'

The film's oddest piece of casting was Harve Presnell in the role of Wade Gustafson. Presnell was a light opera singer, then best known for his work in 1960s musicals such as *Where the Boys Meet the Girls* (Alvin Ganzer, 1965) and *Paint Your Wagon* (Joshua Logan, 1969). He subsequently moved into theatre work, and *Fargo* marked his return to the screen after an absence of more than twenty-five years. 'He actually did a "dancin' in the snow" musical number for us,' says Joel facetiously, 'but we cut it for length.'

The Coens' old chum Bruce Campbell (from *Crimewave* and *The Hudsucker Proxy*) also found his way into the film although he was never on set. The soap opera that Gaear is seen watching at the hideout is a genuine low-budget soap opera from the period and the area, called *Generations*. It ran on a UHF TV channel in Detroit in the 1980s and the clip features the character Campbell played in the show.

PRODUCTION: Understandably, the Coens have been keen to play down the effect that *The Hudsucker Proxy* had on their careers. Warners' total loss on the movie was about $10 million which, as Ethan has pointed out, is not that much for a major studio to lose – 'They were more worried about their $40 and $60 million blockbusters.' Joel concurs: 'They were really good to us, actually . . . [Warner Brothers co-chairman] Terry Semel didn't repossess Ethan's car.' While the Coens were keen as ever to do something different after *Hudsucker*, in this case they didn't have a lot of choice. 'It narrows your options,' says Ethan of producing a dud. 'And that's certainly regrettable and it disappointed us.'

However, *Hudsucker*'s British partners, Working Title, hadn't done anything like as badly out of it. They had been awarded the foreign rights in exchange for their investment and more or less broke even, meaning that executive producers Tim Bevan and Eric Fellner remained enthusiastic about the prospect of working with the Coens. 'During *The Hudsucker Proxy* we all discussed the possibility of working together again on future projects,' Fellner says. 'Of course, Tim and I were thrilled when Joel and Ethan brought *Fargo* to us.' In October 1994 the Coens sent the final draft to Bevan and Fellner, who gave it the green light and supplied the $7 million budget. This was the smallest budget Joel and Ethan had worked with since *Raising Arizona*. 'I don't think it's quite accurate to say that we worked our way up to a big budget,' says Joel, stressing that it was the particular demands of *Hudsucker* that led them to seek more financial backing. 'I guess that we're lucky in that it doesn't bother us to make cheap movies.' The pre-production process was very swift, as it went in front of the cameras on 23 January 1995.

'It was nice doing *Fargo* with them after *Hudsucker*,' says cinematographer Roger Deakins. '*Hudsucker* was quite a big picture. [The budget wasn't] a huge amount of money by today's standards, but that project had its own momentum. *Fargo*, on the other hand, was a small picture, but in a certain sense we could be more flexible because of it. Less pressure, a smaller crew and a more intimate production are advantages in many ways.' Joel agrees: 'It was fun for all of us, and a relief in a way. It was back to working with each other and a small crew in a very controllable environment, which was similar to how we had done *Barton Fink*.' Dennis Gassner, the Coens' regular designer since *Miller's Crossing*, was unavailable, so they engaged the services of Rick

Heinrichs (an old friend of, and regular collaborator with, Tim Burton). The film's minimal look presented Heinrichs with some challenges: 'People ask me, "So you designed *Fargo*? Well, like, what did you *do*?" ' Well, the giant statue of Paul Bunyan, for a start.

In another contrast to *Hudsucker*, which had mostly been shot on sound stages, all of *Fargo* was shot on location with the exception of two small bathroom sets. Also, in keeping with the 'true story' aesthetic, most of the material was shot where the events were supposed to have taken place, rather than having one location stand in for another – hence, most of the Brainerd scenes were actually shot in Brainerd, the Minneapolis scenes were actually shot in Minneapolis and so on. 'It was familiar, although it was also weird,' Ethan says of returning to Minnesota for the shoot. 'We'd been back occasionally, and our parents still lived there, so it's not like we hadn't been back in the interim, but it [had] still changed quite a bit from when we were kids. It was the same, but different.' However, the flat, white landscapes of Minnesota were an integral part of the visual style. 'We were trying to reflect the bleak aspect of living in that area in the wintertime – what the light and this sort of landscape does [to a person], psychologically,' says Joel. 'It was very important for us to shoot on non-sunny days . . . We scheduled the show so that we would be able to avoid blue skies as much as possible.'

This presented another challenge to cinematographer Roger Deakins: 'It's kind of a difficult balance to do something that's bland but not boring . . . In fact, we chose some of the locations because they were particularly bland. Both the designer and I would say, "Well, that's *really* nothing!" I mean, you still have to make it interesting, but they always manage that anyway. I think the Coens could probably make a blank white wall interesting.' The whiteness of the landscapes meant that Deakins was able to use less artificial lighting. 'I was very much working off natural sources. It's not something I always do, but I suppose I do it more often than not.' In any case, the Coens had specified to him that they wanted the film to look dark: even the night-time scenes were shot largely without additional light. 'You usually light up comedies,' Deakins continues, 'but the Coens didn't want to do that. This film was closer to the contrasty style of *Barton Fink*. *Hudsucker*, on the other hand, wasn't necessarily flat-lit, but it was meant to look kind of opulent. *Fargo* is meant to look real and raw.' The whiteout created by the wintry landscape and the blank sky created a sense of disorientation that Joel and Ethan were keen to make use of. 'One of the things we talked about with Roger Deakins,' Joel notes, 'was the idea of not being able to see where the horizon line is, where the land ends and where the sky begins.'

In terms of camera angles the film was more subdued and unobtrusive than the Coens' previous films. 'We wanted the camera to tell the story as an observer,' says Joel. 'It was interesting to try and restrain ourselves . . . We moved the camera far less and used a lot more over-the-shoulders.' The original plan was to keep the camera fixed at all times, but as Ethan says, 'we realised that purist attitude was a little stupid.' Deakins also convinced them to employ the longest lenses they'd ever used, with most shots being done with a 32 mm or a 40 mm lens, despite the Coens' fondness for the wider angle. 'I think it is still a prejudice with us – wanting to go wider more often,' says Ethan. 'It has to do with wanting to enhance the camera moves.' With there being so little movement in *Fargo*, the Coens accepted that longer lenses were the way to go. Deakins' earliest experiences had been on documentary films and he drew on these to give *Fargo* its crisp, distant, 'objective' appearance: 'The impulse here,' says Joel, 'was to de-dramatise things rather than to dramatise things.'

Unfortunately, having assumed the presence of snow and started filming under those conditions, the crew encountered the second mildest winter yet recorded in Minnesota. The snow melted before shooting was completed (described by Ethan as 'a drag') and, although fake snow could be used for some scenes, such as those on the rooftop garage, several others demanded a snowy plain. This forced the production to up sticks at the eleventh hour and move to North Dakota, where snow was still abundant. 'We left Minneapolis on March 9th, and we couldn't have timed it better,' says line producer John Cameron. The move necessitated the erection of a sign reading 'Welcome to Brainerd, Home of Paul Bunyan' outside the town of Bathgate, along with a 25-foot statue of Bunyan, the mythical Minnesotan lumberjack. Joel notes that North Dakota benefited the production in some ways. 'The landscape up there is even flatter and more bleak than it is around Minneapolis. We wouldn't have shot there had the weather been alright in Minneapolis, so in a sense we got more interesting exteriors than we might have got otherwise.' Despite the hiccups, shooting was completed on schedule after a week and a half of shooting in North Dakota. 'We got enough of the "white stuff" to complete the exterior sequence requiring snow,' says Cameron, 'and we were able to return to Minneapolis by March 20th, in order to wrap on the 21st.'

DELETED SCENES: The original scripted opening saw Jerry checking into a Rodeway Inn, where he plans to stay the night after the rendezvous with Carl and Gaear. This would have revealed Jerry's hopelessness even earlier, since he checks in under the name of 'Anderson' but fills out his registration card incorrectly. He automatically writes 'Jerry Lundega–', then crosses out the last name and writes 'Anderson' instead. Jerry then kills time until the rendezvous, watching the local news on TV and drinking coffee in a local restaurant, which would have made his late arrival at the Jolly Troll Tavern funnier. However, using the rendezvous as the opening scene means that the film gets into the plot that much quicker.

There was also to be a scene with Marge telephoning Norm from Minneapolis. Norm is at a fishing hut, speaking on a cellular phone, and Marge tells him what the food is like in the city. This may have been cut because the Coens felt that there were already enough scenes demonstrating Marge's normality, or perhaps because they realised that, this being 1987, Norm would probably not own a cellular phone.

Immediately after Jerry flees the interview, there was to be a scene in which Marge visits a local police station. Another officer tells her more about Jerry and his family while they queue up in the cafeteria. This could easily be cut since it mostly involves

Marge being told things the audience knows already, although it does feature the revelation that Wade's wife is undergoing cancer treatment and a nice coda with the other officer showing Marge pictures of her kids.

Also snipped from the script before shooting was a dream sequence that Rick Heinrichs was really looking forward to, involving Marge, a foetus and a bunch of Native American imagery.

MUSIC: Carter Burwell's approach to the music for *Fargo* was that the film had to balance a straightforward police story and a black comedy. 'I wanted the movie to be bombastic enough that you might just believe it was a real police story and yet, also through bombast, maybe make you just laugh a little bit.' The idea was to create a sense of uncertainty in the viewer, subtly overplaying the mood in order to suggest the possibility of irony. The technique is characteristic of Burwell's work for the Coens. 'It's all stated in the opening theme with harp and solo violin, which bring out the lonely qualities in these characters. Then it gets completely overblown when the orchestra and percussion come in.' This piece aims to lay out the themes of *Fargo* before anything visual has even happened, since all the viewer can see is the subdued image of Jerry's car driving through a blizzard.

After using full orchestra for *Hudsucker*, Burwell stripped it down for *Fargo*, using 'low winds and brass and percussion . . . like film noir *policier* scores'. He also used the same technique that had informed the music for *Miller's Crossing*, looking at the characters' immigrant roots for inspiration. 'I did a fair amount of listening and reading about Scandinavian music, and actually one of the themes for the movie is a Norwegian folk tune called "The Lost Sheep".'

CRITICAL RECEPTION: Following the ambivalent response to *The Hudsucker Proxy*, the Coens' about-face with *Fargo* was hailed as a return to their classic style. 'Joel and Ethan Coen have discarded the pretentiousness of their most recent work (*Barton Fink*, *The Hudsucker Proxy*) in favour of the eerie spirit and deadpan-slapstick of their *Blood Simple* and *Raising Arizona*,' wrote Desson Howe in the *Washington Post* on 14 March 1996. 'Throughout the hypnotised Midwestern atmosphere of this movie . . . Frances McDormand enjoys the comedic role of her career.'

'Following the marketplace debacle of *The Hudsucker Proxy*, the new Coen brothers outing demonstrates an assurance viewing classic themes from a slightly askew perspective,' wrote Leonard Klady in the 12 February 1996 issue of *Variety*. '*Fargo* is a strikingly mature, unique entertainment that plays on many levels . . . all satisfying.' *Newsday*, on 14 March 1996, noted that, with a plot filled with murder and intrigue and dialogue filled with regional tics, 'you know you're in a world that could only spring from the minds of David Lynch or the Coen brothers'. Reflecting the extent to which the critical pendulum had swung away from Lynch since *Twin Peaks* drew to a close, the reviewer continued, 'You're in luck with *Fargo*, it's the Coen brothers.' The review also joined in with the effusive praise for McDormand, stating that she had 'never been better'.

One of the few critics to remain unmoved by *Fargo* was Georgia Brown of the *Village Voice*. 'As usual with the Coens, some hipsters will find *Fargo* fiendishly clever,' she wrote in the 12 March 1996 issue. 'If only some of them hung around the office here, I could've relinquished this thankless task.' Brown acknowledged that the film was of a higher quality than most of the competition, but it didn't work for her. 'A leap over that *Hudsucker* dud, its dark slapstick harks back to *Blood Simple* and *Raising Arizona* (two movies I couldn't get on with either).' Brown was practically a lone voice in a near-consensus of critical opinion: Janet Maslin wrote that, 'The Coens are at their clever best with this snowbound film noir' in the 8 March 1996 issue of the *New York Times*. 'The violence is so quick it appears cartoonish, but there's no mistaking the fact that this tale is fundamentally grim. Yet the film-makers' absurdist humour and beautifully honed storytelling give it a winning acerbity.'

If anything, the British reviews were even better. 'Right from the beginning, the magnificent *Fargo* has that beauty and urgency that can only come from exposure to the real world,' wrote Geoff Brown in the 30 May 1996 edition of *The Times*, suggesting that the film's design as a 'true' story had been beneficial. 'No previous film from the Coen brothers has contained such human characters . . . Warm, dark, grotesque and beautiful all at once, this is the year's best American movie to date.' Many reviewers hedged their bets as to whether they believed that the film was rooted in fact. 'True or not,' wrote Derek Malcolm in the *Guardian* on 30 May 1996, '*Fargo* is the nearest thing the Coens have accomplished to *Blood Simple* . . . The film's style matches and underscores its content so that there is hardly a false note.' Yet again, McDormand was singled out. 'Her performance is remarkable as she plays the comforting wife to her failed artist husband . . . and slowly but surely catches up with her lumpen prey. One feels she could humanise a snake.'

Even the *Daily Mail*'s Christopher Tookey, who had so loathed *The Hudsucker Proxy* and *Barton Fink*, found *Fargo* irresistible. 'The Coens' films tend to be underplotted and anti-climactic. But real events from 1987 have presented them with an extraordinary yarn full of narrative twists to the end.' Tookey had disliked the Coens' previous crime stories, believing that they were too affectionate towards their subjects, but deemed *Fargo* to be 'moral' and was pleasantly surprised. Again, it seems that the film's opening caption card made audiences look differently at it. 'Will it become a mainstream hit? It deserves to be. This is the Coens' most generous-spirited effort yet and the bad language and gruesomeness are justified within the context.' However, Tookey predicted that audiences would ignore it in favour of movies that made crime look cooler, in the vein of Quentin Tarantino. 'Regrettably, there is something out of tune with our times in [*Fargo*'s] tone of civilised detachment and unpretentious moral rectitude.'

Others who had stood by the Coens through their less well-received efforts were just as delighted. 'After the scraper-sized flop that was *The Hudsucker Proxy* (although, let it be known, it remains a work of genius) the Coen brothers return to territory previously found fertile,' Ian Nathan wrote in a five-star review in the June 1996 issue of *Empire*. He described *Fargo* as a snowbound remake of *Blood Simple* with more jokes and, since the Coens were on home territory, a little more affection. 'The Coens are still a million miles from Hollywood staple, but with *Fargo*'s comic felicity, gun-packing coolness and ability to come up with the totally unexpected, they maintain their place among America's most important filmmakers.'

BOX OFFICE: *Fargo* was released in America on 8 March 1996 and, while it made a slow start, it ultimately grossed $24,567,751. It has since been cited as a big hit, but to put it in perspective the Robin Williams comedy *The Birdcage* (Mike Nichols, 1996), which received mixed reviews, was released on the same day and made $124,060,553. *Fargo* was a hit by the standards of a cheap independent movie with no big-name stars, but most Hollywood studio product wouldn't even go into profit with that kind of gross.

After its Oscars, of course, the film reached out to a wider audience, and there was even a TV spin-off under consideration. 'Someone had the idea that it could be turned into a series of one-hour shows, and that Marge could solve a different case each episode,' says Ethan. 'I think they filmed a pilot, directed by Kathy Bates.' One imagines it would have been a kind of cross between *Columbo* and *Northern Exposure*. 'We weren't really involved,' says Joel. 'I can't say that we weren't happy that it died.'

AWARDS: *Fargo* remains the Coens' best showing at the Academy Awards so far. The film picked up seven nominations, for Best Film, Best Director, Best Original Screenplay, Best Actress (Frances McDormand), Best Supporting Actor (William H Macy), Best Cinematography and Best Editing. McDormand picked up the Best Actress Oscar, but the only other award the film managed to bag was Best Original Screenplay. In the public eye this win cemented the Coens' status as successful filmmakers and certainly they haven't suffered a flop since.

The film did even better at that year's New York Film Critics' Circle: not only did McDormand take another Best Actress accolade, but it was declared Best Film and Joel was awarded Best Director. The Screen Actors' Guild voted McDormand Best Actress while the Writers' Guild of America declared the script to be Best Screenplay. *Fargo* also gave the Coens a second Cannes success as they scooped the prize for Best Director, although they were unable to collect the award as they were attending their sister's wedding back home in Minnesota.

DIALOGUE TO SKIP BACK FOR:

Carl: (to the gate operator at the car park) 'You know, these are the limits of *your* life, man. Ruler of your little fucking gate, here. Here – there's your four dollars, you pathetic piece of shit.'

Marge: 'Okay, I want you to tell me what these guys looked like.'
Hooker: 'Well, the little guy, he was kinda funny-lookin'.'
Marge: 'In what way?'
Hooker: 'I don't know, just funny-lookin'.'

ANALYSIS: It has often been said that *Fargo* is virtually a remake of *Blood Simple*. However, is this really the case? The two films have completely different plots: one concerns a desperate man resorting to kidnapping while the other features a cuckolded husband resorting to murder. Both Jerry and Marty hire somebody else to do the job only for that other person to double-cross them later, but where one is murdered in the double-cross the other is simply bullied into acquiescence. *Fargo*'s events originate from deceit where *Blood Simple*'s are because of misunderstandings. None of the same character types recur and they are set in locations which are about as different as any two places within American borders can be. Two undeniable common factors are the presence of Frances McDormand and the scene where a character tries to dispose of a body by the roadside as a car drives past, but even then McDormand plays the character who resolves the situation rather than the one who triggers it and, while Ray simply tries to hide from the truck's oncoming lights, Gaear follows and kills the witnesses. The camera style is also very different to *Blood Simple*, eschewing the earlier film's extreme angles, crash zooms and elaborate tracking shots for a less showy, pseudo-documentary style in keeping with the 'subject matter' (see **GENRE**).

What *Fargo* does have in common with *Blood Simple* is its depiction of crimes as more difficult to carry off than you might think and the criminals as ineffectual buffoons (both discussed at length in **GENRE**), plus its mode of storytelling. As with *Blood Simple*, the story of *Fargo* came before the characters, meaning that the characters are used to tell the story, rather than making the story a vehicle for the characters. Hence, the movie is told from multiple viewpoints. This makes *Fargo* and *Blood Simple* the only Coen films with no lead character, since the others have HI McDonnaugh, Tom Reagan, Barton Fink, Norville Barnes, The Dude, Ulysses Everett McGill and Ed Crane, all of whom appear in the majority of scenes in their respective films and carry the stories through (indeed, Barton and Ed are ever-present). *Fargo* is an ensemble piece with no starring role, and although Frances McDormand receives top billing she does not appear until a third of the way into the film.

Fargo does not have *Blood Simple*'s sense of claustrophobia, due in part to its location (see **EVER AMERICA**) but also because the characters are kept apart whereas in *Blood Simple* they frequently pass close to each other. The story of *Fargo* is divided into three basic areas, with one containing Jerry, his family and his workplace, another containing Carl and Gaear and a third containing Marge. These areas rarely cross over and, when they do, this signals a turning point in the plot. Jerry hiring Carl and Gaear starts the plot running; Carl and Gaear then kidnap Jean; Marge tracks Shep down and speaks to Jerry; Shep beats up Carl; Carl meets Wade and kills him; Marge's presence panics Jerry into giving himself away; Marge finds Gaear and catches him. Most of the film's progress can be summarised in those encounters. The rest is character stuff.

The privileged position of the audience means that they always know exactly what is happening while the characters are left to blunder around in the dark. In *Blood Simple* this means that characters speak at cross-purposes and make mistakes, but as identified above, there are no misunderstandings in *Fargo*, only deceptions. Jerry's plan was to involve the deception of both Wade and Jean, but he goes one further by deceiving Carl and Gaear as well, telling them that the ransom will be $80,000 when in fact he intends to extort $1,000,000 from Wade. Carl does a similar thing with Gaear when he finds out just how much cash is in that bag, having already double-crossed Jerry. All of these lies are motivated by greed (see **EVER AMERICA**).

While Jerry starts off as the antagonist in this situation, he quickly becomes the victim and this appears to be his natural station in life. He is only doing this out of desperation since he is in substantial debt, the source of which is never explained and so the viewer never knows whether it's his own fault. This leaves the viewer uncertain as to how much sympathy they should have for him. His life is dominated by Wade, who is overbearing and selfish, and it seems to be these qualities that have made Wade a success in the business world. Jerry is completely emasculated by Wade's presence, since Wade has manoeuvred Jerry into a job he isn't cut out for (and expects him to be grateful). Wade is also unwilling to let Jerry replace him as the head of Jean's family and makes Jerry redundant and peripheral. The first time Wade appears he's sitting in the armchair in Jerry's living room, drinking beer and watching sports. He dominates the frame, with Jerry reduced to a tiny figure in the background, and Jerry's attempt to strike up a conversation is brusquely brushed aside. At dinner, Wade shows that he is unwilling to help Jerry out, implying that he is waiting for his son-in-law to make a mistake in the hope that Jean will see him for the loser Wade knows him to be. Of course, Jerry has already screwed up with all the debt he's got himself into. Wade's daughter and grandson will be protected from any financial difficulties, but Jerry will be left to fend for himself: this implies that what Wade really wants is to take the father's role once more and gives his competition with Jerry an air of incest.

While Wade is unpleasant it's hard to respect Jerry because he is thoughtless and weak-willed, as seen in the way that he needs

Wade's assistant Stan Grossman to take his side in order to convince Wade to go along with his plan. (He even invokes Stan during his conversation with Scotty – Jerry doesn't even carry authority with his own son.) Fundamentally he is also willing to risk his family to solve his financial problems, which is foolhardy in the extreme. It is true that Jerry might have lost his family anyway, since Wade would have tried to take them away if his financial indiscretions had been revealed, but at least they would all have been alive.

GENRE: *Fargo* opens with the statement that it is a true story, and that, although the names have been changed out of respect for the dead, the rest is a faithful representation of events. That this is not actually the case gives the film much in common with eighteenth-century novels such as Daniel Defoe's *Moll Flanders*, where the text claims to be an account of a person's experiences, transcribed by the author. It also resembles the 'found manuscript' tradition of Gothic novels, where the author abandons any claim on the story, suggesting instead that the text arrived in their hands fully formed.

Authors have often found this a useful technique when they want their own personality to be submerged, and after the heavily stylised *The Hudsucker Proxy* the Coens decided to slot *Fargo* into a format – the true-crime genre – that doesn't allow for any of that. People didn't like their modern American fairy-tale and the true-crime story is pretty much the opposite. The fact that the opening caption is just another part of the fiction is typical of the Coens' love of practical jokes, although it could have badly backfired had this element been revealed prior to the movie's release. To an audience who had felt alienated by *Hudsucker*, this might have seemed like a joke that the Coens were having at the expense of their audience, thereby alienating them again.

You couldn't have blamed them. The true-story claim is a trick, manipulating the audience into expecting a certain type of movie. The true-crime story is a genre in itself, since it creates certain expectations in the audience that are distinct from those created by crime fictions. The beginning of *Fargo* suggests to the audience that this is going to be something different to previous Coen movies. Even though the film is actually made up it *is* something different, and the caption is an efficient (if slightly risky) way of breaking the expectations that the audience will have brought to the movie and substituting different ones. It's as well that the truth was only revealed after the film had already been a success.

For the audience to believe that this is indeed a true story, the plot has to unfold logically and the characters' actions have to remain believable. There is no room here for the speeded-up narrative of *The Hudsucker Proxy* or the flaming corridors of *Barton Fink*. Instead, the audience is given a lurid but believable scenario in which the characters are never given the breaks that fictional characters often get. This is where the approach used in *Blood Simple* returns, as a 'realistic' approach is applied to a traditional crime-story plot. Kidnappings are so frequently carried out in fiction that you'd think they were the easiest thing in the world. However, when Jerry tries to pull one off it turns out to be rather more difficult.

Again, the Coens are presenting characters who are not up to the task they've set themselves. Ethan says that their preference for simple-minded characters comes from a 'desire to go against the Hollywood cliché of the bad guy as a super-professional who controls everything . . . In this sense too, our movie is closer to life than the conventions of cinema and genre movies.' Jerry has been led to believe that he is capable of going through with his plan, but he clearly isn't and it spins out of his control very quickly. Wade, by contrast, is a strong personality who believes he can handle any situation. To his cost, he discovers that this is not the case when dealing with characters like Carl, who negotiate with guns and have no respect for Wade's status.

Then there's Carl himself, a lowlife who fancies himself as a master criminal but comes up short on all the necessary qualities. First of all, he won't shut up, as seen in the scene where he and Gaear are heading for Jerry's house to kidnap Jean and he criticises his cohort for not engaging in conversation. Having said that he's going to give Gaear a taste of his own medicine, Carl proceeds to sit there talking about how he isn't going to talk any more. Carl will also not let things go, and this leads to a lack of subtlety on his part. Subtlety is necessary when committing a crime, but Carl does dumb things like arguing with the tollbooth guy at the car park. He's already acting suspiciously by only staying at the car park for a couple of minutes, so the last thing he should be doing is drawing more attention to himself. (His distinctive 'funny-looking' features don't help either.) And while Carl thinks he's a hard-man he's about as ineffectual as Jerry: his threat to Jean when they are stopped by the police in Brainerd is unconvincing. At the end of the film he tries to argue with Gaear that he should get the car (even though he's already cheated Gaear out of a large share of the money and can afford to let the car go) and this leads to his fitting demise. Gaear is also not an effective criminal, but for quite different reasons: he's not a professional, he's a psychopath.

Not one of these characters is capable of carrying his plan through to the end, and as the plot of *Fargo* unfolds it becomes increasingly clear that nobody is going to get away with anything. This is hardly surprising, since this is supposed to be a true story, so if it were known who was responsible, they would have been caught. The mention of respect for the dead also casts a pall of inevitability over the film. The Coens therefore focus not on whether things will work out, but on how exactly it all goes wrong. 'It's implicit in the construction of the narrative,' says Joel. 'When a character suggests to you, in the first scene, how things are going to happen, you know full well it's going to unfold very differently.'

EVER AMERICA: That this film is geographically closer to the Coens' Minnesota roots than any film they've made before or since perhaps explains the motherly figure of Marge Gunderson, a figure who represents safety and sanity, but also friendliness, in among the chaos of *Fargo*. She's sharp-minded but also possessed of great emotional intelligence, treating others with sensitivity. Both are demonstrated in the scene with Lou as they drive away from the scene of the triple homicide, where she initially came across as naïve. When in the car, not only does she instantly identify that the car had dealer plates, which obviously makes Lou feel a bit dumb, but she follows it up with a joke to make him feel better. Later she also demonstrates the ability to lean on people when the need arises, breaking Shep Proudfoot with ease. Seemingly bereft of negative qualities, she is by far the most sympathetic and likeable character the Coens have created.

However, *Fargo* is hardly a nostalgic tale of the place the Coens once knew. Some emotional distance is achieved by placing the date a long way after the Coens' childhoods, and also by the 'true story' gambit. It's interesting that the Coens don't come from the place that provides the solution (Marge's home, Brainerd), but the city from which the chaos emanates. Minnesota (and North Dakota) is permanently seen under a blanket of snow in *Fargo*, a bleak white landscape against which the characters seem to be lost, such as in the long shot of Jerry returning to his car after work. He can clearly be seen against the white ground, but he seems tiny and insignificant, swallowed by his cold, unfeeling surroundings. It also enhances the sense of isolation, as though this really *is* the middle of nowhere.

There are, however, some benefits to isolation, as seen in the peaceful, uncorrupted nature of Brainerd. The violent events of *Fargo* are an intrusion on this community, as Marge identifies upon discovering the triple murder: she immediately assumes, correctly, that the suspect is from out of town. Brainerd is a strange place, not really the idyllic small-town America that is so often seen in Hollywood movies, but nevertheless depicted as undeserving of this disturbance.

Many characters in this film have Scandinavian names, reflecting the roots of this part of America, and the accents of those original settlers are still in evidence, particularly in Brainerd – 'yes' becoming 'yah' and so on. This did attract some criticism on release, with claims that the Coens were encouraging the audience to laugh at the Minnesotans' peculiar ways. However, the Coens made use of local actors to play most of the roles, and an accent coach was employed for the benefit of those who had come in from outside. Indeed, the film was enthusiastically covered by the local newspaper, the *Brainerd Daily Dispatch*, which was happy to play up the regional modes of speech ('Here's where we tell ya about "*Fargo* da movie", Brainerd and da funny lookin' guys,' the front page of the *Fargo* section of its website announces). One sore point with residents was that the movie was giving the area a reputation for violent acts: 'For the record: no Twin Cities car dealers' wives have been kidnapped

Alienating the audience?

The Coens have frequently been criticised for being aloof and elitist. This is often because their films are viewed as being too arch and containing too many in-jokes, but the charge of condescension towards their characters has also been regularly levelled at them since *Raising Arizona*, with regional stereotyping being the initial charge. 'It's a fundamental misperception,' says Joel, 'because the only people who can answer this is us, and we feel very affectionate towards all of these characters . . . sometimes the more shmucky they are, the more you like them.' The same criticisms returned in force with *Fargo*, perhaps because people are more used to seeing southern hick archetypes in the movies. The part of America that the Coens portrayed in *Fargo* seemed so strange to the rest of the country that many appear to have assumed that it was exaggerated.

Ethan sees the problem as being at least partly associated with the film's mixture of violence and humour. 'A lot of people feel uncomfortable with laughing at horrible situations. They think that if you're laughing at a character, somehow you're condescending to them. And that also makes them uncomfortable.' However, it's also something that's embedded in the style of the Coens' movies: 'We don't give cues about how you're supposed to react.' This *definitely* makes some people uncomfortable and it's the source of much puzzlement over their movies. Not only do Joel and Ethan not write their characters to be representative of anything outside of those characters, but they refuse to guide the viewer's sympathy. This means that when something funny happens, many viewers are unsure whether they're meant to be laughing with a character or at them. This may further explain the view of many commentators that *The Hudsucker Proxy* was insincere and *Barton Fink* meaningless; it might even explain why some suggested that *Miller's Crossing* was anti-Semitic. People just don't know whether they are meant to like a character or not. The answer is that no, you're not *meant* to like the characters: you decide for yourself whether you like them or not. This also points to the fact that the Coens often take inspiration from novels, rather than movies: the unsympathetic protagonist is far more common in literature.

In his excellent book *The Big Lebowski: The Making of a Coen Brothers Film*, William Preston Robertson astutely observes that the problem may be a subtle one of visual style. The Coens' fondness for the wide-angle lens can have the effect of distancing the viewer from the characters, because the character isn't picked out against the background. Stanley Kubrick and Robert Altman – regular touchstones for the Coens – suffered similar criticisms, that their detached styles gave an impression of coldness. 'What you could say is that a very stylised approach with a camera in general will be off-putting to people, because they feel it takes them out of the movie,' is Joel's response to this. 'In the end, it's a combination of things as opposed to only focal length.' Roger Deakins, who is a fan of the wide angle, suggests that it may be because the Coens don't do over-the-shoulder shots. The debate rages on.

and killed in Brainerd . . . hit men do not frequent the city . . . police chief Frank Ball is neither female, nor pregnant.' One rather mean-spirited assessment of the film said that it made the average Brainerd resident look like 'a vapid moron' and suggested burning every copy (although the writer also appears to believe that the movie condones violence, which it clearly doesn't). Later, however, the *Dispatch* declared that the movie 'calls for a lively sense of humour and a quality that can be rare: not taking ourselves too seriously'. Joel stressed that the film was not supposed to lampoon the Minnesotan way of life. 'We were born and grew up in Minnesota, which is one of the reasons why we were interested in that story. We feel very much a part of it, having come from that culture.'

Fargo is set in 1987 and is the first of the Coens' two recent-history period pieces. While only nine years separate the release of the film and its setting, by 1996 people were already looking back at the previous decade and criticising its avarice. *Fargo* is a story of greed, with Marge's speech to Gaear being the closest thing to a moral in any of the Coens' films. At the end, the money buried by Carl is simply forgotten about: after all these events, it isn't important (although one viewer reportedly headed out to Brainerd to try and dig it up, falling for the claim that it was a true story). The final scene sees Marge reassuring her husband that the little things do matter as his artwork is selected for Brainerd's three-cent stamp, and together they look forward to becoming a family. As a reward they are permitted an unambiguously happy ending, a rarity in the Coens' movies.

AVAILABILITY: *Fargo* was released as one of the first clutch of movies on DVD in 1998, when it was still a niche format used mainly by film buffs. The disc featured very little in terms of extras and has since been deleted to make way for a Special Edition. The version currently available features the half-hour documentary *Minnesota Nice* which focuses on the movie's setting, an interview with Joel and Ethan from the Charlie Rose show, a feature on the Coens' regular actors, a behind-the-scenes article from *American Cinematographer*, a pop-up trivia track, a commentary from Tim Bevan and Eric Fellner and another from Roger Deakins, plus the usual trailers, TV spots and photo galleries. It's a good package.

THE COENS' VIEW: 'What're you going to do, you know? I mean, if a movie like *Fargo* succeeds . . . you might as well make whatever kind of movie you want and hope for the best.' (Ethan in 1998)

VERDICT: 'There's more to life than a little money. Don't you know that?' The success of *Fargo* says a great deal about modern cinema audiences. Most people, it seems, consider sincerity a great virtue in art. What you say is less important than whether or not you *mean* it. Even when the Coens revealed that this was not, in fact, a true story, many people maintained that it was more 'honest' than their previous movies.

It's the style of *Fargo* that creates this impression, with the humour and wackiness far more restrained. There are moments of strangeness, but these are kept reasonably subtle (listen for the bells that jingle when Gaear runs towards Carl with the axe) and the humour tends more towards the observational. On reflection, a lot of the film is faintly ludicrous (again, Gaear's murder of Carl, as he feeds him into a wood-chipper) but in telling this particular story the Coens adopt the cinematic equivalent of a straight face. Audiences found their disbelief easier to suspend and therefore they found it easier to get involved.

It seems that many people take it for granted that *Fargo* is the Coens' best film, but to go along with this is to ignore the quality elsewhere in their body of work. It's true that *Fargo* is a great success, accomplished on every level, and it's very difficult to find fault with it. However, one can appreciate why the Coens were surprised at the favourable audience response, since the film is brutal and stark and, while it's basically about a triumph of good over evil, it isn't exactly a feel-good movie. Its blackly humorous tone successfully walks a fine line and the result is minimal, but gripping.

The Big Lebowski (1998)

(Colour – 117 mins)

PolyGram Filmed Entertainment Presents
A Working Title Production
Casting by John Lyons CSA
Supervising Sound Editor: Skip Lievsay
Edited by Roderick Jaynes and Tricia Cooke
Original Music by Carter Burwell
Musical Archivist: T-Bone Burnett
Costume Designer: Mary Zophres
Production Designer: Rick Heinrichs
Director of Photography: Roger Deakins ASC, BSC
Co-producer: John Cameron
Executive Producers: Tim Bevan and Eric Fellner
Produced by Ethan Coen
Written by Ethan Coen & Joel Coen
Directed by Joel Coen

CAST: Jeff Bridges (*The Dude*), John Goodman (*Walter Sobchak*), Julianne Moore (*Maude Lebowski*), Steve Buscemi (*Donny*), David Huddleston (*The Big Lebowski*), Philip Seymour Hoffman (*Brandt*), Tara Reid (*Bunny Lebowski*), Philip Moon, Mark Pellegrino (*Treehorn Thugs*), Peter Stormare, Flea, Torsten

Voges (*Nihilists*), Jimmie Dale Gilmore (*Smokey*), Jack Kehler (*Dude's Landlord*), John Turturro (*Jesus Quintana*), James G Hoosier (*Liam O'Brian*), Carlos Leon, Terrence Burton (*Maude's Thugs*), Richard Gant (*Older Cop*), Christian Clemenson (*Younger Cop*), Dom Irrera (*Tony the Chauffeur*), Gérard L'Heureux (*Lebowski's Chauffeur*), David Thewlis (*Knox Harrington*), Lu Elrod (*Coffee Shop Waitress*), Michael Gomez (*Auto Circus Cop*), Peter Siragusa (*Gary the Bartender*), Sam Elliott (*The Stranger*), Marshall Manesh (*Doctor*), Harry Bugin (*Arthur Digby Sellers*), Jesse Flanagan (*Little Larry Sellers*), Irene Olga López (*Pilar*), Luis Colina (*Corvette Owner*), Ben Gazzara (*Jackie Treehorn*), Leon Russom (*Malibu Police Chief*), Ajgie Kirkland (*Cab Driver*), Jon Polito (*Private Snoop*), Aimee Mann (*Nihilist Woman*), Jerry Haleva (*Saddam*), Jennifer Lamb (*Pancake Waitress*), Warren Keith (*Funeral Director*)

TAGLINE: 'Her life was in their hands. Now her toe is in the mail.' Also: 'They figured he was a lazy time-wasting slacker. They were right.'

SUMMARY: Los Angeles, 1991. Two thugs in the employ of Jackie Treehorn urinate on the rug of Jeffrey Lebowski, known as 'The Dude', in the belief that he is a different, wealthy Jeffrey Lebowski. The Dude visits the other Lebowski asking for compensation, but Lebowski refuses to accept any responsibility. The Dude steals one of Lebowski's rugs. A couple of days later Lebowski calls The Dude back. His wife, Bunny, is being held to ransom for $1 million and he believes that the rug-soilers may be responsible. He will pay The Dude $20,000 to act as courier in order to confirm this. The Dude accepts, although he believes that Bunny 'kidnapped' herself to pay her debts. Back home, his new rug is stolen.

Lebowski gives The Dude a case of money and tells him to follow the kidnappers' instructions. His bowling team-mate Walter insists on coming and, against The Dude's wishes, hands over a false bag so they can keep the $1 million. The nihilist kidnappers leave and The Dude is left holding the money. He is wondering what to tell Lebowski when his car is stolen with the case inside. Lebowski's daughter Maude contacts The Dude: the rug he stole was hers and she took it back. She agrees that the kidnapping is fake and is displeased that her father withdrew the ransom from a charity of which she and Lebowski are co-trustees. She offers The Dude $100,000 to retrieve the money. He accepts, hoping that he will be able to get the case of money back when he finds his car.

Lebowski knows that the kidnappers did not receive the $1 million. He believes that The Dude still has the money and has pointed the nihilists towards him: accordingly, they turn up and threaten The Dude. The police find The Dude's car but the case is gone. The Dude tells Maude that he now believes Bunny was kidnapped by the nihilists, but Maude disagrees. The Dude finds a child's schoolwork, signed Larry Sellars, wedged in the seat of his car, and he and Walter find Larry but don't get the case. Treehorn speaks to The Dude, looking for the money that Bunny owes him. The Dude says that Larry has it but Treehorn doesn't believe him. The Dude finds Maude at his house and she mentions that all Lebowski's money came from her mother. Lebowski just administers the charities and lives on an allowance from Maude. The Dude finally figures it out and heads to Lebowski's.

Lebowski put The Dude in charge of getting Bunny back because he didn't *want* her back. The $1 million was never in the briefcase: he was hoping that the kidnappers would kill Bunny, then he could blame The Dude and keep the $1 million. The Dude and Walter arrive at Lebowski's to find that Bunny has returned. She was visiting friends and didn't tell Lebowski, but the nihilists knew and issued the ransom demand. However, The Dude can't prove anything. The Dude, Walter and their bowling partner Donny are attacked by the nihilists. Walter fights them off but Donny has a heart attack and dies. The Dude and Walter scatter his ashes, then go bowling.

DEVELOPMENT: '*Fargo*, which was allegedly based on real events, in truth contains mostly made-up stuff,' says Ethan. 'Whereas *The Big Lebowski*, which purports to be fiction, actually is based on real people and events.' The story has its roots in the Coens' experiences of being in Los Angeles for the shooting of *Barton Fink* and the two central characters grew from three real people, the first of whom was their friend Pete Exline. The Coens found him, at his rather scruffy abode, in poor spirits. 'So, we complimented him on the place,' says Ethan, 'and he told us about how proud he was of this ratty-ass little rug he had in the living room and how it "tied the room together".' Joel and Ethan expressed their agreement that the rug 'tied the room together', and the phrase bounced back and forth between the Coens and Pete until it became hilarious through sheer repetition.

This suggested some of The Dude's personality to Joel and Ethan. A different element of Pete's background sowed the seeds for another character: 'Pete is a Vietnam vet,' Ethan continues. 'Very bitter. Whenever the subject of Vietnam comes up, he says, "Well, we were winning when *I* left." ' Pete had been known to hold forth on the subject of the Gulf War and how it had been an easier war than Vietnam, and he also had a number of stories about himself and his friend Walter. Joel and Ethan's favourite of these stories concerned the time that Pete and Walter confronted a teenage carjacker who had left a piece of his homework inside the car when he abandoned it. One particular detail stood out: 'They had the homework in a baggie.' (As seen in the finished film, a 'baggie' is a clear plastic bag as used by the police for containing evidence.) The Coens decided to build a character around this semi-mythical Walter figure and bulked him out with elements of John Milius, director of *Conan the Barbarian* (1981), whom they had also met in Los Angeles. 'He's a really funny guy, a really good storyteller. He was never actually in the military, although he wears a lot of military paraphernalia. He's a gun enthusiast and survivalist type.' The Coens had received numerous invites to come to Milius's home and see his gun collection.

Meanwhile, The Dude started to emerge when the Coens met Jeff 'The Dude' Dowd, a producer's rep in Hollywood and the self-styled Pope of Dope. 'He was a member of the Seattle Seven during the Vietnam years,' explains Ethan. The Seattle Seven were tried on charges of conspiracy to riot in 1970, after protesting against the trial of the Chicago Seven (also on charges of conspiracy to riot, this time at the 1968 Democratic Party convention), and this element of Dowd's character was transferred to The Dude. Much of The Dude's character emerged from the real-life Dowd, although the Coens needed to give him a reason to interact with their Walter character. To this end, they brought in another element of Pete Exline, who was 'a member of an amateur softball league, but we changed it to bowling because it was more visually compelling, and it's the kind of sport you can do while you're drinking and smoking,' says Joel. The retro design of bowling alleys and related paraphernalia also suited the characters, who were all designed to be products of another time. Ethan adds, 'It's a decidedly male sport, which is right, because *The Big Lebowski*, which we wrote around the same time as *Barton Fink*, is, like *Barton Fink*, kind of a weird buddy movie.'

The motivation to make this into a crime story was twofold. 'We were really consciously thinking about doing a Raymond Chandler story,' says Ethan, 'as much as it's about LA.' However, the event that spawned the rest of the movie also suggested Chandler. 'I remember when Pete told us the story about the homework in the baggie,' Joel recalls, 'thinking that there was something quintessentially LA about it, but LA in a very Chandlerian way.' He identifies the main Chandleresque aspects of *Lebowski*: 'It moves episodically, and deals with the characters trying to unravel a mystery. As well as having a hopelessly complex plot that's ultimately unimportant.' The Coens drew particularly on *The Big Sleep* (1939), which features a wealthy, wheelchair-bound man who hires Chandler's private eye Philip Marlowe to protect the younger, more flighty and promiscuous of his two daughters. While on the case, Marlowe falls in love with the older, wiser daughter, Vivian. Substitute the younger daughter for a young trophy wife, and the smouldering relationship between Marlowe and Vivian for The Dude's casual tryst with Maude, and you have the set-up for *The Big Lebowski* (see also **EVER AMERICA**).

While the plot did indeed become very complex, the Coens worked on making the individual incidents interesting in themselves. 'The plot is sort of secondary to the other things,' says Joel. 'If people get a little bit confused, I don't think it's necessarily going to get in the way of them enjoying the story.'

REFERENCES: While Larry Sellars's father Arthur Digby Sellars is fictional, the TV western series he is said to have written for, *Branded*, really existed. However, even if Sellars was real he couldn't have written 156 of the episodes because it only ran for 47, between 1965 and 1966. The Dude sings the show's theme song while in the back of the police car that picks him up in Malibu.

Two references to the Coens' own films are present. One is the private detective Da Fino, who has been tailing The Dude in a Volkswagen Beetle – the same car in which Visser tails Abby and Ray in *Blood Simple*. The other is at the top of the faxed ransom note sent to the Big Lebowski, which notes that the paper originated from the Hotel Earl. This Los Angeles establishment appears to have dropped an 'e' since Barton Fink stayed there.

CASTING: 'The part of The Dude wasn't conceived with any particular actor in mind,' says Joel. 'But after the character became focused and developed, we couldn't imagine him as anyone but Jeff Bridges.' The son of Lloyd Bridges had been an actor since the age of eight, with career highlights including *The Last Picture Show* (Peter Bogdanovitch, 1971), *The Fisher King* (Terry Gilliam, 1991) and *Fearless* (Peter Weir, 1993). His performance as The Dude is reminiscent of the student activist he played in the interminable remake of *King Kong* (John Guillermin, 1976).

Again, several roles went to long-time Coen colleagues. The idea of John Goodman as Walter emerged very early and, after taking Steve Buscemi's 'motormouth' persona to the limit in *Fargo*, the Coens decided to give him a complete change of pace by offering him the timid Donny to play. The piece almost became a *Barton Fink* reunion as John Turturro also became involved. The character of Jesus Quintana was in the story from an early stage and was written with Turturro in mind, although the Coens felt that the character still needed something. 'We decided we wanted to give him something a little more meaty to sink his teeth into,' says Joel, 'than, you know, just playing his bowling nemesis who happens to be pretty good.' They were inspired by a play in which Turturro had appeared in the late 1980s, entitled *Ma Puta Vita*: his character had overtones of paedophilia. 'So we thought, well, let's make Turturro a pederast. It'll be something he can really run with.'

Fargo's Peter Stormare made a swift return to play the ringleader of the nihilists, but casting for one of the others was more esoteric. Flea, real name Michael Balzary, was (and still is) the exhibitionist bass player with California punk-funk band The Red Hot Chili Peppers (although he originally hails from Australia). He has done occasional acting work over the years including *Back to the Future II* (Robert Zemekis, 1989) and *My Own Private Idaho* (Gus Van Sant, 1991). Nothing if not versatile, his career also includes voicing Donny Thornberry in the popular children's cartoon *The Wild Thornberrys*.

Among the other newcomers were Julianne Moore and Phillip Seymour Hoffman, both of whom were on the rise when they appeared in *Lebowski* after performing in *Boogie Nights* (Paul Thomas Anderson, 1997). Hoffman had previously appeared mainly in supporting roles in the likes of *Nobody's Fool* (Robert Benton, 1994) and *Twister* (Jan de Bont, 1996), while Moore's CV included *Short Cuts* (Robert Altman, 1993) and *Surviving Picasso* (James Ivory, 1996). Since *Lebowski* they have gone on to be in demand as two of the best character actors currently working in Hollywood. (Ethan notes that Moore's accent in the film 'isn't specifically English – it's a vague, non-specific geographically, swell finishing school for girls in Switzerland accent that she came up with. [She] intuitively grasped that there should be something horribly regal about the character.') *Lebowski* was also a big break for 21-year-old Tara Reid, who came to the film from a regular role as Ashley in the American soap *Days of Our Lives*. Bunny Lebowski was her first film role and she has become a sex symbol since appearing in *American Pie* (Paul Weitz, 1999). Playing her screen husband was David

Huddleston, who had previously starred in the title role of *Santa Claus* (Jeannot Szwarc, 1985).

As well as 'Karl Hungus' and 'Bunny LaJoya', a third actress was needed for the fake porn movie *Logjammin'*. For these purposes, a genuine porn star was employed in the form of Asia Carrera. 'They wanted a porn star to play a porn star,' Carrera, who was one of twelve actresses to audition, explains. '[The casting agent] said I was too beautiful, and that they wanted more of a "girl next door look", which was a rather nice letdown, I thought.' After Carrera left, the Coens looked through the photographs that had been taken at the audition and, according to Carrera, said 'That one! That's the one we want!'

Finally, there was The Stranger – a relic of the Old West and the film's narrator. Accordingly, Sam Elliott, star of TV and film westerns since the 1970s, was cast. 'We really wrote that part for Sam because we like his voice,' says Joel, although the actor was aware of his incongruity in *The Big Lebowski*'s setting. '[Sam] would actually ask us, "What am I doing in this movie?" ' says Ethan. 'We didn't know either.'

PRODUCTION: It took quite some time for the Coens to get their schedules to line up with those of Jeff Bridges and John Goodman, whom they were determined to cast in *The Big Lebowski*. A major problem was that Goodman was still working on *Roseanne* and his time was limited. Hence, while the script was completed shortly after *The Hudsucker Proxy* wrapped, they pressed ahead with *Fargo* instead. (Each works as a contrast to *Hudsucker*: while *Fargo* is small-scale, provincial and downbeat, *Lebowski* has a lazy, listless hero and a disordered aesthetic compared to *Hudsucker*'s ambitious lead character and geometric design.) *Roseanne* came to a close in 1997 and this finally freed Goodman up to take the role of Walter Sobchak at the convenience of the Coens and Bridges. After the success of *Fargo*, securing funding posed no problems: Working Title was more than happy to finance *The Big Lebowski*.

Visually, says Joel, *Lebowski* 'is a weird mix. There are parts of the movie that want to be real and contemporary-feeling, and other things that are very stylised, like the dream scenes. And then there's the bowling stuff.' Cinematographer Roger Deakins notes that 'I'm not sure I ever had a handle on what *Lebowski* was supposed to look like. It's such a mix, I don't think it has one style.' One element of the lighting that Deakins feels is particularly distinctive is the 'orange' quality of the night scenes. 'I decided early on that I would give the night sequences on the street a special look . . . instead of being the usual blue moonlight or blue streetlamp, [they] would have a very orange, sodium-light effect.' When the dailies started coming back from the lab, Deakins noted that the lab was trying to compensate and eradicate the orange during developing, and told them 'It's damn well going back in!'

'Throughout, we wanted to reference a traditional Los Angeles,' says designer Rick Heinrichs, whose second successive film with the Coens this was. He drew heavily upon the architecture and design of the 1950s and 1960s, 'not only to establish the feel of the city, but also to comment on the characters of The Dude and Walter, who are anchored in the past in the way they lead their lives.' Subtlety was an important factor. 'Discussions were always framed with, "We don't want to hit this too hard",' says Ethan. 'No lava lamps or that kind of shit. No Day-Glo posters on the wall of [The Dude's] house. No Grateful Dead music.' Ethan also notes that, while he joked to Jeff Bridges during filming that they were aiming to make something in the vein of Cheech and Chong, they were, in fact, keen to avoid the stoned slacker clichés. (Cheech Marin and Tommy Chong are comedians whose humour largely revolves around marijuana, although they are willing to make jokes about other drugs as well. They starred in *Up in Smoke* (Lou Adler, 1978), *Cheech and Chong's Next Movie* (Thomas Chong, 1980) and *Cheech and Chong: Still Smokin'* (Thomas Chong, 1983), among others; they also appeared in Martin Scorsese's *After Hours* (1985). Ethan stresses that, 'I personally am a Cheech and Chong enthusiast.')

Similarly, Heinrichs stresses that, 'we didn't want to overdo it and hit the audience over the head.' Hence, 'the Lebowski mansion is opulent in a fairly traditional way – we wanted to summon up the greenhouse scene in *The Big Sleep*.' Another example of not 'hitting the audience over the head' occurred when Maude Lebowski's studio was being constructed. The Coens and Heinrichs considered putting together some overtly vaginal art as examples of Maude's work, but decided that this would be too much. Instead the paintings, including the one that she is working on when The Dude arrives at the studio, are egg-themed to suggest her plan to conceive a child with him. Another important consideration throughout, naturally, was the period detail. Nineteen ninety-one was summoned up 'in some of the clunky technology the characters are involved with, the cellular phones, the cars,' says Heinrichs. 'Some things don't change that much, but six years have made quite a difference in that regard.'

Shooting began on 27 January 1997, after a week of rehearsals, in North Hollywood. The first scene to be shot was that of The Dude reclaiming his stolen car from the police pound; from there, the production moved to Beverly Hills, where two estates had been found to double for the Lebowski mansion. One of these was on Charing Cross Road, the other located in Greystone Park. 'At the Greystone Lebowski mansion,' Heinrichs says, 'we ran into a problem that got solved in an unusual way.' Joel liked every aspect of the house except its black and white chequered floor, which jarred with him but he had to accept it. 'But since it grated on him,' adds Heinrichs, 'he used the black and white chequered visual motif in The Dude's dream that occurs later in the film. It appears as an element that has stayed in The Dude's mind.'

The bowling alley scenes were filmed at the Hollywood Star Lanes on Santa Monica Boulevard, a location which had been selected from many. 'We did a study of every bowling alley within thirty miles of Hollywood,' says location manager Robert Graf. 'We wanted a certain size, a look that was a little bit retro but not run-down, with manual scoring tables.' Although the Star Lanes fitted the bill, Heinrichs was required to give it a substantial makeover. 'Since the bowling alley is sort of a lynchpin, visually speaking,' says Ethan, 'we discussed it with Rick more than any other set.' The exterior wall of the building was blank and featureless, and Heinrichs suggested that, rather than painting it, they could affix neon stars to it and reflect that design in the interior. 'Stars are a very '50s thing, which worked well with that '50s–'60s Brunswick look the place had,' says Heinrichs (Brunswick being a long-established bowling company). Remarkably, given that it was called the Star Lanes, there were no stars in the existing decor and they were all added by the production team. Heinrichs worked to keep the budget down by redecorating in a manner that would please the alley's proprietors, thereby avoiding the necessity of painting the alley back to its original colours. He opted for an orange and blue livery.

Also chosen for their retro appearance were the coffee shops frequented by The Dude and his bowling team, as well as the one where the nihilists have pancakes. 'Both of the places we used,' says Heinrichs, 'Johnnie's on Fairfax and Wilshire, and Dinah's in Culver City, are Los Angeles landmarks, prime examples of the Googie style of architecture from the fifties and sixties.' (The Googie style was a commercial mode of architecture which used modern materials and a kind of space-age look.)

One of the most enjoyable scenes to shoot was that of Walter smashing up the Corvette in the mistaken belief that it belongs to Larry – 'Everyone likes to see a Corvette smashed,' says Joel. Two cars were rented for this sequence in order to get all the necessary angles covered, on the understanding that only the bodies would be damaged, not the chassis or engines, and they would be restored before being returned. It was storyboard artist J Todd Anderson who pointed out that Walter would have to smash the side window and flick the headlights up in order to smash them – apparently he is full of such useful information. John Goodman was concerned about the ramifications of screaming, 'This is what happens when you fuck a stranger in the ass' in the middle of a sleeping Los Angeles suburb, particularly because people would be likely to recognise his voice, but Ethan says that the residents were surprisingly amenable to the situation. 'And people whose houses we needed access to,' he adds, 'or who we asked to . . . move their cars, we paid. We'd wake a guy up in the middle of the night and say, "Here's a quarter." ' An interesting note about this scene is that the owner of the Corvette was played by Luis Colina, who worked as an editor on *The Hudsucker Proxy*.

Apart from The Dude's bungalow, which was constructed on a soundstage in West Hollywood, the only other sections not shot on location were the dream sequences, which were shot in a converted aeroplane hangar at Santa Monica airport. The second dream sequence was the more elaborate of the two. 'We wouldn't want to make a full-blown musical,' the Coens say, 'but it seemed a fun thing to make that a musical sequence.' The Dude's drug-induced dream consists of an eroticised Busby Berkeley-style musical number, set to a track by Kenny Rodgers and The First Edition. 'Why wouldn't it?' insist the Coens. 'It makes as much sense as anything else.'

Berkeley was the key influence on this sequence, as choreographers Bill and Jacqui Landrum designed it with particular reference to his work on *Whoopee!* (Thornton Freeland, 1930). 'We put together a tape of various sequences and patterns from the film for Joel and Ethan and they responded,' Jacqui says. 'The feeling was exactly what they wanted.' The reel was also presented to Jeff Bridges and the Landrums worked with him to create a dance routine. 'Jeff's a natural dancer,' Jacqui continues. 'He's uninhibited. We showed him various steps and combinations and he took what he felt most comfortable with, and kind of owned them.' The sequences demanded a contrast from Roger Deakins' usual understated lighting, and accordingly these were lit more brightly and directly. 'We lit The Dude and all the dancing girls as Busby Berkeley would have lit them,' the cinematographer comments. 'I think he would have recognised what we were doing and been quite at home with it.'

Ethan notes that the dancers they hired were somewhat skinnier than they would have preferred. 'In Berkeley movies, the dancers are always dough-faced,' he says. 'Kind of puffy, kind of pudgy. But, you know, in California – good luck. All health, fitness, beauty. They just don't have LA dancers who look like that.' They did, however, specify tall dancers, knowing that Jeff Bridges would have to appear to glide through their legs. The dancers standing on the alley were shot as a separate element, Bridges was shot against a blue screen, and the two elements were combined: however, Bridges was still too large to fit convincingly, so he was shrunk slightly on computer. There was also a point-of-view shot in this sequence of The Dude going down the alley. Deakins had planned to use a small remote-controlled car (developed for use on *Home Alone 2* (Chris Columbus, 1992)) for this and, although it had worked fine in the bowling alley for fast shots, it wouldn't go slow enough for the dreamlike movement of this sequence. So he just pushed the camera down the lane with a big pole.

The dream sequence of The Dude flying over Los Angeles was shot on another soundstage in West Hollywood, including bluescreen work: this was the final scene to be filmed during the eleven and a half week shoot. Production wrapped on 24 April 1997.

DELETED SCENES: In the script, there's a longer ending to the scene where Walter pulls the big Lebowski out of his chair, in the belief that Lebowski is faking his injuries. The Dude and Walter were to have been shown hefting Lebowski back into his chair as Walter apologises to Lebowski. Lebowski seems rather pathetic in this sequence and gives us an insight into his psyche, as he compares Walter to the women whom he believes have been oppressing him all these years. He still resents his first wife for being so much more successful than he is, he resents his daughter for sidelining him by carrying on her mother's work and he doesn't even have the respect of his new, younger wife.

This ending was perhaps cut for matters of taste, since the Coens had already had to pull off the tricky feat of making a joke of John Goodman throwing a disabled man to the floor. Walter describes Lebowski as a 'fucking cry-baby' at one point, which may have been going too far.

MUSIC: At the time, *Select* magazine noted that, with *The Big Lebowski* and *Jackie Brown* (Quentin Tarantino, 1997) it seemed as though Tarantino and the Coens had exchanged scripts and made each other's movies. In the case of *Jackie Brown* this was probably the result of Tarantino's more fluid, low-key camera style. With *The Big Lebowski* it's mostly down to the use of 1970s pop music on the soundtrack. The idea of constructing the majority, if not the entirety, of a film's soundtrack from retro pop songs was popularised by Tarantino with *Reservoir Dogs* (1991) and *Pulp Fiction* (1994) and it's now hard to imagine a time when this was not commonplace.

'The premise of the music in the movie,' says Carter Burwell, 'is that this character, Jeff Lebowski, kind of scores his own life with his 8-track collection.' Burwell therefore aimed to construct a soundtrack out of songs, rather than producing a score, which he did with the assistance of music historian T-Bone Burnett. There were, however, still a few scenes that needed music and, for one reason or another, wouldn't work with archive tracks. Burwell composed various pieces to fit those scenes. 'The pieces that I did were all in song form, even if they didn't have lyrics, and for this reason, they were wildly varying.' Burwell wrote 'about six or seven pieces' for the film, including a pastiche of late 1970s/early 1980s electro-pop that represents the music of Autobahn and the 1940s-style big-band tune that accompanies the appearance of Jon Polito's character, Da Fino.

The movie's theme song, which is also used on the first dream sequence, is 'The Man in Me' by Bob Dylan, drawn from his 1970 LP *New Morning*. One of the other standout tracks is 'Lookin' Out My Back Door' by Creedence Clearwater Revival, which hit number two in the American charts in August 1970. They appear to be The Dude's favourite band, although unlike him they weren't draft-dodgers – the band went on hiatus for a year in 1967 while singer John Fogerty and drummer Doug Clifford did national service. Considering the song's apposite nature, it's a mystery that it isn't included on the soundtrack album. The Gypsy Kings' flamenco version of 'Hotel California' appears to have been included mainly as a dig at The Eagles' original. Certainly The Dude speaks out against the plodding stadium-rock dinosaurs later in the film, which gets him thrown out of a taxi.

CRITICAL RECEPTION: Once again, the Coens suffered for their desire to make each film different from the last. It's very difficult to find a review of *The Big Lebowski* that doesn't feature an unfavourable comparison to *Fargo*. 'Few movies could equal that one, and this one doesn't,' wrote Roger Ebert in the *Chicago Sun-Times*, 'but it's weirdly engaging, like its hero.' Ebert was very fair to the film, anticipating a number of criticisms and countering them before they arose. 'Some may complain *The Big Lebowski* rushes in all directions and never ends up anywhere. That isn't the film's flaw, but its style.' He awarded *Lebowski* three stars out of four.

'Hot directors coming off major successes often follow up with quirky, more idiosyncratic pictures and so it is with the Coen brothers' follow-up to *Fargo*,' wrote Todd McCarthy in the 20 January 1998 issue of *Variety*. While McCarthy thought that there were many very funny ideas and scenes in the film, he felt that it 'nonetheless adds up to considerably less than the sum of its often scintillating parts, simply because the film doesn't seem to be about anything other than its own cleverness.'

It wasn't all lukewarm, though: *Lebowski* even got a good review from the *Village Voice* for a change. 'Have the Coens gone feel-good?' asked J Hoberman on 10 March 1998. '*The Big Lebowski*, their latest perfectly stylised (and pleasingly discombobulated) jape, draws on Jeff Bridges' loser charm.' Hoberman noted that this made it the Coens' second successive film to depend on an affable central character, in contrast to their previous work. 'When it was shown in competition at the recent Berlin Film Festival, *The Big Lebowski* was reportedly attacked for being about itself – which is to say, dialogue, acting, and mise-en-scene.' The *New York Times*, while implying that it wasn't as good as *Fargo*, was also willing to recommend the film. 'The Coens are after something loopier this time,' wrote Janet Maslin on 6 March 1998. 'It's a mode in which they and their actors are supremely comfortable,' although she noted that it would mainly appeal to those who were already attuned to The Dude's sensibilities. Maslin reserved particular praise for the cast: 'Mr Bridges finds a role so right for him that he never seems to have been anywhere else . . . Mr Goodman also fits his role perfectly, ranting with a furious irrelevance.'

The British reaction was more enthusiastic, perhaps because *Fargo* had been less of a revelation in Britain and hence there was less of a backlash when *Lebowski* turned out to be so different. 'Hollywood will be as perplexed by their genius as ever,' declared *Empire*'s Ian Nathan. 'This is a movie that will only make sense if you happen to have Coen genes.' Nathan felt that the transformative power of the Coens was their greatest strength in this film: 'the leisurely pursuit of ten-pin bowling is transformed into something lyrical and wondrous in a stream of elegant longeurs.' He rounded off with the most resounding endorsement ever printed of Ethan and Joel's work: 'In a perfect world all movies would be made by the Coen brothers.'

Alexander Walker was a little less sure. Having enjoyed the Coens' previous films for their invocation of Classic Hollywood values (he even liked *The Hudsucker Proxy*), he found *Lebowski* slightly disappointing. 'If it's possible to enjoy a movie without knowing what the hell's going on, that's the Coen brothers' new one,' he wrote in the *Evening Standard* on 23 April 1998. 'Another *Fargo*, it is not.' Walker considered that the Coens had been a little self-indulgent. 'I think that Joel and Ethan Coen have the sharpest ears in the business. This time, though, they have let their fondness for pastiche run away with them to the extent that they're pastiching themselves.'

Quentin Curtis of *The Daily Telegraph* stated that *Lebowski* was 'as rich, riotous and disorienting as anything they have made' in the 24 April 1998 edition. 'You have always had the feeling in Coen films that the works are not so much thought out, intellectually, as doodled over coffee and doughnuts – pieces of fooling around rather than tracts on human nature.' The film was not, Curtis considered, an intellectual exercise: 'Comic genius of the Coens' order is for enjoyment rather than analysis.' (See **ANALYSIS**.) Matthew Sweet of the *Independent on Sunday* said much the same thing, but he appeared to find it more problematic: 'There's no big idea in *The Big Lebowski* – everything's for show,' he wrote on 26 April 1998. 'Do go and see it – it's so funny that you might get bored of laughing after the first hour. Just don't discuss it afterwards, because there's nothing to say.'

Geoff Andrew, a long-time supporter of the Coens, disagreed. 'It's almost impossible to think of a recent movie more thoroughly enjoyable than this exhilarating comic update of the world crystallised by Raymond Chandler,' he wrote in the 22 April 1998 issue of *Time Out*. 'The film may not have the enigmatic elegance or emotional resonance of *Barton Fink* or *Fargo*, but it's still a marvellous example of the Coens' effortless brand of stylistic and storytelling brilliance.' Rising to the accusations of hollowness, he concluded, 'Far from being shallow pastiche, it's actually about something: what it means to be a man, to be a friend, and to be a "hero" for a particular time and place. Truly terrific.'

BOX OFFICE: *The Big Lebowski* was released in the US on 6 March 1998, opening on 1,207 screens. It took $5,533,844 in its opening weekend and at the end of its twelve-week stint in US movie theatres it had grossed a respectable $17,498,804.

AWARDS: On the comedown from *Fargo*, *The Big Lebowski* scored no notable awards. John Goodman wasn't even nominated for the Best Supporting Actor Oscar. He should have won it.

DIALOGUE TO SKIP BACK FOR:

Dude: 'I'm not Mr Lebowski; *you're* Mr Lebowski. *I'm* The Dude. So that's what you call me. That, or his Dudeness, or Duder, or, you know, El Duderino, if you're not into the whole brevity thing.'

Dude: 'You brought a fucking Pomeranian bowling?'
Walter: 'What do you mean "brought it bowling"? I didn't rent it shoes. I'm not buying it a fucking beer. He's not taking your fucking turn, Dude.'

Walter: 'Smokey, this is not 'Nam. This is bowling. There are rules.'

ANALYSIS: While the Coens prefer to underpin their films with a good deal of wit, *The Big Lebowski* is by far their funniest and achieves this with no sacrifice of plot. This may be because the script draws more heavily on real people whom they met and found amusing. However, it is also worth considering that the difference between mediocre comedy and great comedy often lies in the quality of the delivery.

Up to this point there had been plenty of good performances in the Coens' movies, but it's easy to see that there have been actors they have connected with and actors they haven't. Some have complained, for example, that Joel and Ethan would tend to reject any changes that might suggest themselves on set, not being willing to trust anything that they hadn't had plenty of time to mull over beforehand. (Jon Polito says that, when making *Miller's Crossing*, 'I remember going through it at first, and I got one word wrong. After it was over, [Joel and Ethan] go in stereo, "You missed that word." ') With that in mind, it's noticeable that not only does *The Big Lebowski* feature the best performances that they've ever got out of a cast, but there also seems to be more deviation from the script for *Lebowski* than in the Coens' earlier movies, perhaps indicating that they were becoming more willing to play around with the material more and let it evolve as it was performed. The joke about the rent, for example, does not appear in the script (in the filmed version The Dude misunderstands Allan's hint about the rent, assuming that Allan is commenting on how time flies). Neither, for that matter, does one of the film's finest lines, as The Dude punctuates his accusation: 'All you needed was a sap to pin it on, you'd just met *me*,' with the outburst, 'you, you, human paraquat!'

Some actors who have worked with the Coens have also complained that the brothers are uncommunicative. This is perhaps a consequence of the non-verbal, intuitive communication to which Joel and Ethan are accustomed: they understand each other but don't always put it into words, and perhaps they expect actors to respond the same way. This suggests why they have come to rely on a repertory of actors with whom they find it easy to work: John Turturro, Jon Polito, Frances McDormand, Steve Buscemi and John Goodman. (Hitchcock was much the same, repeatedly using Cary Grant and James Stewart after they grew too old for the roles he was casting them in because he trusted them to do the job without too much instruction.) On *The Big Lebowski* all of the actors seem to click.

Goodman's performance in *The Big Lebowski* remains the pinnacle of his career thus far. He returned to the Coen brothers fold after *Roseanne* came to an end in 1997 and Ethan and Joel wrote a part that was tailor-made for Goodman to play while providing a substantial contrast to the jovial blue-collar husband he'd been playing on TV for the previous nine years. Walter is at once noble and ridiculous, bringing Vietnam into every conversation whether it fits or not: he seems to regard Bunny's supposed extortion of cash from her husband as a personal slight, as though she doesn't appreciate that he fought for her out in Vietnam. He becomes increasingly enraged during this speech, only for The Dude to deflate his argument by pointing out its complete lack of relevance. Walter is also a hypocrite, asking The Dude to use 'Asian–American' instead of 'Chinaman', only to later refer to Burkhalter from the bowling league office as a 'kraut' (ensuring that his slur is accurate by asking the man's name first). He is enraged by Lebowski's suggestion that he planned to steal the money, despite the fact that this is exactly what he intended to do.

The Coens acknowledge that the dynamic of the three members of The Dude's bowling team is based on an archetypal nuclear family, with The Dude as the gentle, sympathetic mother, Walter as the aggressive, domineering father and Donny as the naïve, chattering child. The Dude and Walter do most of the bickering and arguing ('Walter, I love you but sooner or later you're gonna have to face the fact that you're a goddamn moron!') while Walter delivers curt put-downs to Donny to keep him in his place. (This has become an unconscious reflex to Walter, so much so that even when Donny is telling him something that he wants to know Walter starts to reject it before he has even processed the information, as in the scene where Donny brings news of the draw for the next round of the tournament.) The Dude rarely loses his temper because he's too stoned, but Walter frequently seems to hit a nerve with him and their conversations often end with one of them shouting at the other. Generally speaking, two people have to be pretty close before they can vent at each other like this. Walter also automatically acts as the protector: when the trio confronts the nihilists he assures Donny that the nasty men are not going to hurt him.

The effect is slightly subverted when Donny becomes the first of them to die, not least because he suffers a heart attack (an uncommon way for parents to lose a child), but is restored in the funeral parlour. The Dude and Walter are asked if they are the bereaved and they confirm this: Donny does not seem to have any other family and The Dude and Walter are the two most significant people in his life. It is also not until Donny's death that the audience hears Walter apologise to anybody, since he never admits to being wrong (and, indeed, often dares The Dude and Donny to disagree with him). Walter finally says sorry after accidentally covering The Dude with some of Donny's ashes, in a scene that demonstrates just how much they both cared about their team-mate. Ultimately, just as families are held together by their blood relationship, The Dude, Walter and Donny are held together by bowling. They don't seem like people who would ordinarily hang out together: a dope-addled peacenik and a gun-toting patriot? Both were shaped by their experiences in the 1960s (the Summer of Love and Vietnam), but back then they would have been at loggerheads. This seems to be not unusual in bowling teams (Jesus and Liam make a pretty odd couple as well). Walter never gives Donny any credit for anything except his bowling skills and this demonstrates that, as far as bowling goes, the others do have genuine respect for Donny.

This respect is entirely justified, since he gets a strike every time he bowls . . . except on one occasion. Just before the team goes outside to find the nihilists waiting for them, Donny throws a nine on his last bowl of the match. The look on his face tells us that he hasn't had a nine in ages. In a moment of crushing tragedy, it turns out to be the last ball he ever rolls.

GENRE: *The Big Lebowski* is the Coens' finest genre-bending achievement to date. Having constructed an appropriately convoluted Chandleresque mystery, they remove the traditional detective and put in his place a man who is the polar opposite of that character. This makes the plotting of *Lebowski* all the more impressive because there isn't the usual inquisitive detective figure to drive the plot onward.

The traditional American hero is the man of action, but The Dude is a man of inaction. He is contrasted with other slightly skewed versions of typical heroic types, such as the soldier (Walter) and the sportsman (Donny, the only one of the team who is ever seen to bowl), and the Coens throw a cowboy into the mix as the narrator. There is also a more traditional detective figure in the form of Da Fino, the archetypal seedy-looking guy in a suit. Somewhere along the line, his role in the narrative has become mixed with The Dude's: conventional wisdom would slot The Dude in as a colourful supporting character while Da Fino would work on solving the mystery. But that's not how things work out and instead The Dude, the least hard-boiled man in America, becomes the hero of the piece.

The Dude is roped into this story by a dumb coincidence – he shares his name with a rich guy – and at first he is only interested in getting a new rug to replace the soiled one. Then he decides that he can earn some easy money by acting as a courier. However, when this goes wrong and lands him in trouble he doesn't know what he can do. He does not find any leads of his own volition: for instance, it is Maude who gets in touch with him (twice, including one occasion where she impressively tracks him down at the bowling alley despite barely knowing anything about him). The Dude seems to spend most of his time being summoned to places or accosted in his own home. Indeed, his home is invaded on no less than six occasions: three times by Treehorn's thugs (the second time they come back they summon The Dude to Treehorn's place, then they return and trash the place while he's away, making three), twice by Maude and once by the nihilists. As if this wasn't enough, multiple indignities are visited on The Dude's other sanctum, his car. It crashes into a tree when the rendezvous with the nihilists goes wrong, then it is stolen from outside the bowling alley and is found severely damaged by reckless driving. The Dude then crashes it into a post when he drops his joint on the seat, the windows are smashed by the owner of the Corvette that Walter trashes and it is finally set on fire by the nihilists. The Dude has no choice but to remain involved (witness his rather pathetic attempt to wedge his front door shut). Unequipped to deal with a situation that changes more quickly than he can keep up with, The Dude often only manages to keep people from discovering that he doesn't know what has happened to the money by virtue of his meandering, circular mode of speech, more by luck than judgement.

Some label The Dude as a stupid man, but this ignores the fact that he can be very sharp indeed, particularly with his witticisms: when one of Treehorn's thugs holds up the bowling ball and asks, 'What the fuck is this?' The Dude's response is, 'Obviously you're not a golfer.' (That said, he does claim to the police that the case in his stolen car contains his business papers, only to respond to the question of what he does by saying that he's unemployed.) The reason he ends up getting deeper and deeper into this mess is that he moves slowly and events overtake him. The Dude operates at a different pace to the rest of the world: for example Brandt leaves two messages on his answer-phone, believing that The Dude hasn't got in touch because he doesn't want to be collared for stealing the rug. In fact, The Dude has just not picked up the first message yet. Another factor is that The Dude doesn't really care what's going on, but just wants to be left alone (as he tells a number of people). He only pursues the money because he knows that the ramifications for him may be severe if he doesn't.

In some ways The Dude has a good mindset for a detective, since his years of drug abuse have forcibly shifted his perspective so many times that he has no problem looking at a situation from different points of view. (See, for example, The Dude's overly equivocal response to Jesus Quintana's taunts.) When presented with the one piece of evidence that he has been missing – Lebowski is not actually rich, despite the impression he contrives to give – The Dude works out what's going on immediately. He follows the same piece of advice that led him to believe that Bunny had kidnapped herself: look for the person who will benefit. When he realises that Lebowski has something to gain and therefore that his motives are suspect, the mystery is solved.

However, The Dude carries no authority and justice cannot be served. While Lebowski's reaction clearly indicates that The Dude's theory is the truth, there's nothing that The Dude can do about it and Maude will have to deal with her father's embezzlement herself. Genre convention would usually dictate that if the villain cannot be caught then they must die, but neither happens to Lebowski. In fact, this film has a low body count by the Coens' standards, with Donny the only character not to survive to the end credits and even then he dies from natural causes (the other Coen films to feature just one death – *Raising Arizona* and *O Brother, Where Art Thou?* – see the Lone Biker killed by a grenade and a burning cross dropped on Big Dan). This makes *The Big Lebowski*, somewhat surprisingly, the Coens' least bloody film to date. It compensates for the lack of violence by including an enormous number of swear words (the word 'fuck' appears 267 times).

EVER AMERICA: *The Big Lebowski* is the Coens' strangest period piece. The other historical Coen films are set at a remove of at least thirty-five years and are distinct in their evocation of a certain period, apart from *Fargo* which, as a 'true' story, has to be located in the past by default. Just seven years (perhaps even slightly less) separate the setting of *Lebowski* and its release.

The main purpose that this serves is to locate the film within the Gulf War. Apart from providing the joke in the second dream sequence, in which Saddam Hussein hands The Dude his bowling shoes, this provides a backdrop of overseas war that chimes in with the Second World War backdrop of the Raymond Chandler stories from which *Lebowski* draws so much. This is not dissimilar to what Robert Altman did with *The Long Goodbye* (1973), which updates Chandler's novel to a contemporary setting that coincides with the end of the Vietnam War. The Coens noted many years before *Lebowski* that they admired Altman's adaptation, which is no small compliment from two such devoted fans of Chandler's work. ('It's a great movie,' Ethan once said, 'but I read somewhere it's the one he likes least. I can't understand why.' The interviewer told him that this wasn't true: Altman was really pleased with the film. 'Ah! That's OK then,' said a relieved Ethan.) They have acknowledged that *Lebowski* owes a substantial debt to *The Long Goodbye* and William Preston Robertson notes in *The Making of The Big Lebowski* that Altman updated Chandler's LA and made it work in a contemporary setting by turning Marlowe into more of a 'flake', the kind of eccentric character which LA has come to accommodate. The Coens take this to its logical conclusion with The Dude, a man who appears not to care at all about what others think of him.

Another similarity between *Lebowski* and *The Long Goodbye* is that Altman's film mixed its contemporary elements with bits of the 1940s, not only in its deliberately archaic characters but also in some of its props. Marlowe, for example, drives a 1940s car throughout. The Coens' approach in *Lebowski* is even more eclectic, making this a generic Los Angeles in which elements of different eras mingle. Maude's art is akin to the Fluxus movement of the 1960s, while one of the nihilists used to be a member of a 1970s Krautrock group. Jackie Treehorn's pad looks like something out of the 1970s. Bowling had its peak of popularity in the 1950s. The Dude himself is a relic of the late 1960s/early 1970s, and the cowboy dates right back to the previous century. In the way that *The Hudsucker Proxy* is located in a generic New York, so the story of *Lebowski* could take place at almost any time in the twentieth century but is definitely tied to Los Angeles. The one decade that it doesn't really draw from is the 1980s, because The Dude clearly didn't fit in the 1980s (he mentions being a roadie for Metallica during their 'Speed of Sound' tour, describing them as a 'bunch of assholes' – evidently their more confrontational attitude didn't fit with his own outlook). The 1990s are just beginning and The Dude will fit into this decade far more comfortably (the viewer has the benefit of hindsight, watching this film at or after the end of the 1990s).

The Gulf War remains in the background but is often mentioned (note how The Dude echoes George Bush's language in the meeting with Lebowski), casting a light shadow over events that prevents the characters from relaxing. Walter, of course, enthuses about it, making self-righteous proclamations about how the war needs to be fought. (Joel and Ethan noted that this was the main reason they wanted a Gulf War setting, going on to add, 'It's more attractive to make something time specific than just present day, because just what is present day?') It doesn't have the level of austerity of most film noirs but it is noticeable that the majority of the characters in this story would not have met the draft criteria for the Second World War, being either too old, too young, too disabled, too pacifist, too feeble or too female.

Of course, one shouldn't discount the possibility that the Coens wanted to set *The Big Lebowski* in 1991 because they thought it was funny. There are few overt ties to 1991 in the design, but the gigantic mobile telephone that Brant gives The Dude is rather comical. Saddam Hussein is also regarded as a joke, which was possible in 1998. Of course, the wheel turned again very soon afterwards as he became seen as a threat once more during America's 'war on terror', inspired by the attacks on the World Trade Center and the Pentagon on 11 September 2001. In an eerie coincidence, the cheque written by The Dude to pay for his milk at the beginning of the movie is dated 11 September 1991, precisely ten years before the attacks.

AVAILABILITY: Rather laughably, you get more for your money when you buy the VHS of *The Big Lebowski* than you do if you get the DVD. The widescreen version of the VHS includes a good 'making of' documentary at the end of the film, while the DVD gives you no extras whatsoever. Mystifying. There is, however, a booklet in the DVD with some informative production notes.

THE COENS' VIEW: 'Even the things that don't go together should seem to clash in an interesting way – like a Cheech and Chong movie, but with bowling. You sort of do it by feel and not with reasons.' (Ethan in 1998)

VERDICT: 'Ah, fuck it, Dude. Let's go bowling.' *The Big Lebowski* is funny. Very, very funny indeed. But is that enough? What is it trying to say? Where is the human interest? Where is the heart?

It's one of the funniest movies ever made, so who cares? It's actually interesting on many levels – not only as an examination of the detective genre, but also an examination of people who are stuck in the past, of male–female power relationships, of what constitutes worthy achievement – but even if it wasn't, it wouldn't matter because the film is so funny. It's an amazing script, with humour worked into nearly every line by the Coens and their actors. The Coens have a better feel for these characters than any they've ever created (with the possible exceptions of Ed Crane and Barton Fink) and there is immense joy to be found in just listening to them speak. It's a toss-up as to which is funnier, Goodman's self-righteous fury or Bridges's stoned bemusement.

Of all the Coens' films this is the most loveable, with an affable hero whose horizontal demeanour reaches out to the viewer. It can be watched repeatedly and will, in time, attain the status of student video-shelf staples like *Withnail and I* (Bruce Robinson, 1987) and *Monty Python and the Holy Grail* (Terry Jones, Terry Gilliam, 1975): films that can be played at any time, regardless of the viewer's mood. In *Empire*'s all-time great movies poll published in November 2001 it was the highest-placed Coens movie, ranking 35th (*Fargo* was close behind at 39th): its box office performance may have been modest but its stature has grown. A truly great comedy can mean more to people than anything else the cinema can produce, and this is one of the greatest.

The Naked Man (1998)

(Colour – 93 mins)

October Films Presents
A Barenholtz Production
Directed by J Todd Anderson
Written by J Todd Anderson & Ethan Coen
Produced by Ben Barenholtz
Executive Producer: Aida Ashenati
Associate Producer: Mary Schniegenberg

Line Producer: Robert Graf
Director of Photography: Jeff Barklage
Production Designer: Kathleen M McKernin
Costume Designer: Alina Panova
Music by Edward Bilous
Edited by Tricia Cooke, Mark Cretcher
Supervising Sound Editor: Bruce Pross
Music Supervisor: Barry Cole
Casting by Christine Sheaks

CAST: Michael Rapaport (*Dr Edward Bliss, Jr*), Michael Jeter (*Sticks Varona*), John Carroll Lynch (*Sticks's Driver*), Arija Bareikis (*Kim Bliss*), Rachael Leigh Cook (*Delores*), Martin Ferrero (*Sonny*), Joe Grifasi (*Det Lt Albert Karski*), John Slattery (*Ferris*), Peter Thoemke (*Ed Bliss, Sr*), Nancy Plank (*Mrs Marlinda Bliss*), Steve Shaffer (*Dr Preard*), Charles Brin (*Mr Renfrow*), Jessica Shepherd (*Patty*), Jesse Morse (*Betty*), Katherine Pisque (*The Adjusted Woman*), Isabell Monk (*Vice Principal*), Jonathan Rylander (*Middle Eddie – 12 Yrs*), Traci Christofore (*Little Girl on the Playground*), Len Resnick (*Mr Crestifore*), Rick Schleeht (*Cub Scout Leader*), Mick Karch (*Big Time Announcer #1*), Dale Dunham (*Big Time Announcer #2*), Jeff Allin (*Shuffling Man*), April Berquist (*White Wall Woman*), Wayne A Evenson (*Bartender at Hog Heaven*), Terry Hempleman (*Biker*), Jimmy Noonan (*Forklift Thief*), James Gaulae (*Lawyer*), Jay Albright (*Puffy's Manager*), Mark Povinelli (*Little Vic*), Kim Thomassen (*Fat Lady*), Ben Barleniltz (*Biker Cop*), Peter Schmitz (*Police*), Don Hewitt (*Leveranti*), Alex Rizzo (*Martiano*), Doug Fisher (*Viking*), Donald Murphy (*Pilot*), Robert Graf (*Puffy's Counterman #1*), Danny Downey (*Puffy's Counterman #2*), Eric P Notel (*Puffy's Counterman #3*), Joan Sherman (*Referee*), Terry O'Sullivan (*Puffy's Pharamist*), Dennis Carlson (*Schyler*), Charlie 'Thunderblood' Morris (*Wrestling Opponent*), Henry Allen (*Male Model #1*), T Michael Rambo (*Male Model #2*), Scott Soular (*Burglar*), Trump Card (*Young Eddie – 9 yrs*), Eric Haymes (*Mailman*), George R Willeman (*Coroner*), Phil Stockton (*Miles*), Robert Fernandez (*Arthur Fleginheim*)

TAGLINE: 'Chiropractor by day. Wrestler by night.'

SUMMARY: Successful chiropractor Eddie Bliss moonlights as a wrestler named 'The Naked Man' but, owing to his wife Kim's pregnancy, he quits the ring and moves back to his home town, where he plans to set up a practice of his own. He is estranged from his father, who owns a drugstore and was disgusted when Eddie took up chiropractic therapy and wrestling, but they are reconciled when Eddie announces his decision to return to the town. Eddie leaves Kim at his father's drugstore while he goes to pick up the rest of their possessions from the old house, but while he is away the whole family is shot down by a disabled man named Sticks Varona. Sticks owns a chain of drugstores which he uses as a front for drug smuggling: he wants to close down the Bliss drugstore, then take it over for himself.

When Eddie finds his entire family dead he goes insane, vowing revenge on those responsible. His rage leads him to return to the wrestling ring and comprehensively beat up all of his fellow wrestlers; he then goes to a bar, kills a few bikers and gains a companion in the form of young biker chick, Delores. The police catch up with Eddie just as he catches up with Sticks and prepares to mete out justice to the villain. Eddie appears to break Sticks's neck, but in fact his chiropractic skill has cured the criminal of his disability. Sticks then draws a gun and the cops shoot him down. Eddie discovers that Kim is not dead, but merely in a coma. His sanity is restored and he is hopeful of being acquitted of the murders he's committed.

DEVELOPMENT: J Todd Anderson first worked as the Coen brothers' storyboard artist during *Raising Arizona*: having admired *Blood Simple*, he tracked them down to their set in Arizona and asked for a job. He produced the storyboards for all of their subsequent productions and has become part of the 'family' (he played 'Victim in the Field' in *Fargo*, but was credited only with a symbol that parodied the one used by Prince). Nevertheless, he still harboured ambitions of directing, having first become drawn to the industry when making short films in college.

In the early 1990s Anderson made a five-minute short concerning a chiropractor going about his work. Ethan Coen saw this and thought that it had potential as a sequence in a feature. Extrapolating from this, the pair began to collaborate on a script about this chiropractor and added the wrestling element along the way (possibly inspired by *Barton Fink*). Anderson describes the film as a story of 'good intentions gone bad, and the person with the good intentions hasn't been told that they're going bad. Nobody has bothered to inform him.'

REFERENCES: Delores has 'LOVE' tattooed on the top of her right breast and 'HATE' on her left. Robert Mitchum's character in *The Night of the Hunter* (Charles Laughton, 1955) has the same words across his knuckles.

When Eddie names Sticks's driver (an Elvis lookalike) as a special narcotics agent, this is a reference to the fact that Elvis Presley was given that rank by Richard Nixon in the late 1960s.

PRODUCTION: Anderson shot his debut feature in Minnesota in the autumn of 1997, having secured backing of $5 million from Ben Barenholtz, who had helped finance the Coens' first four movies. Post-*Fargo*, the state was keen to encourage filmmakers to consider Minnesota as a location, and accordingly it had passed new legislation that gave out-of-town producers a rebate of 5 per cent on any money spent in-state. In turn, Barenholtz managed to get backing from distributors October Films, who had suddenly found themselves cash-rich following a buyout by Universal.

New York actor Michael Rapaport, best known for *True Romance* (Tony Scott, 1993), took the lead role, while the villain was played by Michael Jeter, who had previously taken a small role in *Miller's Crossing*. Minneapolis native Rachel Leigh Cook, who turned eighteen during the production, was cast as Delores: her later roles would include Josie in *Josie and the Pussycats* (Jasna Stefanovitch, 2001) alongside *The Big Lebowski*'s Tara Reid. Delighted at being given a shot at directing, Anderson was keen not to screw up and he was careful to ensure that the production went off without a hitch. 'I worked six years of my life on this film,' he says. 'I spent a lot of my own money up-front, and then Ethan got involved and we finished the shoot on time and on budget.' He had performed what was required from him and looked forward to the film's release.

BOX OFFICE: A year and a half after shooting wrapped on *The Naked Man*, the movie was still seeking a release. October's keenness for indie flicks had waned after a string of flops during 1998, including *Kicked in the Head* (Matthew Harrison, 1997), *Kiss or Kill* (Bill Bennett, 1997) and *Still Breathing* (James F Robinson, 1998). *The Naked Man* was left floating on their schedule, its release continually postponed. Eventually, after cancelling a Minneapolis premiere at Landmark's Lagoon Cinema, they started to talk about sending it straight to video and cable. Anderson wasn't happy; neither was Ethan. Nevertheless, the film was sold to the Encore channel in January 1999. Shortly afterwards, October was absorbed into fellow indies Gramercy Pictures and Propaganda Films: the new company was christened USA Films. As a result of the problems, Anderson has been unable to launch a second feature of his own.

'October definitely knew what they were getting into,' Ethan says. 'If you read the script, you'd see that the movie is a faithful rendering of it. It's an odd script and it made an odd movie.' He comments that the Coens' own movies have never screen-tested well and he suspects that October got cold feet regarding *The Naked Man* following poor screen-tests. 'I'm just speculating here, but I'd guess that [October] test-screened it hoping against hope that in spite of their expectations some strange thing might happen,' he continues. 'And I'm sure it was uninformative, and did terribly.'

Ultimately, the failure of *The Naked Man* is symptomatic of the hangover from the indie gold rush of 1997, inspired by *Fargo*'s success at the Academy Awards. In early 1997 many thought that a revolution was taking place in Hollywood, that the indie production companies would rise up and overthrow the major studios. By early 1998 the big-budget blockbusters had reasserted themselves with *Titanic* (James Cameron, 1997) taking a record Oscar haul. Odd little movies suddenly didn't seem like such a hot idea any more. 'What this reflects more than anything else is the fact that it has gotten incredibly expensive to release a movie,' says Ethan. 'The cost of release has escalated even beyond the cost of *making* movies.'

DIALOGUE TO SKIP BACK FOR:

Eddie: 'You have seen the many faces of the evil that men do. But what is the single great wrong that poisons human intercourse? I think you all know . . . that it is spinal sacral misalignment.'

ANALYSIS: In many ways *The Naked Man* is not dissimilar to *Crimewave*, not only because it was rejected by its distributor and sank into obscurity, but because it appears that Anderson and Raimi bring similar things to the Coen 'formula' (for want of a more accurate word, hence the inverted commas). Anderson is a storyboard artist and, given the content of *The Naked Man*, it would come as little surprise if he turned out to be an avid reader of comic books (storyboards being not unlike the comic-strip version of a movie). He appears to have drawn Ethan in this direction while retaining the Coen-style figures drawn from hard-boiled crime fiction (the two cops are pure, distilled cliché: one is immaculate and speaks in a monotone, like Jack Webb in *Dragnet*, while the other is dishevelled and shambolic).

The finished film is a confused creature, however, apparently unsure whether it wants to transplant a comic-book-style superhero into the 'real' world or just adopt a stylised aesthetic in order to fit that type of character. In terms of his origins, the Naked Man himself is a straight cross between Spider-Man and Batman. After gaining his powers, Spider-Man first put them to use as a professional wrestler before the violent death of his uncle led him to fight crime: Sam Raimi's film is a pretty faithful rendering of the story. (The wrestling device is useful because it justifies the hero's distinctive costume.) In Batman's case, it was seeing his parents gunned down by a thief that caused him to become a vigilante. While Eddie recovers his sanity upon catching the culprit and being reunited with his wife, for Bruce Wayne the battle is never-ending.

Other motifs of the superhero genre are adopted along the way. Delores adopts the role of the kid sidekick (Robin to Eddie's

Batman), a role that can never become overtly sexual in comics and does not become sexual here. Most interestingly Eddie is given a nemesis who is his polar opposite. Where Eddie is in peak physical condition, believes in holistic medicine and abhors drugs of all kinds (including alcohol, tobacco and pharmaceuticals), Sticks is crippled by spinal problems, owns a chain of drugstores and smuggles drugs. Sticks's own sidekick resembles a 1970s Elvis Presley, a symbol of overindulgence on unhealthy food and over-reliance on drugs. (Just before he dies, Sticks's driver has his belly split open while attacking his drug-smuggling employer and is momentarily transformed into a surrogate of the Naked Man.)

The storyline is therefore surprisingly similar to M Night Shyamalan's fascinating *Unbreakable* (2000), in which an ordinary man discovers that he is a superhero and comes up against a crippled nemesis. In some ways *The Naked Man* seems to be trying to do the same thing by rooting itself in the everyday while adopting the motifs of a superhero comic, but this is undermined because nobody takes it seriously enough. It's full of melodrama and cheap gags (particularly the 'crushed nuts' joke at Sticks's expense, which is one of the oldest in the book), resulting in an uneasy mix of spoof and reinvention.

AVAILABILITY: *The Naked Man* is slightly easier to track down than *Crimewave*, but that's not saying much. There is a VHS edition available in America but the film has never been released in Britain on any format. A DVD is, however, available in France and can be ordered from a number of French DVD websites. There is a choice of dubbed and subtitled versions on the disc so it is possible to watch the film in English. Annoyingly you can't turn the French subtitles off, but they mostly appear in the black border of the widescreen picture and don't encroach too far into the frame.

THE COENS' VIEW: 'I thought J Todd did a great job and, on its own terms, it is a very funny movie. But that's all it has to offer, which, sadly, isn't enough.' (Ethan in 1999)

VERDICT: 'Don't worry. My lawyer says he's never seen a better case for the insanity defence.' *The Naked Man* is a collection of really good ideas that just don't fit together. In parts it is very well conceptualised and plotted, but in others it just feels random. It is possible for a film to get away with this or even make a virtue of it – *The Man with Two Brains* (Carl Reiner, 1982) comes to mind – but the script has to be consistently funny and the filmmakers have to be confident. *The Naked Man* displays neither of these qualities: it's only sporadically amusing and it frequently seems uncertain of its tone.

Why, for example, does Eddie murder the bikers rather than just beat them up like he did with all the others? It isn't funny, it makes a previously sympathetic character much less sympathetic and it makes the resolution much less convincing, so what purpose does it serve? Delores even points out that 'Most of 'em aren't bad people, really, they just have learning disabilities.' If they weren't so bad, why were they disposed of so remorselessly by Eddie? The audience relates to a character differently after they've killed somebody and this has to be handled carefully. Anderson doesn't pull it off in the way that the Coens do in their own films.

That isn't to say Anderson doesn't show talent as a director: the sequence in which Eddie passes out under the influence of Sticks's drugs is superb. Indeed, there are enough directorial flourishes, quality jokes and engaging characters (by the way, what the hell happens to Delores at the end?) to make this a good piece of entertainment and convince the viewer that it was unfairly buried. Like *Crimewave*, however, it doesn't stand up to comparison with the average Coen brothers movie.

O Brother, Where Art Thou? (2000)

(Colour – 106 mins)

Universal Pictures and Touchstone Pictures Present
In Association with Studio Canal

A Working Title Production
Casting by Ellen Chenoweth
Supervising Sound Editor: Skip Lievsay
Film Editors: Roderick Jaynes and Tricia Cooke
Music by T Bone Burnett
Costume Designer: Mary Zophres
Production Designer: Dennis Gassner
Director of Photography: Roger Deakins ASC, BSC
Co-producer: John Cameron
Executive Producers: Tim Bevan and Eric Fellner
Produced by Ethan Coen
Written by Ethan Coen & Joel Coen
Based Upon *The Odyssey* by Homer
Directed by Joel Coen

CAST: George Clooney (*Ulysses Everett McGill*), John Turturro (*Pete*), Tim Blake Nelson (*Delmar O'Donnell*), John Goodman (*Big Dan Teague*), Holly Hunter (*Penny Wharvey McGill*), Chris Thomas King (*Tommy Johnson*), Charles Durning (*Governor Menelaus 'Pappy' O'Daniel*), Del Pentecost (*Junior O'Daniel*), Michael Badalucco (*George 'Babyface' Nelson*), JR Horne, Brian Reddy (*Pappy's Staff*), Wayne Duvall (*Gubernatorial Candidate Homer Stokes*), Ed Gale (*The Little Man*), Ray McKinnon (*Vernon T Waldrip, Penny's Suitor*), Daniel von Bargen (*Sheriff Cooley/The Devil*), Royce D Applegate (*Man with Bullhorn*), Frank Collison (*Washington 'Wash' Bartholomew Hogwallop*), Quinn Gasaway (*Boy Hogwallop, Wash's Son*), Lee Weaver (*Blind Seer on Handcar*), Millford Fortenberry (*Pomade Vendor*), Stephen Root (*Lund, Manager WEZY Radio*), John Locke (*Mr French, Record Company Man*), Gillian Welch (*Soggy Bottom Customer*), A Ray Ratliff (*Record Store Clerk*), Mia Tate, Musetta Vander, Christy Taylor (*Sirens*), April Hardcastle (*Waitress*), Michael W Finnell (*Pete's Interrogator*), Georgia Rae Rainer, Marianna Breland, Lindsey Miller, Natalie Shedd (*Wharvey Gals*), John McConnell (*Woolworths Manager*), Issac Freeman, Wilson Waters Jr, Robert Hamlett (*Gravediggers*), Willard Cox, Evelyn Cox, Suzanne Cox, Sidney Cox (*Cox Family*), Buck White, Sharon White, Cheryl White (*The Whites*), Ed Snodderly, David Holt (*Village Idiots*)

TAGLINE: 'They have a plan . . . but not a clue.'

SUMMARY: Mississippi, 1937. Three convicts – Ulysses Everett McGill, Delmar O'Donnell and Pete – escape from their chain gang. Everett has told Delmar and Pete that there is $1.2 million concealed on land that will be flooded in a matter of days to create a new lake. Along the way, they meet young black musician Tommy Johnson and form a group, The Soggy Bottom Boys. They cut a record called 'I Am a Man of Constant Sorrow' at WEZY Radio and, unbeknown to them, it becomes a hit. The convicts and Tommy are separated during a police raid. The cons go on to encounter a flock of Baptists, meet bank robber George 'Babyface' Nelson and become enticed by three sirens. Pete vanishes and Delmar believes that the sirens have transformed him into a toad. In fact, Pete is being interrogated by the police and confesses where the treasure is. Everett and Delmar meet a one-eyed Bible salesman named Big Dan Teague, who beats them up, steals their money and crushes their toad.

In Everett's hometown, a battle is brewing between current Governor of the state, 'Pappy' O'Daniel, and his challenger Homer Stokes, who is running on an anti-integration ticket. Stokes has the upper hand. Everett and Delmar find Pete and break him out. Pete apologises for blabbing about the treasure and Everett admits that there is no treasure. He knew that his wife, Penny, was getting married again and needed to escape, but Pete and Delmar were next to him on the chain and he needed their help to escape. They happen upon a Ku Klux Klan meeting attended by Stokes and Big Dan, which is about to hang Tommy, so Everett, Delmar and Pete rescue him.

Together, Everett, Delmar, Pete and Tommy infiltrate a political rally and perform 'I Am a Man of Constant Sorrow'. Stokes objects when he realises that The Soggy Bottom Boys are of mixed race, but is ejected from the hall. Pappy pardons the Boys in a vote-winning gesture. Penny agrees to remarry Everett, but insists that he find her old wedding ring. The Boys head to Everett's old home to collect it, but find the police waiting. The police prepare to hang the cons, but at that moment the valley is flooded. Everett, Delmar, Pete and Tommy survive, and Tommy finds the ring. Well, he finds *a* ring . . .

DEVELOPMENT: As far back as 1987 the Coens were talking about making a third movie set in the Deep South to follow *Raising Arizona* and *Blood Simple*, referring to this as their 'Hayseed Trilogy', but they were aware that it would be a long time coming. Thirteen years coming, as it turned out. They started developing the script in the mid-1990s.

Despite getting a credit on the movie, Homer's *The Odyssey* was not the original inspiration for *O Brother, Where Art Thou?* 'We didn't start out with the intention of adapting *The Odyssey* – which sounds funny even as I say it,' says Ethan. 'We started out with the premise of three convicts escaping from a chain gang.' The fact that one of these convicts would be trying to find his way home led the Coens to start drawing from *The Odyssey*, although they did so selectively. There was a very good reason why the adaptation was a loose one: 'We never actually read it,' Ethan admits. 'But we read the comic book version of *The Odyssey* and tarted the movie up with the Cyclops, et cetera.' The Coens included the elements that they felt fitted the story best. When asked about the use of Scylla and Charybdis (*The Odyssey*'s two waterbound perils), Ethan said, 'Scylla and Charybdis? Where were they?' When it was pointed out that they could potentially relate to the flood, he responded, 'Oh, yeah, sure, Scylla and Charybdis.' Nevertheless, the story provided a rich seam of imagery. 'It's an endlessly re-interpretable story,' says Joel. 'Kind of like James Joyce with *Ulysses*.' As with *Ulysses*, *O Brother* places the journey in a far smaller timeframe than Homer's decades-spanning original: the events take place over the course of about five days.

The Coens' attitude towards the period was similarly selective: 'It's all stuff that to one extent or another we were aware of,' says Joel, noting that they didn't purposefully research the period. 'It wasn't like we were trying to create a realistic time and place so much as an imagined world where all those things intersect – real people and made-up people.' (See **EVER AMERICA**.) The period and location also guided the Coens to deal overtly with race politics for the first time, although Joel insists that there is no polemic in the movie. 'The political undercurrent of the movie functions primarily for dramatic purposes, because the politics are frankly pretty primitive. The bad guys are racial bigots and KKK Grand Dragons.'

Yet again, the Preston Sturges movie *Sullivan's Travels* (1941) was an influence from an early stage. 'Because of the Depression-era setting and the chain gang thing, we were thinking about the sequence in *Sullivan's Travels* where he spends time on the prison farm,' says Ethan. 'That suggested the grandeur of the story.' It also provided the title which, if one thinks about it, doesn't seem to relate to any particular aspect of the film. That's because it's the title of the 'serious' picture about human suffering that the main character of Sturges's movie, film director John Sullivan, wants to make after making his name in comedies. Not only did the Coens draw upon its imagery of life on a chain gang, but they also practically lifted a scene wholesale from *Sullivan's Travels*: namely, the one in which Pete's chain gang are permitted an afternoon's rest at the cinema. However, the Coens' *O Brother* does not aim to be some kind of remake of the film that Sullivan might have made, since it does not attempt to engage with grim reality. 'It pretends to be a big important movie, but the grandiosity is obviously a joke,' says Ethan. 'It is what it is, it's a comedy.'

CASTING: After several years of working as a jobbing actor, including recurring roles in such TV shows as *The Facts of Life* and *Roseanne*, George Clooney hit the big time in 1994 playing Dr Doug Ross in *ER*. He seemed set for a successful movie career after roles in *From Dusk Till Dawn* (Robert Rodriguez, 1996) and *One Fine Day* (Michael Hoffman, 1996) but the unmitigated disaster (both creatively and financially) of *Batman and Robin* (Joel Schumacher, 1997) put him off working on blockbusters and he decided to take roles in smaller projects. (By this stage, *ER* was so successful that he was practically guaranteed an income for life from repeat runs alone.) One of the first smaller projects he went to was *Out of Sight* (1998), which became a surprise hit and restored director Steven Soderbergh to the mainstream crossover appeal he had not enjoyed since his debut, *Sex, Lies and Videotape* (1989).

'We'd seen him in *Out of Sight* and we really liked him in that,' says Joel. 'He was the only actor we considered for the part, but the reasons for that are hard to pin down.' Ethan is willing to try: 'As an actor, you never catch him straining for effect . . . you put that little thin moustache on him and you've got the matinee idol look, that mix of Clark Gable and Cary Grant.' Adds Joel, 'He looks like a movie star of the period, and you kind of imagine the character as imagining himself as looking that way.' For his own part, Clooney was so keen to see the film made that, he says, 'I did *O Brother* for nothing.' He agreed to do the film as soon as he was available.

With Clooney in place, many of the other roles were filled by familiar faces. John Turturro returned to the fold in a complete contrast to his cameo in *The Big Lebowski*: 'We like working with John,' says Joel, 'and we like to mix it up with John.' This time it was John Goodman's turn to take the smaller role, as he appeared in support as the one-eyed Bible salesman, Big Dan Teague. Holly Hunter, in her first role with the Coens since *Raising Arizona*, was cast as Penny, while Charles Durning (previously Waring Hudsucker) appeared as 'Pappy' O'Daniel and Michael Badalucco from *Miller's Crossing* returned to play 'Babyface' Nelson.

Other than Clooney, the main newcomers were Tim Blake Nelson and Chris Thomas King. While Nelson started out as an actor, he had already written and directed two features of his own by the time of *O Brother*: *Eye of God* (1997) and *Kansas* (1998). Not only could Nelson sing, which suited what he would be called upon to do as Delmar, he had also studied classical literature. 'Between the cast and us,' says Ethan, 'Tim Nelson is the only one who's actually read *The Odyssey*.' King, meanwhile, came not from an acting background but a musical one. His father, Tabby Thomas, was a noted Delta bluesman and King followed in his footsteps. His music typically mixes traditional blues forms with hip-hop samples and his albums (which include *Me, My Guitar and the Blues*, *Dirty South Hip-Hop Blues* and *It's a Cold Ass World*) often feature covers of songs by Robert Johnson, on whom the Coens based the character of Tommy. *O Brother* was his first acting role and it inspired him to make an album based around Tommy's persona, *The Legend of Tommy Johnson, Act 1: Genesis 1900s–1990s*, charting the history of blues as if through Tommy's lifetime. (This was just one of many musical spin-offs from the film: see **MUSIC**.)

PRODUCTION: The Coens had originally decided to make *The Man Who Wasn't There* as their follow-up to *The Big Lebowski*, but when they decided that George Clooney was the best choice to play Ulysses Everett McGill, it became more important that they do *O Brother* as soon as the schedules could be lined up. Clooney had agreed to do *O Brother* towards the end of the shoot for *Three Kings* (David O Russell, 1999) and he found that he would be available to shoot *O Brother* in mid-1999, so Joel and Ethan dropped *The Man Who Wasn't There* and started work on their hayseed odyssey. Backing for the project again came from Tim Bevan and Eric Fellner of Working Title Films.

The original plan was to shoot *O Brother, Where Art Thou?* in Texas. 'Before I read the script Joel and Ethan told me they had a film they wanted to shoot in the South,' Roger Deakins recalls. 'They imagined something dry, dusty and very hot.' However, when the setting altered to Mississippi, Deakins warned them that they wouldn't get the kind of ambience they were expecting. 'I've worked in Louisiana [on *Passion Fish* (John Sayles, 1992)] and Alabama [on *The Long Walk Home* (Richard Pearce, 1990)] so I knew that the region would be wet and the foliage would be various shades of lush green – and about half the picture would take place in exteriors . . . It would have been a different scenario if we had been shooting in the winter or if we'd been able to take in fall colours, but our film was scheduled for a summer shoot.' The Coens considered switching back to Texas, but had decided that the delta landscapes of Mississippi were exactly right for the film – except for all the green. 'It's very garish in a way,' says Joel, 'and we were looking for a way to de-saturate the colour.'

Deakins was instructed to 'give the images we were going to shoot the feeling of old, hand-tinted postcards'.

Deakins went with Joel and Ethan to Griffith Park in Los Angeles, where they shot some footage of very green trees. He then took this down to Deluxe Labs where he experimented with bleaching techniques and 'diluting' the original colour negative by combining it with a black and white print, but none was quite satisfactory. Deakins was aware of the digital processing work done on *Pleasantville* (Gary Ross, 1998), where the negative had been scanned into a computer so that elements of each frame could be converted into black and white. Other films, such as *Star Wars: Episode I – The Phantom Menace* (George Lucas, 1999) had been digitally scanned for special-effects purposes, but Deakins wasn't sure if the cost could be justified for purely aesthetic reasons. The Coens were intrigued by the suggestion and asked him to process the test footage at Cinesite, which had handled the work on *Pleasantville*. Deakins collaborated with Cinesite's Julias Friede to scan the footage and desaturate the greens, manipulating them into brown and yellow tones. The footage was then transferred back onto film and Deakins screened it for Joel and Ethan, who gave it the thumbs-up. 'They like to try new things,' says Deakins. 'We knew it would be taking a risk, but Cinesite gave us a good price, and quite honestly it was the only way we could see of achieving the look that all three of us wanted.'

Deakins recommended shooting in a widescreen ratio of 2.4:1. All of the Coens' previous movies had been shot in 1.85:1 (the Academy's standard ratio since 1960), but on account of the vast Mississippi landscapes Deakins reckoned that a wider aspect, close to the old CinemaScope ratio, would benefit the picture. He also suggested using a Super 35 camera because he 'didn't want glossy images. The spherical lenses have the effect of pulling the audience closer to the characters . . . the feeling of depth recorded on Super 35 would augment the picture-book quality of the story.' He also used three types of film stock: night scenes were shot on Kodak Vision 500T 5279; the majority of daylight material on Eastman EXR 5248 100-speed emulsion; and the bluescreen work and a number of the forest sequences, where there was a lot of shadow, were shot on Eastman EXR 5293 200-speed. Production commenced in June 1999. Mississippi can be rainy during the summer, and for this reason a couple of sets were built in a warehouse so that work would not have to stop during bad weather. 'We were only rained out once,' Deakins recalls. 'Lucky, I guess!'

This film saw a return to the Coens' drifting camera style after a number of relatively static films, although it remained as 'objective' as possible, an observer of rather than participant in the action. Like *The Big Lebowski*, breakout fantasy moments were also included. 'Those moments aren't structurally necessary for the plot,' says Deakins. 'It is almost an operatic or circus experience, like a Fellini film in many ways.' One of those breakout sequences saw the Baptists march past Everett, Delmar and Pete on their way to the river, and proved to be one of the most challenging shots of the movie. The Coens wanted to go very wide as they pulled away from the three convicts, so they went from shooting with an eleven-foot arm to a reveal shot from an 85-foot Akela crane. 'Trying to track an Akela through a swamp was not an easy thing,' says Deakins. 'We had to cut a road into the forest. My key grip, Mitch Lillian, decided to lay down 100 feet of railway sleepers to support the crane. Even those sank into the mud after a couple of takes.'

While most of the filming was done in Mississippi, some of the larger-scale sequences were shot at the Disney Ranch, just outside Los Angeles, including the effects shot of the flooding valley and the Klan rally. The rally involved around 350 extras and the crew also had to contend with a giant burning cross. 'That sequence posed quite a set of problems,' Deakins says. 'We had a large number of setups to do, and the choreography of the Klan members was going to be time-consuming. We chose a field backed by a tall, wide tree. The scene would be lit as if by the light from a 30-foot burning cross, and I knew I had enough room behind the tree to hide the large construction I would need to augment the firelight.'

Even before the colour processing came into play, *O Brother* was still the Coens' most effects-intensive movie since *The*

Hudsucker Proxy. As they had on the earlier film, the Coens hired Digital Domain for *O Brother* and Eric Nash oversaw the effects. 'The flashy science-fiction stuff is less appealing to me, partly because I spent so many years working on the *Star Trek* TV shows,' Nash says. 'It's a lot more challenging and rewarding to create effects that very possibly could be real; the bar is that much higher to make them invisible.' Most of Domain's work was on the flood sequence at the movie's climax.

First of all, Nash had to create a quarter-size version of the cabin that was destroyed by the flood. This was designed to match the real cabin that had been constructed and shot at the Disney Ranch. 'We told the Coens that the match would never be 100 per cent,' says Nash, 'but that our miniature would be of high enough quality that they could use it for the establishing shot. They were very sceptical.' The miniature and camera were both tilted at a thirty-degree angle in order to ensure that the water would rush through it. Then, two dump trucks poured a collective load of 8,000 gallons of water through the miniature set. Three takes were shot of this, and while the third was the most satisfactory, Nash's team had to do some compositing work in order to remove a piece of roof that stuck to the camera. Nash rates the model as an 80 per cent match for the real cabin, but as he'd promised, the Coens considered that the model was good enough to use for the establishing shot as well as the effects shot.

The next sequence showed a variety of objects floating through the flooded valley. This was a mix of real artefacts and digitally created ones. 'A banjo, a tyre swing, picture frames, a gramophone horn and Clooney, as well as lots of hair-pomade tins, were all shot underwater in Universal's tank,' says Nash. 'Our animation team created a CG bloodhound, which was fun, and we added some digital pomade cans that we could put in specific places and choreograph precisely alongside the film elements of floating cans. The Coens wanted [the audience to] first see one can, then a couple more, with the volume of cans building and building until we get above the surface, where they're all popping out of the water. The real challenge for us was taking these varied underwater elements, which were all shot handheld and varied greatly in water colour and value, and blend them with each other as well as with digital elements into one long, lyrical shot.'

The third and final component of this sequence was the trickiest. The long take of George Clooney, John Turturro and Tim Blake Nelson clinging to a floating coffin could not be shot on a real location and this, too, had to be done in the water tank at Universal. Roger Deakins used a huge overhead silk, which reached down to the waterline in the tank, to reflect light down at the actors and make the scene look as naturally lit as possible. The footage was then passed to Nash's team, who had to create a computer-generated background. 'The real water only extended behind them about 40 feet, and everything beyond that was digital, including the buildings and trees . . . We couldn't use blue- or greenscreen because it would have reflected in the water.' The length of the shot posed some problems, as did the blending of the CG water with the real water, but the team carried it off.

In order for no animals to be harmed during the making of this motion picture, the cow that gets run over on the road during 'Babyface' Nelson's escape from the cops was also digitally created. 'All the cows around it were real and [Digital Domain] inserted a computer-generated cow to get hit by the car,' says Ethan. Digital Domain used the cow they had created for *Lake Placid* (Steve Miner, 1999), in which a cow was consumed by a crocodile. 'I guess once they've got a cow figured out they can be pretty flexible with it,' says Ethan. The other main effects sequence was the moving train near the beginning of the film, which had to be shot against a blue screen for safety reasons.

Despite the fact that the film had to be scanned into a computer for tinting, the Coens used a traditional flatbed machine to cut it together first. 'It's to do with idiosyncratic things about what kind of screen I want to look at all day,' says Joel. 'I like handling the film, too; how I learned to edit was on flatbed editing machines.' The assembled negative was then passed to Deakins.

The colour-tinting process took place over ten weeks at Cinesite, with Deakins again working with Friede on the finished print. 'It was experimental in the sense that it was a learning process for all of us,' says Cinesite's director of digital mastering, Sarah Priestnall. 'Green is the most difficult colour to deal with when you're converting film to digital format.' For his own part, Deakins found that it was best not to get carried away with this new toy. 'We found that the more we tried to manipulate the image, the more noise and electronic artefacts appeared, and then we would have to rescan and retime the image. In the end, we kept the manipulation to a minimum in order to maintain quality overall. We affected the greens and played with the overall saturation but little else.' On one occasion, Deakins toned down an orange-yellow dress worn by an extra because it really stood out when the rest of the picture was desaturated, but he tried to avoid the temptation to meddle where possible. 'You can't take a cavalier approach and just say, "I'm going to change that green to bright red," because you can end up spending your life timing just one picture. The process is not a quick fix for bad lighting or poor photography; it is a tool to be used in the same way as any other tool.'

In the event, Deakins notes that, while he and the Coens found the finished product satisfactory, the process caused a slight loss of definition, which became more apparent when he viewed it on a cinema screen. However, the results speak for themselves. 'To my knowledge [it had] never been done before,' says Joel. 'It was a little bit ridiculous in terms of the time it took, but it was particularly suited to what we wanted to do.'

DELETED SCENES: The script includes a short scene that follows directly on from George Nelson's bank raid. Everett is seen consoling George, who is still upset at having been called 'Babyface' by one of the customers. George cheers himself up by lobbing a stick of dynamite towards the police as they pull up outside the bank.

MUSIC: 'The salient difference between this movie and anything we've done before is the music,' Ethan says. 'We've never used music like this before.' The film was not a musical, but the way that it worked was not dissimilar. 'The songs all sort of figure in the story sort of naturally, they're performed by the characters, not in a musical when the characters sort of burst unmotivatedly into song.'

T-Bone Burnett, who had acted as musical archivist on *The Big Lebowski*, was called in again to help put together a soundtrack that would fit the region, the period and the action as it unfolded. 'Being so heavily involved in roots music, we called him before we'd even finished the script,' says Ethan. 'Both Ethan and I are long-time listeners to and fans of this music,' adds Joel. 'It began to take over the script as we went on . . . It establishes the tone and the flavour.' Burnett was involved throughout the production process, suggesting archive tracks that could be applied and old songs that could be re-recorded. 'We'd get together with him and talk about how certain songs would fit certain scenes,' says Joel, 'or alternative ways in which songs and music would enhance the narrative.' This meant that many scenes could be set up with knowledge of what music would appear there and the songs were often performed by characters on-screen. An example of where this works very well is 'You Are My Sunshine', which was used as a campaign song by the governor of Louisiana in the 1930s and is worked into *O Brother*. There are also the gravediggers towards the end (members of the Fairfield Four, singing 'Lonesome Valley') and the songs performed by Chris Thomas King in the role of Tommy (he sings 'Hard Time Killing Floor Blues'). The Cox Family, bluegrass practitioners since 1976 and Grammy-winners for their 1994 album *I Know Who Holds Tomorrow*, also appeared on-screen to sing 'I Am Weary'.

The film's major song, 'I Am a Man of Constant Sorrow', was first recorded in 1922 and originated in the Appalachians, although the performance heard in *O Brother* is based on a later recording by The Stanley Brothers. While Clooney lip-synched his performances in the finished film, he did make an attempt to record the song himself. 'He came in and had a stab at it and then fired himself,' says Ethan. While Clooney's performance was not bad, Dan Tyminski (of Union Station, backing band for Alison Krauss) recorded a vocal, 'and if you've been steeped in the material like he has, your take on it is a little more authoritative,'

Ethan says. 'But George made a valiant try.' (On being told that her husband was providing Everett's voice, Elsie Tyminski said, 'Your voice coming out of George Clooney's body? Dan, that's my fantasy!') Tim Blake Nelson, however, performed his own lead vocal on the Soggy Bottom Boys' opening number, 'In the Jailhouse Now'. In the studio, artists such as Emmylou Harris and Alison Krauss recorded material suggested by Burnett, who combined these with archive tracks such as 'Big Rock Candy Mountain', recorded by Harry McClintock in 1928 and The Stanley Brothers' 'Angel Band', dating from 1955. As with *The Big Lebowski*, it was necessary to fill a few spaces with score and Carter Burwell was called in to provide some short pieces (these don't appear on the soundtrack album).

With the soundtrack completed, the Coens oversaw a charity concert at the Ryman Auditorium in Nashville on 24 May 2000, seven months before the release of *O Brother* itself. The proceeds went to the Country Music Hall of Fame. The concert featured many of the soundtrack's performers and was filmed by Donn Alan Pennebaker, the director of such legendary concert films as Bob Dylan's *Don't Look Back* (1967) and David Bowie's *Ziggy Stardust and the Spiders from Mars* (1973). The movie that emerged from his footage of the concert was *Down from the Mountain*, which was released in UK cinemas in the same week as *The Man Who Wasn't There* and has since been released on video and DVD, with a CD also available.

The film has become part of the remarkable spin-off industry that surrounds the music from *O Brother, Where Art Thou?* The original soundtrack album made its way to the top of the US Billboard chart, just as the Coens' film had become a sleeper hit (see **BOX OFFICE**). It has been credited with single-handedly reviving the popularity of roots country music and the bluegrass idiom, which was predominant at the time *O Brother* is set but practically died out following the introduction of electric instruments into country. The old-time country sound, epitomised by such acts as The Carter Family, Jimmie Rodgers and Bill Monroe, had long been ignored by both the mainstream American music media and the country-music media, but this all changed when *O Brother*'s popularity spread. (Ralph Stanley of The Stanley Brothers, whose performance of 'O Death' can be heard in the film, had been without a record deal for fifty years when the soundtrack LP came out. His old label re-signed him almost immediately.) The soundtrack has sold more than six million copies to date and was the surprise winner of Album of the Year at the Grammys in 2002.

CRITICAL RECEPTION: For a change, British critics got to air their views on the Coens' offering before their American counterparts. The *Guardian* very much enjoyed it. '*O Brother, Where Art Thou?* has brio, wit and style, and the whole picture is air-cushioned with appealing comedy and its own unassuming good nature,' wrote Peter Bradshaw in the 15 September 2000 edition. 'It is made with a marvellous clarity and fluency, and Joel and Ethan Coen attain a comic simplicity that other film-makers can only dream of.' Bradshaw did pick some faults with the movie, noting that the link with Preston Sturges drew attention to the fact that '*Sullivan's Travels* actually had serious things to say about poverty and what real film-makers can really do about it. For all its accomplishment, there is nothing in the Coens' film which speaks of this concern.' Nevertheless he awarded it four stars, saying, 'Simply: this is a film which is impossible to dislike.'

Not everybody was willing to be so definitive, with Jason Caro giving the film two stars. 'There's no need to pinch yourself – that *is* a two-star rating for a Coen brothers movie,' he wrote in *Film Review*. 'As a massive fan of their work, I so wanted to love this film. But . . . this is easily the weakest and least satisfying film of the pair's extraordinary career.' It wasn't a complete loss – Caro described it as 'still very watchable' – but he mourned that too much time was 'wasted on lame jokes and absurd (within the context of this movie's universe) encounters' and complained that the film hung together poorly, introducing its *Odyssey*-derived episodes without coherence. 'It isn't that bad by anybody else's standards, but considering almost every one of their previous seven films have become instant five-star classics, this weak, wafer-thin tale is simply a massive disappointment.'

Sight and Sound's Kevin Jackson was rather more charitable. '*O Brother* certainly isn't as funny as one of the top-flight Preston Sturges movies – no shame there, since almost nothing is – but it's more than funny enough, and sometimes unexpectedly charming into the bargain,' he wrote in the October 2000 issue. As ever, though, it was 'time to raise and, if possible, lance the old objection levelled against the Coens by unbelievers,' to wit the suggestion that there was no warmth or heart among the cleverness. Jackson didn't feel that the criticism stuck. 'It would be hard for film-makers with no real attachment to Americana to produce a movie so besotted with the bric-a-brac of their nation's half-forgotten folk ways.'

As ever, critics wondered whether they were supposed to be looking for a deeper message. 'Is it just uncool to look for meaning inside their extravagant formal conceits and elaborate jests?' asked Anthony Quinn in the *Independent* on 15 September 2000. 'Great comic filmmakers enlarge our view of the world; the Coens have no ambition beyond poking fun at it.' While watching *O Brother*, Quinn felt, 'One often thinks, "How clever," but hardly ever, "How true." ' This didn't bother Alexander Walker at all. '*O Brother* says everything about the Coens' love of old movie genres and pretty well nothing about anything else,' he declared in the *Evening Standard* on 14 September 2000. 'But most screen entertainment did exactly that 60 years ago, and was no worse for it.' Walker's perception of the film was that, like *Hudsucker*, it was a fine reproduction of Old Hollywood product, and he perceived the Coens as having been 'born out of wedlock with their own times' yet 'smart and successful enough to relive the Golden Age of Hollywood by comic assimilation.'

The American reviews were marginally better. 'As in many of the Coens' movies, the world on screen is one we intuitively recognise, even as its geography seems decidedly askew,' wrote AO Scott in the 22 December 2000 issue of the *New York Times*. '*O Brother* . . . offers a fairy-tale view of an America in which the real brutalities of poverty and racism are magically dissolved by the power of song.' The Coens' vision was aware of its artificiality and used it to poignant effect. 'Rather than wallow in nostalgia for the past, they dare to reinvent it, to make it something strange, beautiful and new.'

Roger Ebert's view on the film was astute, commenting on its roots in the episodic oral tales told by the Greeks. 'In the same spirit, *O Brother* contains sequences that are wonderful in themselves – lovely short films – but the movie never really shapes itself into a whole,' he wrote in the *Chicago Sun-Times* of 29 December 2000. He singled out the surreal Klan rally and the temptation of the sirens for particular praise, 'yet I left the movie uncertain and unsatisfied . . . I had the sense of invention set adrift; of a series of bright ideas wondering why they had all been invited to the same film.' Ebert awarded the film a cautious two and a half stars out of four. J Hoberman of the *Village Voice* refused to be impressed, noting that the title of *O Brother* was 'a jab at anyone who expects the Coens ever to be less than facetious . . . Basically, *O Brother* warms up a gumbo of tepid Deep South clichés.' Yet again, the film was deemed good-looking, yet hollow. 'The art direction is impeccable, but this is a pop-up book that I was impatient to slam.'

BOX OFFICE: In America *O Brother, Where Art Thou?* was released on 22 December 2000 (oddly, more than three months *after* the UK release date of 15 September). Initially it suffered from the glut of other big films released on the pre-Christmas weekend, such as *Cast Away* (Robert Zemekis, 2000) and *Miss Congeniality* (Donald Petrie, 2000), which ultimately grossed $233,630,478 and $106,807,667 respectively and pushed *O Brother* out of many cinemas for the first two weeks. When the movie found its way onto more screens it became a substantial sleeper hit: it opened in just five cinemas, but by its third week this had increased to 165 and from there it snowballed. The film's exposure hit a peak in its ninth week of screenings as it was carried by 847 cinemas. This is not particularly large – *The Big Lebowski* opened in 1,207 theatres after the success of *Fargo* – but it is unusual for a film to build over so many weeks from such a small opening. It finished its run with $45,506,619, by far the Coens' biggest ever gross at the US box office.

AWARDS: George Clooney took home a prize from the annual festival of categories and sub-categories that is the Golden Globe Awards, winning the 2001 award for Best Actor in a Comedy or Musical. The only other notable award garnered by the film was for Best Cinematography, as presented by the Las Vegas Film Critics Society in 2000, although it did get an Oscar nomination for Best Adapted Screenplay.

DIALOGUE TO SKIP BACK FOR:
Everett: 'What'd the devil give you for your soul, Tommy?'
Tommy: 'Well, he taught me to play this here gee-tar *real* good.'
Delmar: 'Oh, son. For *that* you traded yer everlastin' soul?'
Tommy: 'Well I wasn't usin' it . . .'

Big Dan: 'I generally refrain from speech during gestation. Well, those who attempt both at the same time . . . I find it coarse an' vulgar. Where were we?'
Delmar: 'Makin' money in the Lord's service.'

Everett: 'Why are you tellin' my gals I was hit by a train?'
Penny: 'Lots of respectable people been hit by trains. Judge Harvey over in Cookville was hit by a train.'

ANALYSIS: There really wasn't any need for the Coens to apply the credit 'Based Upon "The Odyssey" by Homer' to *O Brother, Where Art Thou?* As the Coens themselves have noted, the film is a loose interpretation, based around the concept of *The Odyssey* plus its iconic moments and characters, rather than the story itself. It's *The Odyssey* presented as enduring myth, a story that is buried deep in our culture and emerges in all kinds of new forms.

Like *The Odyssey*, *O Brother* features a character called Ulysses (among the grand Biblical names so common in the Deep South, names drawn from Greek literature don't seem too out of place), trying to reach his wife, Penelope. Big Dan, of course, represents a Cyclops whose eye is nearly put out by a spear and who has a burning cross dropped on his head (Homer's Cyclops was blinded by a flaming spear). The Baptists who lure the cons into the water parallel the Lotus-Eaters. The sequence in which

Pete becomes separated from Everett and Delmar not only features sirens, but also invokes Circe (who turned men into beasts). When Everett makes it home, he wears a false grey beard (Homer's Ulysses was disguised as an old man), he must fight off Penny's suitors, and then Penny gives him a test: just as Ulysses was tested with his bed, Everett must locate Penny's wedding ring.

In addition to the two rival candidates (Menelaus and Homer), there's also an Oracle in the form of the old guy who works the handcart. He is also a kind of representative of Homer himself: he's blind, as Homer is said to have been, and he reflects the oral tradition of these epic poems by outlining the plot to the three convicts before it even begins. He's an American version of the archetype, however, and as such he resembles wise drifters such as Moses in *The Hudsucker Proxy* and the cowboy in *The Big Lebowski*, two other characters who possess a wider perspective on events than seems possible.

There is a degree of reflection between Homer's culture and that seen in *O Brother*. While the Greeks passed oral narratives from one generation to the next, in 1930s Mississippi the concept of recording music had only recently become commonplace and live music was still the more common form of entertainment. The songs that people still sing to each other have been passed down though the generations and, notably, most of the soundtrack comes not from original recordings but new versions. The songs have been remade and reinterpreted down the years just as Homer's story has.

While there are ways in which *O Brother* provides a contrast to the Coens' previous film, the dynamic between the three central characters is not unlike that in *The Big Lebowski*. They resemble a nuclear family, with Everett as the father who won't be argued with and assumes he is in charge, Pete as the mother who, denied an active role, resists by tending towards martyrdom and Delmar as the child, filled with wonder, forever asking questions and deferring to the authority of his colleagues. Furthermore, the central character, Ulysses Everett McGill, is another variation on the loveable loser, although he struggles to remain the right side of loveable considering his selfishness. His lie to Pete and Delmar about the treasure, though born out of desperation and love for his neglected wife, is ill considered and Pete's cry of 'You ruined my life!' is not unjustified. Most of their problems are directly Everett's fault: the authorities manage to track them by the scent of his pomade (which he refuses to change for Fop when Dapper Dan proves unavailable). He also bears links with other Coen characters: from his mode of speech he could easily be an ancestor of *Raising Arizona*'s Hi. Seeing the way that he bamboozles the less well educated (Pete and Delmar, chiefly) with such convoluted, grandiose speech, it's no surprise that he turns out to be a crooked lawyer rather than an armed robber.

Another thing that Everett has in common with Hi is that, while he may be incompetent and a crook, he *is* funny and the audience is willing to cut him some slack for that reason, even if they're laughing at him rather than with him. The Coens have often defended their use of unlikeable characters in central roles: 'It's absurd to think the only stories you can tell or the only stories worth telling involve likeable characters,' Joel says. 'It's as artificial a constraint as one can imagine.' True, but whether a character is likeable or not will affect the audience's satisfaction with the ending. If they are negative characters and they all get their just deserts (as in *Fargo*), that's fine. However, if you want to give your characters a happy ending then they need to be at least partly likeable or the audience won't feel any involvement in the denouement and so, to a degree, a lowlife like Everett needs to be likeable. Clooney is accustomed to loveable rogue parts and yet this one does represent a departure for him: usually he plays guys who are disreputable but cool, and Everett is clearly *not* cool. Effectively, George Clooney here plays a guy who *thinks* he's George Clooney.

GENRE: While the Coens' intent to make the more downbeat *The Man Who Wasn't There* as their follow-up to the comic *The Big Lebowski* was scuppered by practicalities, there is still a sense in which *O Brother, Where Art Thou?* is a substantial contrast to the movie that preceded it. While *The Big Lebowski* is tautly plotted and rather convoluted, *O Brother* is loosely constructed. It identifies that the road movie is the twentieth-century American equivalent of *The Odyssey*, and whereas the road movie and the detective story are both episodic narratives, *Lebowski*'s are all linked by the story, whereas *O Brother*'s are largely random occurrences on a journey.

In road movies the journey is what gives the narrative its structure. It doesn't matter what the characters encounter along the way, as long as the incidents are interesting and make the journey either more challenging or teach them something. In the case of *O Brother* it's mostly the latter, on the principle that the tougher a ride the characters have, the more rewarding it is when they get to where they're going and/or find what they are looking for. This is what gives the Coens the freedom to pick and choose so freely from *The Odyssey*: the events do not have to occur in any particular order. Whatever order you put the trials in, they will add up to the same thing. The fact that Everett is lying about the treasure is symbolic of the road movie as a genre, because when Delmar and Pete get to where they're going they don't find what they (and the audience) expect. Everett gets what he sets out for, but he does not win Penny merely by finding her again. She initially rejects him, but when she sees what the journey has done to her former husband – he has made a hit record, saved an innocent man from death and found favour with the Governor – she agrees to take him back.

The Coens also play with expectations at the end: as identified by Rob Content in *Film Quarterly*, the film has 'a full three happy endings, complete with a big musical number, a pardon from the Governor, a wedding, and even a miracle'. Having used the conventions of the musical throughout the film without ever making it into one – music is so big a part of these characters' lives that there is no need to contrive the presence of music in the narrative – other generic conventions come into play. Redemption, in the form of a pardon and a miracle here, is the standard ending for a confessional narrative, while the traditional way to conclude a comedy is to do so with a wedding. Such generic conclusions are often adopted by writers to provide a satisfying denouement while drawing attention to its fictionality, and that is what Content suggests is happening at the end of O

Brother (rather like in Shakespeare's *Measure for Measure*, in which a contrived final act highlights the fact that the play's situation is, in fact, irreconcilable). This points towards the fantastic quality of *O Brother*'s 1930s (see **EVER AMERICA**).

EVER AMERICA: As with *The Hudsucker Proxy*'s depiction of 1950s New York, the vision of 1930s Mississippi seen in *O Brother* is an idea of what it was like, based on old novels, movies, paintings and the like, rather than any serious attempt to recreate the period. However, while *Hudsucker* consciously drew from a range of periods and sources, creating a composite of the most memorable elements, *O Brother* presents a fantasy of what Mississippi in the 1930s might have been like. Joel and Ethan's unfamiliarity with the area is demonstrated by their notion that it would have a yellowish aspect, when in fact it is very green (it's worth, if possible, checking out photos from the *O Brother* set to see just how much Deakins manipulated the colour in the post-production process).

Their awareness of both place and period is purely based on what they have picked up from old movies, novels and suchlike: this is also true of *Miller's Crossing* and *Hudsucker*, but while those films were direct pastiches of other works and genres, adopting the perspectives of Hammett, Sturges and Capra, *O Brother* is an overall impression gleaned from myriad sources. This also accounts for the appearance of real and quasi-real figures like George 'Babyface' Nelson (who had, in fact, been dead for three years in 1937), 'Pappy' O'Daniel (historically real, O'Daniel made use of country music in his campaigns, although he ran for governor in Texas, not Mississippi) and Tommy Johnson (who derives from Robert Johnson, the blues player reputed to have gained his prowess on the guitar from a pact with the Devil).

This is not a time or place that ever existed. As noted, the Coens draw on the race politics of the era but they do not comment on it, merely using it as a story point: Homer Stokes is finally defeated by the power of music, which causes people to overcome whatever prejudices they may have and come together. (There may be an element of satire in this, in the way that one can read satire around the edges of Frank Capra. For example, the ease with which the voters are swayed from one political candidate to another does not place the electorate in a good light, just as Capra seems to fear what might happen to American politics should no equivalent to his Jefferson Smith, from 1939's *Mr Smith Goes to Washington*, emerge.) Life is by no means as tough for America's black population in this film as it undoubtedly was in reality, although as Rob Content notes, the three cons do seem to possess a certain affinity with the black population. They have escaped from Parchman Farm, a real prison camp that was almost exclusively populated by black prisoners, and they are mistaken for blacks more than once: they also address the old seer on the handcart as 'grandpa' and he refers to them as 'my sons'. The point of this, Content says, is 'that the natural solidarity of brotherhood arises out of shared suffering' – and, in this context, the title does make some sense. Any real suffering in *O Brother* is far from explicit but the connection between its disenfranchised characters is certainly interesting.

Ultimately, however, this is a fantasy and it knows it's a fantasy, which prevents it from becoming a nostalgia-fest for a time the Coens never knew. It's a sepia-tinted daydream of the 1930s that is perhaps edged with a slight sadness at the knowledge that the world was never really like this and it never will be. Nevertheless, *O Brother* is one of the Coens' more escapist efforts, resembling the kind of movie that somebody might have made during the Depression in order to take people's minds off it – which is exactly what John Sullivan set out to do at the end of *Sullivan's Travels*. In that sense, perhaps this *is* the *O Brother, Where Art Thou?* that Sullivan would have made.

AVAILABILITY: The available versions of *O Brother, Where Art Thou?* are particularly frustrating. A Region 1 DVD is available with some 'making of' footage and interviews, the music video for 'I Am a Man of Constant Sorrow', deleted scenes and the facility to flick between the movie and the original storyboards. The original Region 2 release was poor by comparison, with just the interviews plus a trailer and TV spots (not included on the Region 1). However, the Region 2 was then reissued on two discs with all the features from both the Region 1 version and the old Region 2 edition, including a featurette on *Down from the Mountain* but (and this is the frustrating bit) omitting the deleted scenes.

THE COENS' VIEW: 'As we were making this we sort of decided that we were probably making the *Lawrence of Arabia* [David Lean, 1962] of hayseed movies.' (Joel in 2000)

VERDICT: 'We was beat up by a bible salesman, and banished from Woolworths . . . I don't know, Everett, was it the one branch or all of 'em?' Hmm. This has become a cliché in reviews of Coen brothers films down the years, and is only stated here with great caution: while *O Brother, Where Art Thou?* is visually astonishing, it is slightly lacking in substance. This criticism is usually used to lambast the Coens for not investing enough in their characters or providing a coherent message to their films, but here it is applied to *O Brother* because the film's meandering plot is unsatisfying. It ambles along amiably enough but there isn't enough of a story for the viewer to get their teeth into. This is all the more striking by comparison with the films either side of it, *The Big Lebowski* and *The Man Who Wasn't There*, both of which have ingenious plots at their cores.

Nevertheless, it is still very good, with a typically witty script, and it certainly scores over previous Coen films in terms of its visual and aural spectacle. For a change it isn't the camera work that makes each shot fascinating, but the breathtaking landscapes, beautifully framed and colour-tinted. The lengthy process that went into creating the film's unique look was more than worthwhile: it achieves what the Coens set out to do way back in *Raising Arizona*, when they spoke of creating a film that looked like a storybook. The tailoring of the music to every scene was no less meticulous and the results are equally impressive. As suggested by its stellar sales, the soundtrack album is full of neglected gems and the revival of this brand of country music is one of the Coens' widest-ranging achievements. There's also a watershed performance from Clooney: his ongoing desire to challenge himself cannot be commended too highly and in him the Coens seem to have found a bona fide star who fits their style.

It's a good thing that the Coens made *O Brother, Where Art Thou?* because it's probably their most accessible film to date, as borne out by its strong box-office performance. It's light, it looks and sounds great and, by their standards, it's positively feel-good. In that sense it's the film that they wanted *The Hudsucker Proxy* to be and it makes for a good introduction to the Coens for the uninitiated. But it isn't one of their best.

The Man Who Wasn't There (2001)

(Black and White – 116 mins)

USA Films Presents
A Working Title Production
Directed by Joel Coen
Written by Joel Coen & Ethan Coen
Produced by Ethan Coen
Executive Producers: Tim Bevan and Eric Fellner
Co-producer: John Cameron
Director of Photography: Roger Deakins ASC, BSC
Production Designer: Dennis Gassner
Costume Designer: Mary Zophres
Original Score: Carter Burwell
Film Editors: Roderick Jaynes and Tricia Cooke
Supervising Sound Editor: Skip Lievsay
Casting by Ellen Chenoweth
Unit Production Manager: John Cameron
First Assistant Director: Betsy Magruder
Second Assistant Director: Jonathan McGarry
Associate Film Editor: David Diliberto
Associate Producer: Robert Graf
Visual Effects Supervisor: Janek Sirrs

CAST: Billy Bob Thornton (*Ed Crane*), Frances McDormand (*Doris Crane*), Michael Badalucco (*Frank Raffo*), James

Gandolfini (*David Allen 'Big Dave' Brewster*), Katherine Borowitz (*Ann Nirdlinger*), Jon Polito (*Creighton Tolliver*), Scarlett Johansson (*Rachael 'Birdy' Abundas*), Richard Jenkins (*Walter Abundas*), Tony Shalhoub (*Freddy Riedenschneider*), Christopher Kriesa (*Persky*), Brian Haley (*Krebs*), Jack McGee (*Burns*), Gregg Binkley (*The New Man*), Alan Fudge (*Diedrickson*), Lilyan Chauvin (*Medium*), Adam Alexi-Malle (*Jacques Carcanogues*), Ted Rooney (*Bingo Caller*), Abraham Benrubi (*Young Man*), Christian Ferratti (*Child*), Rhoda Gemignani (*Costanza*), EJ Callahan (*Customer*), Brooke Smith (*Sobbing Prisoner*), Ron Ross (*Banker*), Hallie Singleton (*Waitress*), Jon Donnelly (*Gatto Eater*), Dan Martin (*Bailiff*), Nicholas Lanier (*Tony*), Tom Dahlgren (*Judge #1*), Booth Colman (*Judge #2*), Stanley DeSantis (*New Man's Customer*), Peter Siragusa (*Bartender*), Christopher McDonald (*Macadam Salesman*), John Michael Higgins (*Doctor*), Rick Scarry (*District Attorney*), George Ives (*Lloyd Garroway*), Devon Cole Borisoff (*Swimming Boy*), Mary Bogue (*Prisoner Visitor*), Don Donati (*Pie Contest Timer*), Arthur Reeves (*Flophouse Clerk*)

TAGLINE: 'The last thing on his mind is murder.'

SUMMARY: Santa Rosa, 1949. A barber named Ed Crane suspects his wife Doris of committing infidelity with her boss, Big Dave. A customer named Creighton Tolliver tells Ed about a business venture – a store trading in a new concept called dry-cleaning – for which he needs a silent partner to invest $10,000. Ed agrees to put up the money, then writes Dave an anonymous letter threatening to reveal his affair with Doris and demanding $10,000. Dave believes that the blackmailer is Tolliver, but he pays up, embezzling the money from the business. Ed hands the cash over to Tolliver. A few days later, Doris is drunk and Ed puts her to bed, then Dave calls Ed to his office. Dave has discovered that Ed put up the cash for Tolliver's venture and has realised that Ed is the blackmailer. He attacks Ed, who stabs out with Dave's cigar-cutter and kills him. Ed flees the scene.

To Ed's surprise Doris is arrested for Dave's murder. He hires an expensive lawyer named Freddy Riedenschneider, who struggles to come up with a defence for Doris. Ed tells them the truth, but Riedenschneider rejects his version of events as unconvincing. Tolliver appears to have skipped town. The day before the trial commences, Doris hangs herself. Ed discovers that Doris was pregnant with Dave's baby. He determines to help young Birdy Abundas become a successful pianist and takes her to see piano teacher Jacques Carcanogues, who is unimpressed. Nevertheless, Birdy appreciates what Ed is doing and suggests they have sex on the drive home, distracting him from the road and causing him to crash.

When Ed regains consciousness he is arrested for the murder of Tolliver, who has been found at the bottom of a lake, beaten to death by Dave. In Tolliver's briefcase are the partnership papers that confirm Ed's payment. The District Attorney believes that Ed got Doris to steal the money, but Tolliver realised it was dirty cash and Ed killed him to cover up. Ed can't use the true story of what happened because it fingers him for Dave's murder. The judge sentences him to the chair for the murder of Tolliver. Ed's narration turns out to be an article he's been writing for a men's magazine. Ed goes to his death with hope for the next life.

DEVELOPMENT: 'We started thinking about the movie actually because we had this piece of set dressing from *The Hudsucker Proxy*,' Ethan says, referring to the scene in which Norville visits a barbershop. 'There was a poster on the wall with all the different 1940s haircuts.' The Coens took this poster away when the set came down and put it up in their office, and looking at it every day started them thinking about writing a story with a barber as the central character. 'The barber thing is really just a backdrop,' deadpans Ethan. 'The story didn't catch fire until we added the dry-cleaning to the mix. Then we knew we had something that we could pitch to all the studios.'

Joel and Ethan started work on the screenplay for *The Man Who Wasn't There* during the mid-1990s, then put it to one side while shooting *The Big Lebowski*. After *Lebowski* they picked it up again with the intention of shooting it next. Frances McDormand was appearing in *A Streetcar Named Desire* at the Gate Theatre, Dublin, and Joel, being between projects, decided to join her in Ireland. Ethan also travelled over so that they could work on the script together and they finished it off during their stay.

Having taken James M Cain as the starting point for *Blood Simple*, the Coens returned to their favourite crime writer for the tone, themes and structure of *The Man Who Wasn't There*. 'This movie is heavily influenced by Cain's work,' says Joel. 'It's kind of his story.' Ed's existence as a barber originated from Cain's use of characters with banal lives. 'Cain was interested in people's workaday lives and what they did for a living,' Ethan continues. 'He wrote about guys who worked as insurance salesmen, or in banks, or building bridges. We took that as a cue.' Having selected a protagonist with a very ordinary job, the Coens found that the Cain style was well suited to this particular story. (See **GENRE** for more.)

'Even though there is a crime in the story,' Ethan says, 'we were still very interested in what this guy, who's a barber, does as a barber.' Ed's day-to-day life became the background for the plot's driving force, the blackmail and murder of Big Dave, as an alternative to setting the crime story in an underworld setting and having the crime committed by career criminals. Nevertheless, the banal life of Ed Crane was to be completely destroyed by his single venture beneath the level of the law. '*The Man Who Wasn't There* is about ordinary middle-American people who get into a situation that spirals out of control. The crime element here is sort of inadvertent. The hero sort of stumbles into it.'

The title arrived very late in the day and until shortly before its exhibition at Cannes the film was simply referred to as *The Barber Project*. A number of alternative titles are listed in the introduction to the screenplay (although since this was written by 'Roderick Jaynes' some or all of the titles may be false): *Pansies Don't Float*; *I, The Barber*; *The Nirdlinger Doings*; *Missing, Presumed Ed*; *I Love You, Birdy Abundas!* (rejected for being 'too '60s'); *The Barber, Crane*; *The Other Side of Fate* (rejected 'because of their uncertainty as to whether Fate had more than the one side'); *None Know My Name*; *I Will Cut Hair No More Forever* and *Ed Crane, You So Crazy!* In the end they settled on *The Man Who Wasn't There* since it represented Ed's perceived innocence of Big Dave's murder and his actual innocence of Tolliver's, as well as being a comment on Ed's silent, unobtrusive existence. The Coens used this even though it had already been the title of a Steve Guttenberg comedy from 1983, directed by Bruce Malmuth.

REFERENCES: There are two nods to the murder victim from James M Cain's novel *Double Indemnity*, filmed by Billy Wilder in 1944. In the book, the victim is called Nirdlinger, which provides the name for the family department store at which Big Dave and Doris both work. In Wilder's film he's called Dietrichson, a name which is appended to the county medical examiner in *The Man Who Wasn't There* (see **GENRE**).

The name of Tolliver's hotel, the Nobart Arms, is an anagram of the Barton Arms in *Miller's Crossing*.

CASTING: 'With this one, we wrote the part for Fran, and we wrote the part that Michael Badalucco plays, but that was about it,' says Joel. 'We didn't know who was going to play the lead character.'

The Coens knew how important the central performance of *The Man Who Wasn't There* was to the success or failure of the film, and Billy Bob Thornton was not an actor who they originally had in mind. However, they did know him socially and he had recently worked with Sam Raimi, performing in the *Fargo*-aping *A Simple Plan* (1998) and providing the screenplay for *The Gift* (2000). 'I don't know why [Thornton] occurred to us, because he's not our image of the character. [But] on the other hand, Billy Bob's such a transformative actor.' The Coens got in touch with Thornton to discuss the picture and, as tends to be the case with actors, he jumped at the chance to work with them. 'I was on the phone with Joel,' Thornton says, 'and I said, "What's the movie about?" and he said, "It's about a barber who wants to be in the dry-cleaning business." And I said, "I'll take it".' The actor had few concerns about playing such a subdued role. 'To play a character like this is easy for me . . . It's easy to just sit there and watch and look around me as the rest of the world goes by and these people talk.'

These were the qualities that led Joel and Ethan to adjust their ideas of who Ed should be and fit Thornton into the role. 'He certainly has the confidence to do this kind of character,' Joel says, noting that most actors would have problems giving a performance that involved doing so little on-screen. 'Ed says very little, he's very still, and that would drive most actors crazy. They'd be very insecure about it, thinking they weren't doing enough; we had a feeling that Billy Bob would understand.' Ethan cites Montgomery Clift as a comparison, describing both actors as 'soulful': 'If this movie was being made in 1949, when it's set, Clift would have been the man to do it. He had the same quality that Billy Bob has.'

The film also provided Frances McDormand with her third major role in a Coen movie. 'I know that when Joel and Ethan write a script, they often have certain actors in mind because they want to offer these actors a challenge – and I must say that this role is a challenge for me.' Other actors whom the Coens had previously used made appearances in *The Man Who Wasn't There*: Michael Badalucco (from *Miller's Crossing* and *O Brother, Where Art Thou?*), described by Ethan as 'an actor who fills the frame with excitement', took the role of Frank Raffo, Tony Shalhoub (from *Barton Fink*) was cast as Freddy Riedenschneider and Jon Polito (of *Miller's Crossing*, *Barton Fink*, *The Hudsucker Proxy* and *The Big Lebowski*) took the part of Creighton Tolliver. One of the smaller roles, that of Anne Nirdlinger, went to John Turturro's wife, Katherine Borowitz.

Unusually, the Coens encountered a little resistance when they offered the part of Big Dave to James Gandolfini, an actor who had received increasing critical acclaim for his television work in the lead role of HBO's gangster series *The Sopranos*. 'He'd been working a lot and was just wrapping another movie [*The Mexican* (Gore Verbinski, 2001)] and about to return to his television series,' says Joel. 'We sort of had to twist his arm, but he finally agreed to join up.' Gandolfini's initial reticence was because he had wanted to take a break before launching back into *The Sopranos*. However, he was highly conscious of being typecast as a result of the series' success and ultimately accepted *The Man Who Wasn't There* because it was so different to the other work he'd done.

PRODUCTION: While the Coens had planned to put *The Man Who Wasn't There* into production during 1999, this plan was disrupted by George Clooney's sudden availability for *O Brother, Where Art Thou?* Not wishing to lose momentum on *The Man Who Wasn't There*, they moved directly to their 'Barber Project' as soon as they finished their final edit of *O Brother*. Production began on 26 June 2000 with a budget of almost $20 million, backed once more by Working Title's Tim Bevan and Eric Fellner.

In the run-up to production, the major decision made by the Coens was that *The Man Who Wasn't There* would be their first movie to be shot in black and white. 'For a lot of intangible reasons that aren't easy to explain, it seemed as if black and white was appropriate,' says Joel. '[It] is evocative in ways for a story like this that colour photography isn't.' Joel also expresses his regret that there is a degree of stigma attached to making black and white movies, since colour has become the default option and black and white is only considered in particular circumstances. 'Black and white is a whole different kind of photography that nobody uses any more and when you do, there's a chance you can get stigmatised,' Joel adds. 'It's seen as "arty", and it becomes an issue.' The Coens discovered a different way of looking at the things they were about to put on film, thinking in terms of what light they would get from an image when the colour element was removed. They resorted to using black and white Polaroid cameras on set, taking pictures of sets, costumes, actors and lighting set-ups.

Roger Deakins, on board as cinematographer once again, was delighted to get the opportunity. 'I love the process. I'd shot black and white footage in film school, and even recently photographed material in black and white for *The Hurricane* [Norman Jewison, 1999] that was used on a TV screen.' Deakins also notes that colour can be 'a distraction' and make images 'too pretty', whereas black and white permits more manipulation of the image because lighting contrasts are more marked. Accordingly, in the black and white era of Hollywood, cinematographers tended to use direct light and shoot for contrast, but Deakins decided to tend towards the European method of softer light, used by the likes of Jean-Luc Godard. 'We aimed for less contrast and used few but larger light sources. What we mainly did is separate things tonally and use little diffusion so we didn't create a lot of those hard shadows.' Deakins considers that the objects in the frame look fuller as a result.

Deakins shied away from making the film look too much like the films of the past merely because it was monochrome, but he did hark back to Alan Ladd's movies of the 1940s, particularly *This Gun For Hire* (1942) and *The Blue Dahlia* (1946), and he also cites noirs such as *Touch of Evil* (Orson Welles, 1958) and *Kiss Me Deadly* (Robert Aldrich, 1955). He particularly rates *Hud* (Martin Ritt, 1963) for its black and white lighting. 'In many ways it's easier to create an image in colour that the audience finds interesting, but it might not necessarily be the point of what the story's about or the shot's about,' he says. 'Black and white is about light and composition.'

However, the movie wound up being shot on colour film stock and printed in black and white. 'The decision to shoot on colour stock was a bit convoluted,' notes Deakins. The problem was that, with black and white having fallen out of mainstream use, it was a long time since anybody had developed new types of black and white film. The Coens and Deakins performed some tests, and Deakins could see the benefits of both, but the decision was made for them when they discovered that they were contractually obliged to provide a colour version of the movie for overseas video release. 'It's a compromise we had to make,' says Joel. Hence, Deakins used colour 5277 low-contrast stock and Beverley Wood at Deluxe Labs worked out a way of getting a good print from this on black and white 5269 title stock. These were sent back to the set to serve as dailies, but Wood worked for months in post-production to make the best possible release print. The crew also had to keep the colour version in mind at all times, ensuring that it would look acceptable. 'I made sure that we were balanced in terms of colour temperature, and Dennis [Gassner] designed everything in the tones we wanted without resorting to bright colours that would distract viewers in the colour version. We worked mainly in browns and greys – tones that represented the time period and would reproduce equally well in either version.' Despite the compromise, Deakins actually rates the look of the colour printed onto black and white title stock as being slightly better than the look of regular black and white film.

While it has often been said of *The Man Who Wasn't There* that its black and white photography gives it the look of classic Hollywood cinema, Ethan notes that their sources were more esoteric. 'For some reason it's an object of interest among critics, what our influences are, and you tell 'em important stuff 'cause that's what they wanna hear, but it's really like high school hygiene movies.' Joel adds that they were also looking at 'science fiction films from the 50s, all the postwar paranoia things. You get the pulpier, cheesier elements of American postwar culture, as reflected in men's magazines, and health movies you'd see in school.' Civil defence films, Driver's Ed films and other public information cinema were also influential. Designer Dennis Gassner reflected the UFO theme, introduced in Ann Nirdlinger's surreal revelation to Ed, in his own work. 'It even manifests itself into some of the sets as an element in lighting fixtures, doorknobs, decorative ornaments, and so on. But it still exists on a subliminal level.'

The first scenes to be shot were on location at the Lincoln Heights Jail in Los Angeles. The scene in which Riedenschneider talks about the Uncertainty Principle is rated by Deakins as 'the hardest scene to get right – although it was also the easiest scene because it had just one light source.' They cut a piece of card to serve as a window and lit Doris's prison cell with a single light. 'We had something really graphic, you know, a shaft of sunlight kind of bleaching out. I thought that worked pretty well – we wanted it to look sort of B-movie-ish, in a way.' This heightened the surreal quality of Riedenschneider's musings.

While the film is almost all set in Santa Rosa, North California, much material was shot around Los Angeles. Musso and Frank's, a Hollywood steakhouse, stood in for the restaurant where Ed meets Riedenschneider for the first time; the bingo hall material was shot in a Presbyterian church on Wilshire Boulevard; the hotel lobby was in fact the entrance hall of an apartment complex in downtown LA; and Ed's visits to the bank were shot at an abandoned branch of the Bank of America, also in downtown LA. However, the town of Orange in California's Orange County was selected by Joel and Ethan to double for most of the exteriors of Santa Rosa. The exteriors were all shot in one day, although it took more than two weeks to modify the streets of Orange to give the appearance of 1949, an effort which included replacing and altering street signs, remodelling store fronts and even repainting street markings. Other than this, the main sequence to be shot outside LA was the wedding reception, which was filmed over two days in Thousand Oaks, also in California.

Much of the film was shot on location, although in some cases the locations needed to be substantially dressed. Nirdlinger's Department Store, for example, was represented by an abandoned furniture shop in Glendale. 'We had to retrofit it in a way, keeping what was already there in the architecture and making it work for a 1949 *moderne* style,' says Gassner. He used many of the existing wall fittings and took advantage of various fixtures that reflected art deco design. 'Once we dressed the space with period display cases and merchandise from the era, it all came to life.' When shooting the scene in which Ed meets Birdy for the first time, upstairs at the store, Deakins 'arranged the pianos with their covers open and silhouetted them against the back wall, which I kept as much light off as possible. Then we set one incredibly bright practical on the piano next to Birdy, whilst keeping everything else in the room dark. The practical is really bright, but it works because it draws your attention straight to her.'

The exterior of the Cranes' home was shot in Pasadena. In order to exemplify the mid-twentieth-century setting, an area known as 'Bungalow Heaven', filled with Craftsman bungalows, was selected. 'The Craftsman bungalow was pretty much standard in the middle-class California community of the period,' says Gassner, noting that a bungalow with a lower than average roof was used in order to suggest that Ed and Doris were not among the wealthiest of Santa Rosa's citizens. 'The sense that the space inside the house was a little pinched served to underline the characters' emotional state as well – that was another reason we chose it.' Also shot in Pasadena were the scenes in Jacques Carcanogues's studio, which was a dressed top-floor apartment in the Castle Green complex.

The barbershop was constructed by Gassner as a complete building, interior and exterior, on the Paramount backlot. Prior to shooting on this set the Coens needed to so some soundstage work at Universal Studios (including the underwater scenes), and both Thornton and Badalucco took the opportunity to train with real barbers (the shop at which Thornton trained was the delightfully named Dirty Dan's Clip Joint). Ethan notes that all the cast and crew were entertained by watching Badalucco and Thornton's attempts to cut hair for the camera, although it wasn't as much fun for the extras in the barbershop chairs. 'The sad thing is that Billy Bob actually thinks he's good at it,' Ethan says, likening Thornton to 'one of those guys who trains to be a boxer for a boxing movie and then thinks he can beat people up.' With these scenes completed, and numerous extras given 'gruesome' haircuts, production wrapped on 1 September 2000, a day ahead of schedule.

The production process had repercussions for its star. 'I was still smoking at the time we shot the film so it was fine to me,' says Thornton, 'but it should have been called *The Man Who Smoked Too Much*.' During the takes he smoked non-filter Chesterfield cigarettes that were appropriate to the period, and on top of that he smoked his regular Marlboros during the breaks. 'After the movie I quit. I was so sick of smoking. It was the thing that drove me to quit, thank God.'

DELETED SCENES: The flying saucer from Ed's dream towards the end of the movie was originally set to make another appearance earlier in the film, but the scene in question was cut from the script prior to shooting. After Ed's return home from killing Big Dave (as seen in the finished film) he gets into bed next to Doris and goes to sleep. Upon waking, Ed hears what Ethan describes as a 'theramin classic fifties flying saucer effect' and goes outside to see a spaceship descend. The hatch opens and numerous tiny ant-people swarm out and over Ed's veranda and front lawn. He goes inside, finds a towel, wedges it under the bedroom door and calmly goes back to sleep. 'It's one of those scenes that's so fantastic that you wish you'd put it in,' says Thornton, 'but you know it doesn't fit the movie.'

The deleted scenes included on the DVD are mostly very brief. Three of them are shots of haircuts – the 'Timberline', the 'Duck Butt' and the 'Alpine Ropetoss' – that ended up not being used in the sequence where Ed demonstrates the various cuts he is required to do. There's also an unused shot of a salad. The most substantial shows Riedenschneider's opening defence of Ed in its entirety, which was not cut in the finished movie but its dialogue was obscured by Ed's voice-over.

MUSIC: One of the main things that ensures that *The Man Who Wasn't There* doesn't slip into mere 1940s pastiche is the score. Carter Burwell likes to examine other options rather than merely using the standard full orchestra, and in this case he reflects James M Cain's enthusiasm for classical music with a selection of piano-based pieces drawn from Beethoven and Mozart. The score is centred around Beethoven's Piano Sonata No. 8 (*Pathétique*), although his No. 14 (*Moonlight*), No. 23 (*Appassionata*) and No. 25 are also incorporated by Burwell and used as springboards for his own contributions, much as he did with the score for *The Hudsucker Proxy*. The closing theme is also Beethoven: a section of the Piano Trio No. 8 (*Archduke*). Of Mozart's work, *Che Soave Zeffiretto* makes an appearance. Burwell's own compositions are in the same style as the classical pieces (with the exception of one diagetic piece, the big band tune heard during the party at Nirdlinger's). Because these pieces soundtrack Ed's constant monologue, it makes sense that Birdy's performances of Beethoven strike such a chord with him.

CRITICAL RECEPTION: Your average movie critic is not one to be put off by a film being presented in monochrome, and this aspect of *The Man Who Wasn't There* passed with little or no negative comment. However, many reviewers were dubious about the rather stately pace of the film. 'The first time I saw it at Cannes,' noted Roger Ebert in the *Chicago Sun-Times* of 2 November 2001, 'I emerged into the sunlight to find Michel Ciment, the influential French critic, who observed sadly, "A 90-minute film that plays for two hours".' Ebert feared that Ciment might be correct, but he was willing to give the film a second chance. After further consideration, he described the film as 'so assured and perceptive in its style, so loving, so intensely right, that if you can receive on that frequency, the film is like a voluptuous feast.' And of the pacing? 'Yes, it might easily have been shorter. But then it would not have been this film, or necessarily a better one.'

Variety was not overly impressed by the film but acknowledged that it had many good qualities. 'Beautifully made picture is one of the brothers' second-tier efforts artistically and commercially,' wrote Todd McCarthy in the 13 May 2001 edition. He noted that the film 'has all the ingredients at hand for an enticing film noir' but 'the way the Coens have decided to tell their story . . . uncommonly mutes the action and saps it of its potential heat and tension; the viewer is largely told about what happens rather than being shown.' This, McCarthy felt, meant that there were nowhere near enough scenes of dramatic conflict and prevented the Coens from playing to their strengths: 'snappy, wildly imaginative regional and period dialogue'.

The *Village Voice* reacted more positively. 'A tediously sub-Lynchian UFO subplot notwithstanding, the Coens have not lost their cleverness,' wrote J Hoberman in the 6 November 2001 issue. 'This fastidiously hyperreal neo-noir suggests a sadder but wiser remake of the Coens' rambunctious debut *Blood Simple*.' Again, however, the pace was a sore point for many critics.

'There's a fine distinction between cool and comatose and, punishingly slow, *The Man Who Wasn't There* repeatedly drifts over the line. Were the Coens asleep at the wheel or presciently mourning the death of irony?'

The British reviews were slightly better, although Kim Newman did advise a degree of caution. 'Slowly paced for a thriller and with a hero many will find off-putting,' he noted in *Empire*'s November 2001 issue, 'this is nevertheless a gripping, unusual and challenging work from the most consistently brilliant filmmakers of the last decade.' While he found Thornton's toupee 'somewhat disturbing', Newman seemed pleased to discover 'a chilly film, in stark black and white, as if the brothers want to get back to their core audience'.

In some quarters the reception was highly enthusiastic. 'What a stunning, mesmeric movie this is,' Peter Bradshaw wrote in the *Guardian* on 26 October 2001. '[It] is quite simply the Coen brothers' masterpiece . . . I can only hope that on Oscar night the Academy are not so cauterised with dumbness and cliché that they cannot recognise its originality and playful brilliance.' (See **AWARDS**.) Bradshaw also hailed 'a classic performance from Thornton, displaying the kind of maturity and technical mastery that we hardly dared hope for from this actor,' and noted the film's mix of noir with 'the atmospheric crackle of a tale from *The Twilight Zone*.' Phillip French of the *Observer* concurred – '*The Man Who Wasn't There* is as good a film as I've seen this year' – and *Time Out*'s Geoff Andrew again found much to enjoy. 'A brave, mostly very successful attempt to explore the inner life of an impassive, deeply internalised man who simply doesn't feel the way most of us do,' he wrote in the 24 October 2001 issue. 'Richly imaginative, resonant, rewarding . . . and, of course, admirably weird.'

Jason Caro of *Film Review* was also favourably disposed towards the film, describing it as 'easily [the Coens'] most unique, intriguing and textured movie since *Fargo*.' Like many reviewers, Caro was impressed by the Coens' resurrection of a lost cinematic aesthetic – 'it's not hard to convince yourself that this is a re-discovered noir gem from 1944' – but was aware that the film would not suit all tastes. 'Not as accessible as the Coens' recent successes and sometimes guilty of indulgent over-fleshing, the many pleasures here aren't easy to isolate. Perhaps that's what makes it a Coen brothers' movie.' He awarded the film four stars.

Even so, the criticisms of style over substance and empty formalism continued to follow the Coens. Tim Robey of the *Daily Telegraph* declared the film to be 'perfectly executed' on 26 October 2001, but added that 'it is a perfectly executed illustration of what is not, quite, great about the Coen brothers, which is a kind of grandstanding, and another kind of weirdly alienating insincerity.' He seemed to imply that Joel and Ethan had declined slightly: 'It is typical of the Coens these days that they've borrowed the trappings of Cain's work but then balk at committing themselves to its clammy fatalism, which is really the whole point.' Robey also criticised the shapelessness of the Coens' shaggy-dog stories. 'The fact that some of their movies have tragic endings doesn't mean much, either: they're just shaggy-dog stories in which the dog happens to die.'

Worse was in store. 'Whilst the film is technically accomplished,' wrote Phillip Kerr in the *New Statesman* on 22 October 2001, 'this is film noir without the heroes and heroines, the sociopaths, the crooked cops, the expressionist and avant-garde effects, and the witty, hard-boiled poetry of great screenwriters such as Phillip Yordan, Ben Hecht and Harry Kleine.' Not only was Kerr critical of the Coens, he was hostile to their fans. 'It's axiomatic that Coen-heads – the people who get off on "getting it" – will like *The Man Who Wasn't There*. Coen-heads get off on the mechanics of film-making: the flashy stylistics, the look of the picture . . .' The Coen fan was characterised as valuing style over any kind of substance. 'They are the people who walk out of the cinema talking not about the great dialogue, or a great scene, but the great lighting. I know, because . . . I heard some of them.'

BOX OFFICE: *The Man Who Wasn't There* was released in America on 31 October 2001, less than a year after *O Brother, Where Art Thou?* but unfortunately its performance was nowhere near as good. Autumn is traditionally a good time to release 'worthier' pictures (somewhere between the blockbuster season and the Oscar nominations) but some of its audience may have been drawn to the surprise French hit *Amelie* (Jean-Pierre Jeunet, 2001). The release of kids' favourites *Monsters, Inc.* (Harley Jessup, Bob Pauley, 2001) and *Harry Potter and the Philosopher's Stone* (Chris Columbus, 2001) during November pushed a lot of smaller films out of theatres too. On the other hand it could just be because it's so damned difficult to get people to come and see a black and white movie. *The Man Who Wasn't There* grossed $7,494,849 over a seventeen-week run, which fell a long way short of the $20 million budget.

AWARDS: Joel took yet another Best Director prize at Cannes for *The Man Who Wasn't There*, joking on his acceptance that they decided to shoot the movie in black and white 'to let people know how important this film is'. He had to share it though as the panel decided, not unfairly, that David Lynch was equally deserving for his typically twisted thriller *Mullholland Drive*. Does that count as three Best Director awards or two and a half?

The Oscars yielded far fewer rewards, with just one nomination for Best Cinematography. Although the film didn't win, Roger Deakins did – he also worked on *A Beautiful Mind* (Ron Howard, 2001), which scooped most of the prizes that year, including Cinematography.

DIALOGUE TO SKIP BACK FOR:

Ed: (on Doris) 'It was only a coupla weeks later she suggested we get married. I said "Don't you want to get to know me more?" She said "Why, does it get better?" '

Ed: 'This hair . . . d'you ever wonder about it? How it keeps on coming. It just keeps growing . . . It's part of us, and we cut it off and throw it away.'

ANALYSIS: More so than any other Coens film, *The Man Who Wasn't There* rests on the success of a single performance. Ed

Crane is so out of step with the characters around him, and the film follows him so closely, that it can be easy not to notice anybody else (there are often point-of-view shots and almost-point-of-view shots from Ed, especially when he's in an unusual position, and the use of slow motion shows us the world at his speed). This is in spite of fine performances from McDormand, Polito, Gandolfini and especially Shalhoub and Scarlett Johansson. *The Man Who Wasn't There* is the Coens' second film to be entirely based around a single character, after *Barton Fink*, and shows us a character who is even more closed off from other people than Barton is. Indeed, it could be argued that everything in the movie is an externalisation of Ed, since it is he who tells us the story (Barton never got a narrative voice of his own; clearly it'd be a bad idea to give him any storytelling authority) and his surroundings do sometimes seem to reflect him. (Note that *Life* magazine, which Ed is shown reading at one point, is actually about Ed's life, with stories about alien abduction and dry-cleaning.) In the case of this particular character, however, identifying so closely with him is a risk for the Coens to take because it isn't easy to sympathise with someone who never betrays much emotion and doesn't say much.

Watch this movie on the DVD with the commentary from Joel, Ethan and Billy Bob Thornton on and you realise two things. One is how much affection they, as his creators, all have for him. The other is that, with the dialogue largely obscured by the commentary, your attention focuses on the non-verbal acting and it becomes clear just how hard Thornton is working. Every apparently blank facial expression, every pose, every drag on a cigarette is inherently Ed. 'Sometimes when I would ask what to do in a scene,' says Thornton, 'they'd say, "Be like Ed," and I knew what they meant.' He also says that the Coens agree with Riedenschneider's suggestion that Ed is 'modern man'. Joel notes on the commentary that Ed seems to have developed a life with them all outside of the film, which is unsurprising because he is so thoroughly conceptualised. Yet the audience knows little about him: Ed is more of a state of being than a character. He's just 'modern man', meaning he could be *any* man.

Ed is a blank slate, a nothing trying to become something. He doesn't feel attached to his job, noting that although he worked in a barbershop he didn't think of himself as a barber. He's only there because his brother-in-law owns the shop. (That said, the old habits die hard: even in his last moments in the electric chair, Ed examines the haircuts of the witnesses at the window.) There is nothing in his marriage: they have no children and their relationship has developed little since their first meeting. Ed almost forgets to mention her when describing his home life at the beginning and it is later revealed that they had not had sex in a long time. Even when he suspects that Doris is having an affair his reaction is, 'It's a free country.' The only thing that does move him into action is the chance to invest in dry-cleaning, which catches whatever imagination he may have. But why does he want to be a dry-cleaner? Why does Ed do anything, for that matter?

Ed says very little, not unlike the Coens themselves. Not only do they prefer a kind of intuitive, largely non-verbal communication on-set ('You wouldn't believe how much we *don't* talk with Roger [Deakins],' says Ethan), but journalists often note that the Coens are reticent interviewees and they prefer to talk about the process of writing and making the film rather than addressing wider issues. In the latter case this seems at least partly to be because they like to leave some ambiguity for the viewer and it may be why they work so well with Ed, because he leaves nothing but ambiguity. The viewer never knows what he's thinking. On a first viewing it comes as a complete surprise when he decides to blackmail Big Dave because he hasn't shown any inclination towards blackmail up until that point. It's also hard to believe that he doesn't on some level want to kill Dave, even though the murder is not premeditated. Not only has Dave been sleeping with his wife, he's also been undermining Ed by constantly talking about his military service (despite this Ed bests him in combat, and indeed Dave is revealed to have lied about his army career). It's no use trying to divine precisely what Ed thinks or why he does what he does.

Even at the end, with a death sentence hanging over him, Ed doesn't seem to mind that much. 'Maybe the things I don't understand will become clearer there, like when a fog blows away,' he says, contemplating the next life. And his final words put a rather different spin on our view of Ed, perhaps giving us more of an insight into his thinking than anything he's said thus far: 'Maybe Doris will be there. And maybe there I can tell her all those things they don't have words for here.'

GENRE: As ever, the Coens have not been influenced so much by film noir itself as by the novels that those movies were based on. When combined with the Coens' love of stylising the image, the result is very noirish, although as Joel says, 'there are ways in which it's not film noir. For one thing, the main character couldn't be further from your conventional film noir hero, in terms of his obsessions and personality . . . but, it's got all that modern dread, that feeling of disassociation and paranoia about what's happening in the world around you.'

James M Cain's novels were enthusiastically seized upon by Hollywood when such crime dramas became popular and three of them were made into movies in consecutive years: *Double Indemnity* (Billy Wilder, 1944), *Mildred Pierce* (Michael Curtiz, 1945) and *The Postman Always Rings Twice* (Tay Garnett, 1946). The books tend to focus around working-class characters who are often contrasted with wealthier types, much as the Coens often do. There's often a get-rich-quick scheme involved, centring around murder, blackmail and/or an insurance scam, and there's always a doomed romance. *Blood Simple* features the kind of story that Cain might have written: it inverts his narratives where one man falls for another's wife and together the two adulterers plot to murder the husband, so instead he plots to kill the lovers out of bitter jealousy. However, the story is told in a very different way. Cain tends to use the first person when writing ('If I in the third person faltered and stumbled, my characters in the first person knew perfectly well what they had to say,' he wrote in the preface to *Double Indemnity*, although he did use the third person when writing *Mildred Pierce*). Most importantly, the voice he takes tends to be that of the criminal. The key to the way that *Blood Simple* works is that the audience is shown all points of view, then watches the characters talk and act at cross-purposes. Despite Visser's opening narration he is not our only guide through the story. This isn't how Cain works: he shows us the perpetrator, the character who thinks he holds all the cards and is trying to keep everybody else from seeing them. There's usually a nasty surprise in wait for the narrator, but it's as much a surprise for us as it is for him.

The Man Who Wasn't There models its structure directly on Cain's 1934 debut novel, *The Postman Always Rings Twice*. In this, drifter Frank Chambers gets a job at a roadside service station and falls in love with the proprietor's wife, Cora Papadakis. Together they murder her husband, Nick, and make it look like an accident. The problem is that, unbeknown to either of them, Nick had life insurance to the value of $10,000 and this makes their actions look far more suspicious. The District Attorney tries to turn Frank and Cora against each other in his pursuit of a conviction, but a brilliant lawyer named Katz gets them off the hook and they receive the insurance money. They've got away with it. However, the knowledge of what they both did, plus the fact that they turned on each other during the investigation, sours their relationship. They reconcile after fighting off a further threat of their actions being uncovered, but while out driving Frank accidentally crashes the car, killing Cora. This time the court believes that it was on purpose and Frank is sentenced to hang for Cora's murder.

While the structure is similar, the story itself is very different to *The Man Who Wasn't There*. The Coens' version takes place from the viewpoint of the cuckolded husband rather than the adulterers, and Ed has no intention of killing anybody at first. He just wants the money so that he can make the business deal. What's really distinctive about the plot structure of Cain's novel and the Coens' film is that the plot seems to be over about two-thirds of the way through, with the murder investigation wrapped up and the main character getting away scot-free. What else can happen? In both cases, however, they wind up being collared and condemned for a murder they *didn't* commit. It is also revealed at the end of both narratives that the narrator is writing his account on Death Row: Frank gave his account to a priest as a confession and for possible publication, where Ed sells his story to a men's magazine. Cain often reveals that the narrator is writing an account of events when he is close to death. Ed even echoes Walter Huff's comments in *Double Indemnity* after Huff delivers his novel-length account of the murder he committed to his insurance company: 'It'll be more than he bargained for, but I wanted to put it all down.' Ed's excuse, that 'They're paying me five cents a word, so you'll pardon me if I've sometimes told you more than you wanted to know,' is not convincing. He's going to die, and he has no heirs – what does he need money for? Like Cain's guilty men, Ed needs to spill his guts before he dies.

This isn't the only motif that the Coens draw from *Postman*. A car crash plays an important role in both plots. Just before her death, Cora reveals that she is pregnant with Frank's child. The inquest into Doris's death reveals that she too was pregnant, although in this case Ed knows that the kid wasn't his. There's also the amount of money that Ed tries to get out of Big Dave, $10,000. In *Postman* the life insurance policy pays out to the tune of $10,000, and don't forget that in *Blood Simple* Marty pays Visser $10,000 to take out Abby and Ray. (Note that both Marty and Big Dave have to embezzle the cash from their own businesses, laying crime on top of crime.) Whether it's 1934, 1949 or 1984, $10,000 remains the Cain shorthand for a large sum of money.

The figure of the lawyer in *Postman* is also similar to the lawyer in *The Man Who Wasn't There*. *Postman*'s lawyer, Katz, delights in the seemingly impossible nature of Frank's case and the (admittedly ingenious) way that he wins it: 'Oh, Chambers, you did me a favour all right when you called me in on this. I'll never get another one like it.' Similarly, Riedenschneider doesn't believe that there's a case he can't win and keeps working in the face of overwhelming evidence. Ironically, he is defending somebody who didn't do it and he should be able to create a reasonable doubt if he's such a great lawyer, but the truth is actually more difficult to prove, even when it is laid before him by Ed. That's because, while Katz really is an excellent lawyer, Riedenschneider talks gibberish in a clever way, completely misapplying the Uncertainty Principle: relating to certain types of particle, it says that an observer may affect the things they observe by their very presence, but for it to be relevant the observer has to be there as the event occurs, whereas Riedenschneider applies it to examining events that have already happened. Riedenschneider never stops talking and is therefore the opposite of Ed. And, just as Katz knows he'll never get another case like this again, the fact that Doris kills herself before her case comes to trial is regarded by Riedenschneider as 'The biggest disappointment of his professional career.'

It's here that the Coens pull off their real twist. Because Ed is the originator of the plot, he doesn't have a co-conspirator. The main point of *Postman* is that murder is too big a secret for two people to keep between each other. No matter how implicitly they trusted each other before, the scale of their deed means that each one finds they can't rely on the other not to betray them. (This theme, of course, emerges in an altered form in *Blood Simple*, and while the idea that murder changes a person and makes them go 'blood-simple' comes from Hammett, it is also central to Cain's work.) After the trial, the remainder of *Postman* sees Cora and Frank's relationship fall apart and the book turns out to be less about the murder and more about its consequences. However, *The Man Who Wasn't There* does an odd feint. After Doris hangs herself Ed is left alone with his guilt and realises what a mess he's made of his life, but he seems to be in the clear and decides to try and help somebody else – Birdy – make the most of theirs. At this point it really isn't clear where the movie is going, but then Ed is collared for the murder he *didn't* commit. It's necessary to show how Ed would have reacted if he had never been found out, even if it doesn't flow as naturally out of the main body of the plot. One sense in which *The Man Who Wasn't There* is slightly more elegant than *Postman* is that Frank Chambers is eventually found out for the murder he committed and this casts him in a bad light when he is tried for the murder he didn't commit. Ed, however, is never fingered for the murder of Big Dave. He is assumed to have been connected to it but ultimately they can't touch him for it.

However, he is instantly connected with the murder of Tolliver and nobody else has a motive – the same thing that led the police to arrest Doris.

Cain often wrote about people who try to commit the perfect murder, working it out meticulously in advance but falling down on some small detail they haven't considered, or finding that their own guilt overwhelms them. They have to fail in order to show that crime does not pay. However, Ed Crane commits a murder without intending to, with no pre-planning at all, and gets away with it (note that after he kills Big Dave, Ed looks down at his hands and sees that they are clean). When he tries to confess to his wife and to Riedenschneider, the story is dismissed for not being credible. Ed has committed the perfect murder by accident because there is a far more obvious suspect. Unfortunately, it's his wife, the one person who, as he later discovers, he didn't want to lose.

EVER AMERICA: The 1949 setting of *The Man Who Wasn't There* does not merely serve to position it closer to the era which Cain lived in and wrote about. Such a setting is not vital in order to make a Cain-style narrative work: the fact that *Blood Simple*, which takes its inspiration from the same source, works just as well in the 1980s demonstrates that Cain's stories are more universal than, say, Hammett's (*Miller's Crossing* wouldn't have felt much like Hammett if its plot had been relocated to the present day). *The Man Who Wasn't There* is set fifteen years after the publication of *The Postman Always Rings Twice* and accordingly it brings in a number of themes and concerns that were not part of Cain's world. 'We set the film [in 1949] because of this idea, which you see in a lot of work from that period, of the fear of the modern,' says Joel.

As noted above, the Coens refer to Ed as 'modern man', as does Riedenschneider during his defence. The most important element of this is that Ed himself doesn't understand what this means. Riedenschneider's speech about the Uncertainty Principle may be gobbledegook but uncertainty is what governs the characters' lives. 'It's like he stands outside, looking at himself,' says Ethan, suggesting that in that sense Ed 'fits the post-war era: laymen going around saying "Einstein says light is curved" and wondering what it means, where they fit in, feeling like they're cast adrift.' The Second World War made substantial changes to life at every level, not least of which was that after the nuclear attacks on Japan, and the onset of the Cold War, people were aware that the world could end at any moment – and if that could happen, *anything* could. *The Man Who Wasn't There* features a number of characters living under the nuclear shadow who have not reconciled their identities with this new world yet. Ed doesn't even have an identity to begin with, refusing to think of himself as a barber, but he knows that he doesn't want to work in the shop all his life and tries to change his future. Big Dave, by contrast, copes by inventing elements of his past.

The Cold War also carried with it the threat of America being overwhelmed by communism, and this paranoia manifested itself in the greater popularity of science fiction and particularly alien invasion stories. The Coens, who have never shown any interest in making a science fiction movie ('We've never really thought about doing one of those,' says Ethan. 'I don't know . . . Something about space suits . . .') make use of retro sci-fi imagery in order to communicate this sense of unease. Dennis Gassner contributes to this in his designs, which subtly suggest the contours of spacecraft (see **PRODUCTION**) and the Coens suggest both alien invasion paranoia and fear of earthbound threats by adopting the visual style of cheap sci-fi movies and public service films. The look of the film is an adaptation of the Coens' usual detached style, the lack of colour giving it a sterile, dispassionate air, as though it is designed to instruct rather than entertain. (In the typical Coen manner, this effect is undercut by the comic touches and the result means that it *is* entertaining.)

This sort of paranoia was usually located in small towns (easier to take over, presumably) and the Coens have selected just such a location for *The Man Who Wasn't There* in the form of Santa Rosa. The town's previous claim to fame is that it was the setting for Alfred Hitchcock's 1943 thriller *Shadow of a Doubt*, often cited by the director as his favourite of his own films. Although the plot of *The Man Who Wasn't There* is very different, the Coens acknowledge that *Shadow of a Doubt* influenced their thinking and the slow pace of both movies gives them a not dissimilar atmosphere.

AVAILABILITY: At long last, a Coen brothers movie on DVD which has both a decent selection of features and the same ones in both territories. *The Man Who Wasn't There* comes with a commentary by Joel, Ethan and Billy Bob Thornton, a 'making of' documentary (which is actually an unvarnished selection of interview clips and on-set footage but one shouldn't quibble), an interview with Roger Deakins about his superb cinematography (which proves to be very illuminating, haha), the aforementioned deleted scenes, filmographies, a photo gallery, a trailer and two really cheesy TV spots. Let's hope this one sets the standard.

THE COENS' VIEW: 'The film distributor doesn't want us to flog it as film noir. So, we're saying it's about existential dread. Maybe that'll sell a few more tickets – at least in France.' (Ethan in 2001)

VERDICT: 'Sooner or later everybody needs a haircut.' *The Man Who Wasn't There* is so bleak and yet so beautiful. Most obviously there's the subdued black and white photography, accentuated by elegant design, and Carter Burwell's halting, wistful score makes a tremendous contribution. It also must be said that this is a wonderful script: I cannot understand why several reviews found the dialogue wanting. Like the Cain novels that inspired it, its beauty is in its economy, making a hard, impassive central character into a tragic figure as dreadful events unfold around him. The more delicate treatment of the other aspects of the production, meanwhile, lend the film the exquisite desolation of F Scott Fitzgerald.

Although there is little of his personality for the audience to grasp, Ed is one of the Coens' most sympathetic characters because his lack of personality is, perversely, part of the crisis that defines him. His struggle for identity in a society he doesn't understand, brilliantly communicated by Thornton, is deeply moving, and his acceptance of the various misfortunes that befall him – from the infidelity of his wife to being sentenced to death – create a crushing sense of inevitability around those events. In the context of what has already transpired, Ed's final lines are the most evocative the Coens have ever written, signifying a tiny ray of hope and a desperate desire for understanding in a cruel, unfeeling world.

Hence, *The Man Who Wasn't There* is light years away from the film noir pastiche that its Cainisms and monochromania might suggest. It takes the concerns of other times and other writers and runs with them. It carries off its apparent contradictions with ease: it's a thriller that doesn't aim to thrill; it's an immensely sophisticated exploration of an unsophisticated man. The film that ultimately emerges ranks among the Coen brothers' very finest work.

Intolerable Cruelty (2003)

(Colour – TBC)

Universal Pictures Presents
An Alphaville/Imagine Production
Casting by Ellen Chenoweth and Rachel Tenner
Supervising Sound Editor: Skip Lievsay
Edited by Roderick Jaynes
Music by Carter Burwell
Costume Designer: Mary Zophres
Production Designer: Leslie McDonald
Director of Photography: Roger Deakins ASC, BSC
Co-producers: John Cameron and Grant Heslov
Executive Producers: Jim Jacks and Sean Daniel
Produced by Ethan Coen and Brian Grazer
Written by Ethan Coen & Joel Coen and Jonathan Demme,
Robert Ramsey & Matthew Stone
Directed by Joel Coen

CAST: George Clooney (*Miles Massey*), Catherine Zeta-Jones (*Marylin Rexroth*), Geoffrey Rush (*Donovan Donnelly*), Billy Bob

Thornton (*Howard Doyle*), Cedric the Entertainer (*Gus Petch*), Paul Adelstein (*Wrigley*), Edward Herrmann (*Rex Rexroth*), John Bliss (*Mr MacKinnon*), Emmy Collins (*Himself*), Barbara Kerr Condon (*Meyerson's Nurse*), Mia Cottet (*Romona Barcelona*), Allan Trautman (*Convention Lawyer*), Steven Hack (*Lawyer #2*), Alonzo F Jones (*Yet Another Guy*), Wendle Josepher (*Massey Secretary*), Michael A Tessiero (*Slot Jockey*), Stacey Travis (*Bonnie Donovan*), Camille Anderson (*Tart #1*), Kitana Baker (*Tart #2*), Tamie Sheffield (*Tart #3*), Susan Yeagley (*Tart #4*), Dale E Turner (*Yet Another Man*)

SUMMARY: The scene is contemporary Los Angeles. Miles Massey, the best divorce lawyer in the business, sabotages a case in order to save developer Rex Rexroth from having to pay a settlement to his wife Marilyn, who has filed for divorce on the grounds of infidelity. Marilyn plots her revenge on Miles, which involves drawing him into marriage without a prenuptial agreement so that she can take his money. However, when Rex dies, Marilyn discovers that he never got around to writing her out of his will, meaning that her fortune is now greater than Miles's. Miles and Marilyn plot and counter-plot to extricate themselves from the marriage, each wanting to take the lion's share of the money.

DEVELOPMENT: In 1994 the Coens were hired to redraft a script that had been languishing in development hell for a couple of years. Called *Intolerable Cruelty*, it was based on an original concept by John Romano, author of *The Third Miracle* (Agnieszka Holland, 1999) and had been developed into a screenplay by Robert Ramsey and Matthew Stone, who wrote *Big Trouble* (Barry Sonnenfeld, 2002) and *Life* (Ted Demme, 1999). For Joel and Ethan it carried echoes of Howard Hawks romantic comedies where the couple are at loggerheads for most of the movie before falling in love. It was the Coens' first job as writers-for-hire and they were apparently happy to leave it behind after completing work on it.

Intolerable Cruelty continued to float around Hollywood, drifting past directors such as Ron Howard and Andrew Bergman and going through countless further rewrites. (It's said that every time a new writer came to the project, they worked not from the most recent draft but from Joel and Ethan's version, presumably because they felt it was the best.) Eventually, Jonathan Demme – director of the Talking Heads concert film *Stop Making Sense* (1984) and winner of the Best Director Oscar for *Silence of the Lambs* (1990) – picked it up as his next project. The script went through more drafts, including one by Jay Kogen, who wrote *The Wrong Guy* (David Steinberg, 1997), and Barbara Benedek, author of *Sabrina* (Sydney Pollack, 1995) and *The Big Chill* (Lawrence Kasdan, 1983). Demme kept the project on the back burner for some time, planning to direct it in late 2001 after *The Truth About Charlie* (2002), but eventually dropped out. At this point, *The Man Who Wasn't There* had just come out and Joel and Ethan were looking for a new project after the collapse of *To the White Sea* (see **Still in the Drawer**). When the studio pointed out to them that *Intolerable Cruelty* was in need of a director, they dug out their original draft and took the film on.

CASTING: Before it became a Coen brothers production, *Intolerable Cruelty* was under consideration by Richard Gere and Julia Roberts, who were looking to reunite as romantic leads in order to emulate the success of *Pretty Woman* (Garry Marshall, 1990). However, they eventually settled on *Runaway Bride* (Garry Marshall, 1999) for this purpose. After this the project was suggested for Tea Leoni (who had been in talks to star in *Runaway Bride*) and Will Smith, then Hugh Grant was slated for the male lead. At this point Universal saw another chance to pair Julia Roberts with a previous co-star, since she appeared alongside Grant in *Notting Hill* (Roger Michell, 1999) and they talked to her about returning to the project. This was dependent on fitting her schedule in with Grant's and Demme's, which proved difficult. After Demme left the project, the Coens' first move was to cast George Clooney. While this offered possibilities *yet again* for Roberts to team with an old co-star (she and Clooney paired up in *Ocean's Eleven* (Steven Soderbergh, 2001)), in late 2001 Universal confirmed that Catherine Zeta-Jones would be the female lead.

For the benefit of American readers, it is worth noting just how strange the rise of Catherine Zeta-Jones seems in Britain. In the mid-1990s this Welsh actress was practically the stuff of 'Where are they now?' columns, having been in the public eye during the early 1990s due to her role in the TV comedy-drama *The Darling Buds of May* and her relationship with John Leslie, a children's TV presenter. Her first attempt to crack Hollywood, *The Phantom* (Simon Wincer, 1996) slipped by unnoticed, but she found success with *The Mask of Zorro* (Martin Campbell, 1998), married Michael Douglas and has worked with the likes of Steven Soderbergh. Some people can scarcely believe that it's the same Catherine Zeta-Jones.

Billy Bob Thornton was obvious casting for the Texan oil magnate Howard Doyle, but the rest of the roles were filled from outside the Coen repertory. Australian Geoffrey Rush was cast as daytime TV soap opera director Donovan Donnelly: Rush came to prominence after winning Best Actor at the Oscars for his role in *Shine* (Scott Hicks, 1996). His other work includes *Shakespeare in Love* (John Madden, 1998) and a turn as the Marquis de Sade in *Quills* (Phillip Kaufman, 2000). The role of private investigator Gus Petch went to comedian Cedric the Entertainer, whose film work has mainly comprised cameos in the likes of *Big Momma's House* (Raja Gosnell, 2000) and *Dr. Dolittle* 2 (Steve Carr, 2001). He has also hosted his own sketch show, *Cedric the Entertainer Presents*.

PRODUCTION: Photography on *Intolerable Cruelty* finally began on 20 June 2002, having been delayed further by George Clooney's schedule: he was working on his directorial debut *Confessions of a Dangerous Mind* (2002) when the call came to work with the Coens again, by which time he was already lined up to make a third film with Steven Soderbergh, *Solaris* (2002).

It was the Coens' third film to be set in Los Angeles and the fourth to be made there, with most of the location work taking place around Beverly Hills. Footage was also shot in Las Vegas during a week at the end of production, including a scene at Caesar's Palace in which Miles operates a row of slot machines and gets a jackpot on every one. The exteriors for Miles and Marilyn's wedding scene were shot at the tragically named Wee Kirk O' the Heather Wedding Chapel, with the interiors being completed in an appropriately tartan-decked studio. The shoot was completed on 11 September 2002.

BOX OFFICE: At the time of writing, *Intolerable Cruelty* is scheduled for release in America on 10 October 2003. 'Mean Mr Mustard' reviewed the film for *Ain't It Cool* on 22 January 2003 following a test screening and predicted that the film would find favour with the movie-going public 'because it's one of the lightest and most audience-friendly films that the Coen brothers have ever made, and because it has two genuine movie stars at the top of their form'. He went on to suggest that it would be the first film from the Coens to gross over $100 million.

Still in the drawer: the Coens' as-yet unrealised projects

Many of the Coens' movies have lain dormant as scripts for several years before heading in front of the cameras. That being the case, one shouldn't rule out the possibility that some project they fleetingly referred to in an interview in 1992 will suddenly roll into production. Here's a few that may, or may not, see the light of day eventually.

Coast to Coast

This was Joel and Ethan's first serious attempt at a feature film script, written when they were still at college. 'We never really did anything with it,' Joel reflects. 'It was sort of a screwball comedy.' Ethan describes the plot thus: 'It had 28 Einsteins in it. The Red Chinese were cloning Albert Einstein.'

Suburbicon

A murder mystery that the Coens started writing shortly after Ethan moved to New York. This one may still be a going concern in some sense, as George Clooney has mentioned that it was going to be his first film with the Coens until they decided to offer him *O Brother, Where Art Thou?* 'It was a small part, and I was going to get beaten to death with a shovel. I liked it. It was a great part.'

Old Fink

The Coens have occasionally spoken of their desire to make a sequel to *Barton Fink*, which would see John Turturro's eponymous character some years down the line, in the late 1960s. The idea is that Barton would have become a kind of Allen Ginsberg figure, an elder guru to the hippie generation. Having covered most decades of the twentieth century during their career, it would be great to see the Coens' version of the 1960s, and to see whether Barton ever did manage to grow up. The project has never reached a stage of serious development: perhaps they're waiting for John Turturro to get a little closer to the right age, so they won't have to bother with make-up? On a similar note, Turturro has noted that the Coens have spoken to him occasionally about the possibility of a vehicle for his Hispanic pederast bowler from *The Big Lebowski*, Jesus Quintana, although whether a full-length Jesus movie would be a remotely viable idea is a matter for conjecture.

To The White Sea

While in Cannes to pick up the Best Director prize for *The Man Who Wasn't There*, the Coens took the opportunity to talk about their next movie. This would be an adaptation of *To The White Sea*, the novel by *Deliverance* author James Dickey, with Brad Pitt attached to star and described by the Coens as their first 'without any jokes at all'. The book concerns a US airman in WWII crash-landing in the Japanese countryside and making his way back to civilisation, an experience which drives him to shocking acts of violence.

The script was originated not by Joel and Ethan but by the husband-and-wife writing team David and Janet Peoples, best known for their work on *Twelve Monkeys* (Terry Gilliam, 1995), and it had been drifting around Hollywood in search of backing since 1993. Unsurprisingly, when the Coens came to the project they did a rewrite, and in the process set themselves a challenge. They dumped the expository voice-over (basically large chunks of the book that explained the main character's reactions to his predicament and surroundings) and decided to communicate everything through the nuances of the camerawork and Pitt's performance. (*IGN FilmForce*'s script reviewer would have agreed – they had found the voice-over to be the only questionable element of the Peoples' script.) In order to create the sense of a wilderness that felt totally alien to the protagonist, the Coens considered it very important to have the shoot actually take place in Japan.

This proved to be the project's downfall. It had already been a struggle for the Coens to convince 20th Century Fox to take this brutal, experimental movie on (no doubt the interest of Pitt helped). However, when Fox realised the cost of shooting in Japan (the budget was set for $60 million) the studio decided that it was too much of a risk and pulled out. 'It's hard for someone to lose money as long as the movies are done very cheaply,' Joel says. 'But . . . *To The White Sea* is quite a bit more expensive and very difficult subject matter.' This may account for the Coens' decision to return to the more studio-friendly *Intolerable Cruelty*, which had suddenly found itself in need of a new director. As for *To The White Sea*, Joel's conclusion is, 'I think it's dead.'

Cuba Libre

Another direct adaptation of a novel completed by the Coens and sitting in a drawer, *Cuba Libre* is a version of the Elmore Leonard book of the same name. If this does go ahead it will be their first venture into pre-twentieth century territory, as it concerns the bank-robbing activities of an 1890s cowboy. On some occasions they have suggested that they aren't interested in directing it themselves, but at the present moment neither is anybody else, apparently.

The Ed Harris Project

The brothers have, thus far, refused to elaborate any further on this one. It's a script that they wrote with Ed Harris in mind. Mr Harris has had a lengthy and varied acting career, including roles in *Glengarry Glen Ross* (David Mamet, 1992), *Nixon* (Oliver Stone, 1995), *The Truman Show* (Peter Weir, 1998) and *A Beautiful Mind* (Ron Howard, 2001). None of this sheds any light on what the Coens might have written for him. Sorry.

Bad Santa

This one *will* see the light of day, but not as a Coen brothers movie. John Requa and Glenn Ficarra have written a script based on Joel and Ethan's concept of a department store Santa who robs a shopping mall every Christmas Eve and it has been realised by Terry Zwigoff (director of one of the outstanding movies of 2001, *Ghost World*). Billy Bob Thornton took the lead role of Willy T Soke. The Coens acted as producers on the film, which has been put back from a Christmas 2002 release to late 2003.

The Ladykillers

Cited, at the time of writing, as the Coens' next movie after *Intolerable Cruelty*, this would be a remake of the 1955 Ealing comedy about five robbers who plot to kill an elderly lady after she discovers their crimes. The Coens' remake would revolve around Professor Goldthwait Higginson Dorr, an expert in dead languages and Renaissance music, and his plot to steal the takings of a riverboat casino in the town of Saucier, Mississippi. The original was directed by Alexander Mackendrick and starred Alec Guinness and Peter Sellers: Tom Hanks is up for the role of Professor Dorr in the new version.

A review of the Coens' script has been posted on *FilmJerk.com* by Edward Havens. This includes the script's description of the opening sequence, in which a garbage boat makes its way along the Mississippi: 'No sound, except for an incongruously heroic score. The coverage is a little rough, coarse-grained; along with the overbearing score it almost suggests an industrial film rather than a feature.' The elderly lady is Marva Munson, an African–American churchgoer, and Professor Dorr's gang is made up of demolitions expert Clark Pancake, custodian Gawain MacSam, former General of the Vietnamese Army turned doughnut shop proprietor Nguyen Pham Doc and failed football player Lump Hudson, along with Clark's girlfriend Mountain Girl. Havens gave the script an unequivocal thumbs-up: '*The Ladykillers* could easily become [the Coens'] first blockbuster hit. On their terms, naturally.'

Guess Who's Coming To Dinner?

Sometimes you really don't know whether the Coens are joking or not when they say things like 'we've both talked about doing a remake of *Guess Who's Coming To Dinner?*' They've certainly mentioned more than once tackling Stanley Kramer's 1967 Oscar-winner, about a wealthy white girl from San Francisco bringing her black fiancé home to meet the parents. Ethan suggested that the remake would 'be an interesting exercise in post-modern aesthetics'.

On one occasion the subject came up at the end of a string of clearly untenable projects, after Joel reiterated his desire to make a dog movie – 'Like *Old Yeller*,' he elaborated. Ethan's response to this was, 'We keep arguing. Joel wants to do a dog movie and I want to do a farm comedy like *Ma And Pa Kettle* . . . you know, we'd cast David Straithairn and Kathy Bates.' It has to be said that the Coens are so wilfully perverse that you couldn't rule any of those out entirely. But they won't happen. Probably.

Index of Quotations

NB: All quotations from French-language sources are drawn from the translations prepared by Paul Buck and Catherine Petit for *Joel & Ethan Coen: Blood Siblings*, edited by Paul A Woods.

All material from *American Cinematographer* is reprinted with permission of *American Cinematographer* C1985, 1996, 2000, 2001, 2003, 2004. More information about the American Society of Cinematographers (ASC) can be found at http://www.theASC.com.

Introduction

1 'they have to write a . . .' The Coens, quoted in *The Coen Brothers* by Ronald Bergan

3 'There's no point in making . . .' Joel, interview with Geoff Andrew for *Time Out*, 5 February 1992

4 'We tend to do period stuff . . .' Ethan, interview with Jonathan Romney for the *Guardian*, 19 May 2000

4 'Strangely, the subjects that come . . .' Joel, interview with Michel Ciment and Hubert Niogret for *Positif*, September 1996

Early Life

5 'My mother once wrote an . . .' Joel, interview with David Edelstein for *American Film*, April 1987

5 'There's three years difference in . . .' Joel, interview with Michel Ciment and Hubert Niogret in *Positif*, July/August 1987

6 'We started writing scripts for . . .' Joel, interview with Andrew Pulver for the *Guardian*'s *Weekend* magazine, 13 October 2001

Blood Simple

8 'The inspiration [for *Blood Simple*] was . . .' Ethan, quoted in *My First Movie* edited by Stephen Lowenstein

8 'When we did *Blood Simple* . . .' Ethan, interview with Paul Fischer for *Dark Horizons*

8 'the poet of the tabloid . . .' Edmund Wilson, quoted in *The Five Great Novels of James M Cain*

8 'seemed tailor-made for something . . .' Ethan, interview with Nathan Rabin for *The Onion AV Club*, 19 July 2000

9 'These types of stories are . . .' Ethan, interview with Paul Fischer for *Dark Horizons*

9 'was also very much inspired . . .' Joel, interview with Anthony C Ferrante for *IF Magazine*, 7 July 2000

9 'It is very difficult, very . . .' Alfred Hitchcock, quoted on the *Blood Simple* trailer

9 'What we asked ourselves was . . .' Ethan, quoted in the production notes on the *Blood Simple* DVD

10 'We met Holly Hunter and . . .' Ethan, quoted in *My First Movie* edited by Stephen Lowenstein

10 'But she and Fran were roommates . . .' Joel, quoted in *My First Movie* edited by Stephen Lowenstein

10 'Holly went back and told . . .' Joel, quoted in *My First Movie* edited by Stephen Lowenstein

10 'I went in and they . . .' Frances McDormand, interview with James Mottram for *BBC News Online*, 22 October 2001

10 'They were chain-smoking with a . . .' Frances McDormand, interview with James Mottram for *BBC News Online*, 22 October 2001

10 'I thought they were weird . . .' Frances McDormand, interview with James Mottram for *BBC News Online*, 22 October 2001

11 'because nobody was going to . . .' M Emmet Walsh, quoted in *The Coen Brothers* by Ronald Bergan

11 'I saw the storyboards and . . .' M Emmet Walsh, quoted in *The Coen Brothers* by Ronald Bergan

12 'We knew no one would . . .' Ethan, interview with Eric Breitbart for *American Film*, May 1985

12 'We followed the example of . . .' Joel, quoted in *My First Movie* edited by Stephen Lowenstein

13 'The trailer was our selling . . .' Barry Sonnenfeld, 'Shadows and Shivers for *Blood Simple*' in *American Cinematographer*, July 1985

13 'small business people [who] related to . . .' Joel, quoted in *My First Movie* edited by Stephen Lowenstein

13 'A lot of [the investors] said . . .' Ethan, interview with Eric Breitbart for *American Film*, May 1985

13 'We couldn't get people to . . .' Joel, interview with Eric Breitbart for *American Film*, May 1985

14 'We had a short discussion . . .' Joel, interview with Eric Breitbart for *American Film*, May 1985

14 'We decided to do it . . .' Ethan, interview with Eric Breitbart for *American Film*, May 1985

14 'You've got to *really* want . . .' Ethan, interview with Eric Breitbart for *American Film*, May 1985

14 'I'd lived in Texas for . . .' Ethan, interview with Nathan Rabin for *The Onion AV Club*, 19 July 2000

14 'Essentially, don't pay [the crew] . . .' Joel, interview with Anthony C Ferrante for *IF Magazine*, 7 July 2000

14 'Tom taught us a lot of . . .' Barry Sonnenfeld, 'Shadows and Shivers for *Blood Simple*' in *American Cinematographer*, July 1985

14 'Joel and I decided early . . .' Barry Sonnenfeld, 'Shadows and Shivers for *Blood Simple*' in *American Cinematographer*, July 1985
15 'We had to be able . . .' Joel, interview with Anthony C Ferrante for *IF Magazine*, 7 July 2000
15 'The first day of shooting . . .' Joel, quoted in *My First Movie* edited by Stephen Lowenstein
15 'even on this little low . . .' Ethan, interview with Anthony C Ferrante for *IF Magazine*, 7 July 2000
15 'The real surprise was that . . .' Joel, interview with Anthony C Ferrante for *IF Magazine*, 7 July 2000
15 'The one thing we did . . .' Joel, interview with Anthony C Ferrante for *IF Magazine*, 7 July 2000
15 'cannot be beat at any . . .' Barry Sonnenfeld, 'Shadows and Shivers for *Blood Simple*' in *American Cinematographer*, July 1985
16 'It was a very enjoyable . . .' Barry Sonnenfeld, 'Shadows and Shivers for *Blood Simple*' in *American Cinematographer*, July 1985
16 'too self-conscious.' Joel, quoted in 'Praising *Arizona*' by Jack Barth in *Film Comment*, March/April 1987
16 'This whole *movie* is self-conscious.' Ethan, quoted in 'Praising *Arizona*' by Jack Barth in *Film Comment*, March/April 1987
16 'For *Blood Simple* the lighting . . .' Barry Sonnenfeld, 'Shadows and Shivers for *Blood Simple*' in *American Cinematographer*, July 1985
17 'I'd be perfectly happy never . . .' Joel, interview with Smriti Mundhra for *IGN FilmForce*, 2 November 2001
17 'The fact that we separate . . .' Joel, interview with Jim Emerson for *Cinepad*, 1991
17 'Joel talks to the actors more . . .' Ethan, interview with Jim Emerson for *Cinepad*, 1991
17 'Psychologically, it's sort of important . . .' Joel, interview with Jim Emerson for *Cinepad*, 1991
17 'That's sort of why we . . .' Joel, interview with Jim Emerson for *Cinepad*, 1991
18 'almost thirty years.' 'Roderick Jaynes', foreword to the *Barton Fink and Miller's Crossing* screenplays
18 'struggling to make simple match cuts . . .' 'Roderick Jaynes', foreword to the screenplay for *The Man Who Wasn't There*
18 'the actors had been issued proper . . .' 'Roderick Jaynes', foreword to the *Barton Fink and Miller's Crossing* screenplays
18 'He's probably at some BAFTA . . .' Joel, interview with Damon Wise for *Filmfestivals.com*, 2001
18 'Joel, Ethan and I felt . . .' Barry Sonnenfeld, 'Shadows and Shivers for *Blood Simple*' in *American Cinematographer*, July 1985
19 '[Something] which we had no idea . . .' Ethan, interview with Anthony C Ferrante for *IF Magazine*, 7 July 2000

33 'I really think our film . . .' Joel, interview with Eric Breitbart for *American Film*, May 1985

Crimewave

37 'a fiasco'. Bruce Campbell, quoted in *Halliwell's Film & Video Guide 2000*

37 'beefed up the Heel role'. Bruce Campbell, interview with *Insound*

38 'It was a blessing in . . .' Bruce Campbell, interview with *Insound*

38 'It's no big deal for . . .' Ethan, interview with Paul Zimmerman for *FilmZone*, 1996

38 'We like it lost.' Joel, interview with Paul Zimmerman for *FilmZone*, 1986

38 'A boisterous, goofy, cartoonish comedy . . .' uncredited review of *Crimewave* in *Variety*, 22 May 1985

38 'Both of those films displayed . . .' Tim Pulleine, 'Crimewave' in *Films and Filming* issue #379, April 1986

39 'Overacted and overwrought, *Crimewave* . . .' Marjorie Bilbow, 'Crimewave' in *Screen International* issue #546, May 1986

39 'Occasionally, *Crimewave* hits the genuinely . . .' Steve Jenkins, review of *Crimewave* in *Monthly Film Bulletin*, April 1986

42 'We've always let Sam make . . .' Joel, interview with David Edelstein for *American Film*, April 1987

Raising Arizona

45 'Essentially, after having finished *Blood Simple* . . .' Ethan, interview with Michel Ciment and Hubert Niogret in *Positif*, July/August 1987

45 'Holly in uniform hurling orders . . .' Ethan, interview with Michel Ciment and Hubert Niogret in *Positif*, July/August 1987

45 'We weren't that interested either . . .' Joel, interview with Michel Ciment and Hubert Niogret in *Positif*, July/August 1987

45 'was a way of talking . . .' Joel, interview with Michel Ciment and Hubert Niogret in *Positif*, July/August 1987

46 'I guess you can detect . . .' Joel, interview with Michel Ciment and Hubert Niogret in *Positif*, July/August 1987

46 'Most of what we know . . .' Ethan, interview with Kevin Sessions for *Interview*, April 1987

46 'There are people who find . . .' Joel, interview with Michel Ciment and Hubert Niogret in *Positif*, July/August 1987

46 'The script was incredible, one . . .' Nicolas Cage, quoted in *The Unauthorised Biography of Nicolas Cage* by Ian Markham-Smith and Liz Hodgson

47 'It looks great but where . . .' Francis Ford Coppola, quoted in *The Unauthorised Biography of Nicolas Cage* by Ian Markham-Smith and Liz Hodgson

47 'There is no pretence to . . .' Joel, interview with Jack Mathews for *American Film*, December 1989

48 'It's a coincidence. We chose . . .' Joel, interview with Michel Ciment and Hubert Niogret in *Positif*, July/August 1987
48 'They both had these faces . . .' Joel, quoted in *The Unauthorised Biography of Nicolas Cage* by Ian Markham-Smith and Liz Hodgson
48 'He's not really an actor . . .' Joel, interview with Michel Ciment and Hubert Niogret in *Positif*, July/August 1987
48 'He's less an actor than . . .' Joel, interview with Michel Ciment and Hubert Niogret in *Positif*, July/August 1987
49 'Nathan Junior is supposed to . . .' James Jacks, quoted in *The Unauthorised Biography of Nicolas Cage* by Ian Markham-Smith and Liz Hodgson
49 'We figured twins would allow . . .' James Jacks, quoted in *The Unauthorised Biography of Nicolas Cage* by Ian Markham-Smith and Liz Hodgson
49 'It was a risk, but . . .' James Jacks, quoted in *The Unauthorised Biography of Nicolas Cage* by Ian Markham-Smith and Liz Hodgson
49 'We learned a lot between . . .' Joel, interview with Smriti Mundhra for *IGN FilmForce*, 2 November 2001
50 'There was nothing on paper . . .' James Jacks, interview with John H Richardson for US *Premiere*, October 1990
50 'We trusted them, it was . . .' Joel, interview with Michel Ciment and Hubert Niogret in *Positif*, July/August 1987
51 'accept another artist's vision'. Nicolas Cage, interview with David Edelstein for *American Film*, April 1987
51 'Nic's a really imaginative actor . . .' Joel, interview with Michel Ciment and Hubert Niogret in *Positif*, July/August 1987
51 'We shot it static. We . . .' Joel, quoted in 'Praising *Arizona*' by Jack Barth in *Film Comment*, March/April 1987
51 'The shot was done in . . .' The Coens, interview with Paul Zimmerman for *FilmZone*, 1996
52 'I don't know if I . . .' Joel, interview with Paul Zimmerman for *FilmZone*, 1996
52 'Every time I put on . . .' Barry Sonnenfeld, quoted in 'Praising Arizona' by Jack Barth in *Film Comment*, March/April 1987
52 'like you're shooting them in . . .' Barry Sonnenfeld, quoted in 'Praising Arizona' by Jack Barth in *Film Comment*, March/April 1987
52 'colourful and beautifully lit'. The Coens, quoted in 'Praising Arizona' by Jack Barth in *Film Comment*, March/April 1987
53 'A major pain of using . . .' Barry Sonnenfeld, quoted in 'Praising Arizona' by Jack Barth in *Film Comment*, March/April 1987
53 'It's grainy, low-contrast and has . . .' Barry Sonnenfeld, quoted in 'Praising Arizona' by Jack Barth in *Film Comment*, March/April 1987
53 'The blacks are richer and . . .' Barry Sonnenfeld, quoted in 'Praising Arizona' by Jack Barth in *Film Comment*, March/April 1987

53 'The lower a camera, the . . .' Barry Sonnenfeld, quoted in 'Praising Arizona' by Jack Barth in *Film Comment*, March/April 1987
54 'The Coens are control freaks . . .' Barry Sonnenfeld, quoted in 'Praising Arizona' by Jack Barth in *Film Comment*, March/April 1987
54 'The attitude on *Blood Simple* . . .' Barry Sonnenfeld, interview with David Edelstein for *American Film*, April 1987
54 'I have very fond recollections . . .' Carter Burwell, interview with Doug Adams for *Film Score Monthly*, October/November 1998
55 'connect the characters through the . . .' Ethan, interview with Michel Ciment and Hubert Niogret in *Positif*, July/August 1987
55 'I have a problem with . . .' Roger Ebert, review of *Raising Arizona* in the *Chicago Sun-Times*, 20 March 1987
55 'The amazing thing about *Raising Arizona* is . . .' Sheila Benson, review of *Raising Arizona* in the *Los Angeles Times*
55 'talented – up to a point . . .' Vincent Canby, review of *Raising Arizona* in the *New York Times*, 11 March 1987
55 'Quite possibly there has never been . . .' uncredited review of *Raising Arizona* in *Variety*, 4 March 1987
56 'This broad farce is no big deal . . .' Pauline Kael, review of *Raising Arizona* in the *New Yorker*
56 'The co-writing Coens are like . . .' Rita Kemply, review of *Raising Arizona* in the *Washington Post*, 20 March 1987
56 'More comedy than thriller, *Raising Arizona* . . .' Tom Milne, review of *Raising Arizona* in *Sight and Sound*, Summer 1987
56 'Whilst *Raising Arizona* is much . . .' Steve Jenkins, review of *Raising Arizona* in *Monthly Film Bulletin*, July 1987
63 'It encourages people to view . . .' Mike Zink, quoted in *The Unauthorised Biography of Nicolas Cage* by Ian Markham-Smith and Liz Hodgson
63 'His endorsement by the authorities . . .' Timothy Wright, 'Hope in the Midst of the Nuclear Threat: A Critical Examination of the Imagery in *Raising Arizona*'
64 'This movie is about parenting . . .' Joel, quoted in *The Unauthorised Biography of Nicolas Cage* by Ian Markham-Smith and Liz Hodgson
65 'It's like a real cheap . . .' Ethan, interview with David Edelstein for *American Film*, April 1987

Miller's Crossing

68 'Big guys in overcoats in . . .' The Coens, quoted in the production notes for *Miller's Crossing*
68 'We couldn't think of a . . .' Ethan, interview with John H Richardson for US *Premiere*, October 1990
68 'We weren't thinking so much . . .' Joel, quoted in the production notes for *Miller's Crossing*
68 'In Hammett, the plot is . . .' Joel, quoted in the production notes for *Miller's Crossing*

68 '[Tom is] the quintessential Hammett . . .' Joel, quoted in the production notes for *Miller's Crossing*
68 'He's got principles and interest . . .' Ethan, quoted in the production notes for *Miller's Crossing*
69 'a small man, short and . . .' from *The Glass Key* by Dashiell Hammett
70 'When I read the script . . .' Gabriel Byrne, quoted in the production notes for *Miller's Crossing*
70 'The part was originally an . . .' Gabriel Byrne, interview with Angie Errigo for *Empire*, March 1991
70 'We were sceptical, but we . . .' Joel, quoted in the production notes for *Miller's Crossing*
70 'as Ethan says, they "got . . ." ' Gabriel Byrne, interview with Angie Errigo for *Empire*, March 1991
70 'When we sat down and . . .' Gabriel Byrne, interview with Angie Errigo for *Empire*, March 1991
70 'It seemed like a comic . . .' Albert Finney, quoted in the production notes for *Miller's Crossing*
70 'What's strange is that the . . .' Ethan, interview with Jean-Pierre Coursodon for *Positif*, February 1991
71 'I read the script in . . .' Jon Polito, quoted in *The Coen Brothers* by Ronald Bergan
71 'It's amazing how he allows . . .' The Coens, quoted in 'Someone to Lean On' by Suzie Mackenzie in the *Guardian*, 2 September 2000
72 'New Orleans is sort of . . .' Ethan, interview with Steven Levy for US *Premiere*, March 1990
73 '*Raising Arizona* was low and . . .' Barry Sonnenfeld, quoted in the production notes for *Miller's Crossing*
73 'With longer lenses, you can . . .' Barry Sonnenfeld, quoted in the production notes for *Miller's Crossing*
74 'We wanted this movie to . . .' Barry Sonnenfeld, quoted in the production notes for *Miller's Crossing*
74 'The colours in *Miller's Crossing* . . .' Joel, quoted in the production notes for *Miller's Crossing*
74 'because Fuji greens are much . . .' Barry Sonnenfeld, quoted in the production notes for *Miller's Crossing*
74 'Ethan said, "Yeah, right, that's . . ." ' Dennis Gassner, quoted in the production notes for *Miller's Crossing*
74 'The boys phoned me from . . .' Jimmy Otis, quoted in the production notes for *Miller's Crossing*
75 'I like to provide as . . .' Dennis Gassner, interview with Rachel Altman for US *Premiere*, April 1990
75 'the emotional state of Tom's . . .' Dennis Gassner, interview with Rachel Altman for US *Premiere*, April 1990
75 'Dennis is very low-key and . . .' Joel, interview with Rachel Altman for US *Premiere*, April 1990

75 'It's about time at that . . .' Ethan, interview for Stephen Levy for US *Premiere*, March 1990

75 'You have to sell that . . .' Ethan, interview for Stephen Levy for US *Premiere*, March 1990

76 'All kinds of fun things . . .' Joel, interview for Stephen Levy for US *Premiere*, March 1990

76 'He got a very high . . .' Ethan, interview for Stephen Levy for US *Premiere*, March 1990

76 'The gun is incredibly loud . . .' Joel, interview for Stephen Levy for US *Premiere*, March 1990

76 'without really knowing how it . . .' Ethan, quoted in the production notes for *Miller's Crossing*

76 'The hat really becomes a . . .' Ron Neter, quoted in the production notes for *Miller's Crossing*

77 'Joel said, "Ethan, come here . . ."' Gabriel Byrne, interview with Angie Errigo for *Empire*, March 1991

77 'you don't *have* to know . . .' Gabriel Byrne, interview with Angie Errigo for *Empire*, March 1991

77 'When we were finishing the . . .' Ethan, quoted in the production notes for *Miller's Crossing*

78 'The song on which Carter . . .' Joel, quoted in the production notes for *Miller's Crossing*

78 'In *Miller's Crossing*, we all . . .' Carter Burwell, quoted in *The Coen Brothers* by Ronald Bergan

78 'Because it's emotional and overwrought . . .' Joel, quoted in the production notes for *Miller's Crossing*

78 'The pleasures of the film . . .' Roger Ebert, review of *Miller's Crossing* in the *Chicago Sun-Times*, 5 October 1990

79 '*Miller's Crossing* wants to be . . .' Vincent Canby, review of *Miller's Crossing* in the *New York Times*, September 21 1990

79 'Joel and Ethan Coen may represent . . .' Gary Giddins, review of *Miller's Crossing* in the *Village Voice*, 25 September 1990

79 'Substance – the missing ingredient in . . .' uncredited review of *Miller's Crossing* in *Variety*, 3 September 1990

80 'a very clever, stylish story of . . .' uncredited review of *Miller's Crossing* in *Empire* issue #21, March 1991

80 '[The Coens'] latest operates . . .' Geoff Andrew, review of *Miller's Crossing* in *Time Out*, 13 February 1991

80 'The film's particular strength derives . . .' Steve Jenkins, review of *Miller's Crossing* in *Monthly Film Bulletin*, February 1991

80 'Words dominate . . . a masterful piece . . .' Geoff Brown, review of *Miller's Crossing* in *The Times*, 14 February 1991

81 'I love it, but the . . .' Joel, interview with Jean-Pierre Coursodon for *Positif*, February 1991

81 'It's difficult to analyse why . . .' Joel, interview with Michel Ciment and Hubert Niogret for *Positif*, September 1991
89 'The hat in *Miller's Crossing* . . .' Joel, interview with Simon Braund for *Empire* issue #136, October 2000

Barton Fink

92 'It was just going really . . .' Ethan, interview with Jim Emerson for *Cinepad*, 1991
92 'It's not exactly writer's block . . .' Joel, interview with Jim Emerson for *Cinepad*, 1991
92 'rattling around for a time'. Joel, interview with Geoff Andrew for *Time Out*, 5 February 1992
92 'It actually got written very . . .' Joel, interview with Jim Emerson for *Cinepad*, 1991
92 'We didn't do any research . . .' Ethan, interview with Jim Emerson for *Cinepad*, 1991
92 'It was one of the . . .' Joel, interview with Jim Emerson for *Cinepad*, 1991
92 'We thought it was like a joke . . .' Ethan, interview with Jim Emerson for *Cinepad*, 1991
93 '[John Mahoney] really does resemble . . .' Joel, interview with Jim Emerson for *Cinepad*, 1991
93 'Barton *is* based on Clifford Odets . . .' Joel, interview with Jim Emerson for *Cinepad*, 1991
94 'did go to Hollywood in . . .' Roger Ebert, review of *Barton Fink* in the *Chicago Sun-Times*, 23 August 1991
94 'Hollywood, like Midas, kills everything . . .' Clifford Odets, quoted in *Halliwell's Who's Who in the Movies*
94 'When Barton awoke and discovered . . .' Joel, interview with Michel Ciment and Hubert Niogret for *Positif*, September 1991
94 'We were conscious that the . . .' Ethan, interview with Michel Ciment and Hubert Niogret for *Positif*, September 1991
94 'The world he has to . . .' Joel, interview with Geoff Andrew for *Time Out*, 5 February 1992
94 'The starting point wasn't that . . .' Joel, quoted in the production notes for *Barton Fink*
95 'the idea of a big . . .' Joel, quoted in the production notes for *Barton Fink*
95 'When we first talked, they . . .' John Turturro, quoted in the production notes for *Barton Fink*
95 'This was specifically something we . . .' Joel, quoted in the production notes for *Barton Fink*
95 'just to be in touch . . .' John Turturro, quoted in the production notes for *Barton Fink*
95 'but it's also not like . . .' Ethan, quoted in the production notes for *Barton Fink*

96 'It's really good writing. It . . .' John Goodman, quoted in the production notes for *Barton Fink*

97 'Shooting in LA was a . . .' Ron Neter, quoted in the production notes for *Barton Fink*

98 'New York is black and . . .' Richard Hornung, quoted in the production notes for *Barton Fink*

98 'the chaos of the USO . . .' Richard Hornung, quoted in the production notes for *Barton Fink*

99 'We wanted an art-deco style . . .' Joel, interview with Michel Ciment and Hubert Niogret for *Positif*, September 1991

99 'At the end, when Goodman . . .' Joel, interview with Michel Ciment and Hubert Niogret for *Positif*, September 1991

99 'We wanted the whole thing . . .' Joel, quoted in the production notes for *Barton Fink*

99 'We used a lot of green . . .' Ethan, interview with Michel Ciment and Hubert Niogret for *Positif*, September 1991

99 'We got a letter from . . .' Joel, interview with Jim Emerson for *Cinepad*, 1991

99 'The shot was a lot . . .' Joel, quoted in *The Coen Brothers* by Ronald Bergan

99 'After that, every time we . . .' Joel, quoted in *The Coen Brothers* by Ronald Bergan

100 'In *Barton Fink*, the camera . . .' Roger Deakins, interview with Ryan Mottesheard for *indieWIRE*

100 'Nearly everything was used. I . . .' Joel, interview with Michel Ciment and Hubert Niogret for *Positif*, September 1991

100 'We filmed other shots . . .' Joel, interview with Michel Ciment and Hubert Niogret for *Positif*, September 1991

101 'To someone who has not . . .' Vincent Canby, review of *Barton Fink* in the *New York Times*, 20 May 1991

101 'It was said by some . . .' Vincent Canby, review of *Barton Fink* in the *New York Times*, 18 August 1991

101 '*Barton Fink* is one of . . .' uncredited review of *Barton Fink* in *Variety*, 27 March 1991

101 'The Coens mean this aspect . . .' Roger Ebert, review of *Barton Fink* in the *Chicago Sun-Times*, 23 August 1991

102 'Whatever this oddball odyssey . . .' Edmond Grant, review of *Barton Fink* in *Films in Review*, November/December 1991

102 'You can imagine it peopled . . .' Joel, interview with Michel Ciment and Hubert Niogret for *Positif*, September 1991

102 'I'm not sure there is . . .' Arthur Miller, review of *Barton Fink* in US *Premiere*, October 1991

103 'So is *Barton Fink*, which . . .' Shaun Usher, review of *Barton Fink* in the *Daily Mail*, 14 February 1992

103 'Despite its setting, *Barton Fink* . . .' Steve Jenkins, review of *Barton Fink* in *Sight and Sound*, February 1992
103 'Logical plotting and character development . . .' Christopher Tookey, review of *Barton Fink* in the *Sunday Telegraph*, 16 February 1992
103 'almost as baffling as it . . .' Angie Errigo, review of *Barton Fink* in *Empire* issue #33, March 1992
104 'The more perversely weird the . . .' Geoff Andrew, review of *Barton Fink* in *Time Out*, 12 February 1992
104 'kind of ironic'. Ethan, interview with Jim Emerson for *Cinepad*, 1991
104 'It's no coincidence. If they . . .' Spike Lee, quoted in *Empire* issue #25, July 1991
108 'We're certainly hard on Barton . . .' Joel, interview with Geoff Andrew for *Time Out*, 5 February 1992
109 'Somewhere in a book, I . . .' Preston Sturges, quoted in *Between Flops: A Biography of Preston Sturges* by James Curtis
109 'was Sullivan's conclusion, not mine . . .' Preston Sturges, quoted in *Between Flops: A Biography of Preston Sturges* by James Curtis
109 'That question about a larger . . .' The Coens, interview with Sheila Johnston for the *Independent*, 22nd May 1991
110 'If somebody goes out to . . .' Joel, interview with Hal Hinson for *Film Comment*, March/April 1985
110 'There is apparently only one . . .' Roger Ebert, review of *Barton Fink* in the *Chicago Sun-Times*, 23 August 1991
113 'By trying to reduce the . . .' Michael Dunne, 'Barton Fink, Intertextuality, and the (Almost) Unbearable Richness of Viewing' in *Literature/Film Quarterly* volume 28 number 4, 2000
114 'One of the things the . . .' Richard T Jameson, review of *Barton Fink* in *Film Comment*, September/October 1991
114 'would make sense as . . .' Richard T Jameson, review of *Barton Fink* in *Film Comment*, September/October 1991
114 'careless melange of Faulkner-bio minutiae . . .' Richard T Jameson, review of *Barton Fink* in *Film Comment*, September/October 1991
115 'We are conscious of the . . .' The Coens, interview with Phillip Bergson for *What's on in London*, 10 February 1992

The Hudsucker Proxy

118 'Our comedy begins with a . . .' Ethan, interview with Kim Newman for *City Limits*, 25 January 1985
119 'that does take place in . . .' The Coens, interview with Kevin Sessions for *Interview*, April 1987
119 'From there it was a . . .' The Coens, quoted in the production notes for *The Hudsucker Proxy*
119 'We were having fun. The . . .' Ethan, quoted in the production notes for *The Hudsucker Proxy*

119 'But it was bigger and . . .' Ethan, quoted in the production notes for *The Hudsucker Proxy*
119 'There is Capra in the . . .' Joel, interview with Jonathan Romney for the *Guardian*, 25 August 1994
119 'with certain common mythical elements – the . . .' Joel, interview with Jonathan Romney for the *Guardian*, 25 August 1994
120 'We had to come up . . .' Joel, interview with John Naughton for UK *Premiere*, September 1994
120 'the design element that drives . . .' Joel, interview with John Naughton for UK *Premiere*, September 1994
121 'The scale of *Hudsucker* was . . .' Joel, quoted in the production notes for *The Hudsucker Proxy*
121 'It became clear that it . . .' Joel, interview with John Naughton for UK *Premiere*, September 1994
121 'although it continued to interest . . .' Joel, quoted in the production notes for *The Hudsucker Proxy*
121 'There are certain movies that . . .' Joel, interview with John Naughton for UK *Premiere*, September 1994
122 'We talked over our ideas . . .' Joel, quoted in the production notes for *The Hudsucker Proxy*
122 'I jumped at the chance . . .' Tim Robbins, quoted in the production notes for *The Hudsucker Proxy*
122 'When I finished *The Player* . . .' Tim Robbins, quoted in the production notes for *The Hudsucker Proxy*
123 'And when we met him . . .' The Coens, interview with Howard Maxford for *What's On in London*, 7 September 1994
123 'a road company Machiavelli – and . . .' Paul Newman, quoted in the production notes for *The Hudsucker Proxy*
123 'I'm not a comic actor . . .' Paul Newman, quoted in the production notes for *The Hudsucker Proxy*
123 'The script was the most . . .' Joel Silver, quoted in the production notes for *The Hudsucker Proxy*
124 'big, glass-shattering action movies'. Joel, quoted in *The Coen Brothers* by Ronald Bergan
124 'When we heard he was . . .' Joel, interview with Jonathan Romney for the *Guardian*, 25 August 1994
124 'You hear all this stuff . . .' Joel, interview with John Clark for US *Premiere*, April 1994
124 'They like being quirky, artistic . . .' Joel Silver, interview with John Clark for US *Premiere*, April 1994
125 'He's a real enthusiast. Once . . .' The Coens, interview with Howard Maxford for *What's On in London*, 7 September 1994
125 'The ambition . . .' Joel, interview with Jonathan Romney for the *Guardian*, 25 August 1994

125 'You see, we wanted things . . .' Dennis Gassner, quoted in the production notes for *The Hudsucker Proxy*
125 'We also transformed a huge . . .' Dennis Gassner, quoted in the production notes for *The Hudsucker Proxy*
125 'Ethan and Joel wanted an . . .' Dennis Gassner, quoted in the production notes for *The Hudsucker Proxy*
126 'The men's clothes reflect the . . .' Richard Hornung, quoted in the production notes for *The Hudsucker Proxy*
126 'but rather a stylised version . . .' Michael J McAlister, interview with WC Odien for *Cinefex*
126 'We took all our favourite . . .' Michael J McAlister, quoted in the production notes for *The Hudsucker Proxy*
127 'Marrying a live-action image . . .' Michael J McAlister, interview with WC Odien for *Cinefex*
127 '*that* was state-of-the-art . . .' Michael J McAlister, interview with WC Odien for *Cinefex*
127 'The buildings had been designed . . .' Michael J McAlister, interview with WC Odien for *Cinefex*
128 'I got to shoot all the . . .' Sam Raimi, interview with John Clark for US *Premiere*, April 1994
128 'They weren't reshoots. They were . . .' Joel, interview with John Clark for US *Premiere*, April 1994
128 'We're really unambitious, to be . . .' Joel, interview with Jonathan Romney for the *Guardian*, 25 August 1994
129 'This is the best-looking movie . . .' Roger Ebert, review of *The Hudsucker Proxy* in the *Chicago Sun-Times*, 25 May 1994
130 '*The Hudsucker Proxy* is no doubt . . .' Todd McCarthy, review of *The Hudsucker Proxy* in *Variety*, 31 January 1994
130 '*Hudsucker*, for all its ultrasavvy . . .' Georgia Brown, review of *The Hudsucker Proxy* in the *Village Voice*, 22nd March 1994
130 'Why do I think *The Hudsucker Proxy* . . .' Christopher Tookey, review of *The Hudsucker Proxy* in the *Daily Mail*, 2nd September 1994
131 '*The Hudsucker Proxy* is one . . .' John Lyttle, review of *The Hudsucker Proxy* in the *Independent* London Supplement, September 1994
131 'As usual, the Coen brothers . . .' Geoff Brown, review of *The Hudsucker Proxy* in *The Times*, 1 September 1994
132 'No one could say that . . .' Derek Malcolm, review of *The Hudsucker Proxy* in the *Guardian*, 1 September 1994
132 'An archetypally populist story . . .' Kim Newman, review of *The Hudsucker Proxy* in *Empire* issue #64, October 1994
132 'While the earlier Coen films went . . .' Kim Newman, review of *The Hudsucker Proxy* in *Sight and Sound*, September 1994
132 'The sad thing about all . . .' Alexander Walker, review of *The Hudsucker Proxy* in the *Evening Standard*, 1 September 1994

138 '*Hudsucker* truly is a comment on . . .' Joel, quoted in *The Coen Brothers* by Ronald Bergan
140 'The kind of terrific verbal slam-bang . . .' The *New Yorker*, quoted in *Halliwell's Film & Video Guide 2000*
141 'It's not anachronistic as much . . .' Ethan, interview with Jonathan Romney for the *Guardian*, 25 August 1994
141 'Nominally, it's New York – but . . .' Ethan, interview with Jonathan Romney for the *Guardian*, 25 August 1994
141 'The world created in [Sturges's] films . . .' John Harkness, 'The Sphinx Without a Riddle' in *Sight and Sound*, August 1994
141 'There isn't enough weird logic . . .' John Harkness, 'The Sphinx Without a Riddle' in *Sight and Sound*, August 1994
142 'There was a lot of press . . .' Ethan, interview with John Naughton for UK *Premiere*, September 1994

Fargo
146 'Everything we have done before . . .' Joel, quoted in the production notes for *Fargo*
146 'the characters of Jerry and . . .' Ethan, quoted in the production notes for *Fargo*
146 'In this case, however . . .' Joel, quoted in the production notes for *Fargo*
146 'I could tell you, but . . .' Ethan, quoted in the *Brainerd Daily Despatch*
146 'We heard about it through . . .' Ethan, interview with Michel Ciment and Hubert Niogret for *Positif*, September 1996
146 'Generally speaking the movie is . . .' Joel, interview with Michel Ciment and Hubert Niogret for *Positif*, September 1996
146 'But, by telling the public . . .' Joel, interview with Michel Ciment and Hubert Niogret for *Positif*, September 1996
147 'We wanted to do something . . .' Joel, interview with Peter Biskind for US *Premiere*, March 1996
147 'The impetus was the previous . . .' Joel, interview with Michel Ciment and Hubert Niogret for *Positif*, September 1996
147 'We began it before shooting . . .' Ethan, interview with Michel Ciment and Hubert Niogret for *Positif*, September 1996
147 'my whole association with Minnesota . . .' Ethan, interview with Michel Ciment and Hubert Niogret in *Positif*, July/August 1987
147 'I remember having meetings with . . .' Joel, interview with Graham Fuller for *Interview*, March 1996
147 'Sometimes the way we approach . . .' Ethan, interview with Peter Biskind for US *Premiere*, March 1996
148 'almost a verbatim transcript of . . .' Ethan, interview with Lizzie Francke for *Sight and Sound*, May 1996
148 'Marge and Jerry are both . . .' Joel, interview with Lizzie Francke for *Sight and Sound*, May 1996

148 'We wanted to give another . . .' Joel, interview with Michel Ciment and Hubert Niogret for *Positif*, September 1996
148 'Our intention was to show . . .' Ethan, interview with Michel Ciment and Hubert Niogret for *Positif*, September 1996
148 'It's literally the sound of . . .' Ethan, interview with Michel Ciment and Hubert Niogret for *Positif*, September 1996
149 'I don't get that from . . .' Joel, quoted in *The Coen Brothers* by Ronald Bergan
149 'Now it doesn't matter. If . . .' Frances McDormand, quoted in *The Coen Brothers* by Ronald Bergan
149 'We are aware of his . . .' Joel, interview with Lizzie Francke for *Sight and Sound*, May 1996
150 'Peter's an old friend of . . .' Ethan, interview with Michel Ciment and Hubert Niogret for *Positif*, September 1996
150 'We imagined him a sloven . . .' Joel, interview with Lizzie Francke for *Sight and Sound*, May 1996
150 'Casting Bill we went in . . .' Joel, interview with Lizzie Francke for *Sight and Sound*, May 1996
150 'Bill refused to do a . . .' Ethan, interview with Lizzie Francke for *Sight and Sound*, May 1996
150 'He actually did a "dancin' . . ." ' Joel, quoted in *The Coen Brothers* by Ronald Bergan
151 'They were more worried about . . .' Ethan, interview with Peter Biskind for US *Premiere*, March 1996
151 'They were really good to us . . .' Joel, interview with Peter Biskind for US *Premiere*, March 1996
151 'It narrows your options, and . . .' Ethan, interview with Peter Biskind for US *Premiere*, March 1996
151 'During *The Hudsucker Proxy* we . . .' Eric Fellner, quoted in the production notes for *Fargo*
151 'I don't think it's quite . . .' Joel, interview with Peter Biskind for US *Premiere*, March 1996
151 'It was nice doing *Fargo* . . .' Roger Deakins, interview with Chris Probst for *American Cinematographer*, March 1996
151 'It was fun for all . . .' Joel, interview with Chris Probst for *American Cinematographer*, March 1996
152 'People ask me, "So you . . ." ' Rick Heinrichs, quoted in *The Big Lebowski: The Making of a Coen Brothers Film* by William Preston Robertson and Tricia Cooke
152 'It was familiar, although it was also . . .' Ethan, interview with Nathan Rabin for *The Onion AV Club*, 19 July 2000
152 'We were trying to reflect . . .' Joel, interview with Chris Probst for *American Cinematographer*, March 1996
152 'It's kind of a difficult . . .' Roger Deakins, interview with Chris Probst for *American Cinematographer*, March 1996

152 'I was very much working . . .' Roger Deakins, interview with Chris Probst for *American Cinematographer*, March 1996
152 'You usually light up comedies . . .' Roger Deakins, interview with Chris Probst for *American Cinematographer*, March 1996
153 'One of the things we . . .' Joel, interview with Peter Biskind for US *Premiere*, March 1996
153 'We wanted the camera to . . .' Joel, quoted in *The Coen Brothers* by Ronald Bergan
153 'We moved the camera far . . .' Joel, interview with Chris Probst for *American Cinematographer*, March 1996
153 'we realised that purist attitude . . .' Ethan, interview with Michel Ciment and Hubert Niogret for *Positif*, September 1996
153 'I think it is still . . .' Ethan, interview with Chris Probst for *American Cinematographer*, March 1996
153 'The impulse here was to . . .' Joel, interview with Chris Probst for *American Cinematographer*, March 1996
153 'a drag'. Ethan, quoted in the production notes for *Fargo*
153 'We left Minneapolis on March 9th . . .' John Cameron, quoted in the production notes for *Fargo*
154 'The landscape up there is . . .' Joel, interview with Chris Probst for *American Cinematographer*, March 1996
154 'We got enough of the . . .' John Cameron, quoted in the production notes for *Fargo*
155 'I wanted the movie to . . .' Carter Burwell, interview with Doug Adams for *Film Score Monthly*, October/November 1998
155 'It's all stated in the . . .' Carter Burwell, interview with Doug Adams for *Film Score Monthly*, October/November 1998
155 'low winds and brass and . . .' Carter Burwell, interview with Doug Adams for *Film Score Monthly*, October/November 1998
155 'I did a fair amount . . .' Carter Burwell, interview with Doug Adams for *Film Score Monthly*, October/November 1998
155 'Joel and Ethan Coen have . . .' Desson Howe, review of *Fargo* in the *Washington Post*, 14 March 1996
156 'Following the marketplace debacle of . . .' Leonard Klady, review of *Fargo* in *Variety*, 12 February 1996
156 'you know you're in a . . .' anonymous review of *Fargo* in *Newsday*, 14 March 1996
156 'As usual with the Coens . . .' Georgia Brown, review of *Fargo* in the *Village Voice*, 12 March 1996
156 'The Coens are at their . . .' Janet Maslin, review of *Fargo* in the *New York Times*, 8 March 1996
156 'Right from the beginning, the . . .' Geoff Brown, review of *Fargo* in *The Times*, 30 May 1996
157 'True or not, *Fargo* is . . .' Derek Malcolm, review of *Fargo* in the *Guardian*, 30 May 1996

157 'The Coens' films tend to . . .' Christopher Tookey, review of *Fargo* in the *Daily Mail*, 31 May 1996
157 'After the scraper-sized flop that . . .' Ian Nathan, review of *Fargo* in *Empire* issue #84, June 1996
158 'Someone had the idea that . . .' Ethan, interview with Mike Goodridge for *Screen International*, 30 January 1998
158 'We weren't really involved. I . . .' Joel, interview with Mike Goodridge for *Screen International*, 30 January 1998
163 'desire to go against the . . .' Ethan, interview with Michel Ciment and Hubert Niogret for *Positif*, September 1996
164 'It's implicit in the construction . . .' Joel, interview with Michel Ciment and Hubert Niogret for *Positif*, September 1996
166 'Here's where we tell ya . . .' from the front page of the *Brainerd Daily Dispatch*'s *Fargo* site
166 'For the record: no Twin Cities . . .' Steve Waller, 'Fargo nominated for best picture Oscar' in the *Brainerd Daily Dispatch*, 14 February 1997
166 'It's a fundamental misperception, because . . .' Joel, interview with Peter Biskind for US *Premiere*, March 1996
166 'A lot of people feel . . .' Ethan, interview with Peter Biskind for US *Premiere*, March 1996
166 'We don't give cues about . . .' Ethan, interview with Peter Biskind for US *Premiere*, March 1996
167 'What you could say is . . .' Ethan, quoted in *The Big Lebowski: The Making of a Coen Brothers Film* by William Preston Robertson and Tricia Cooke
167 'a vapid moron'. editorial in the *Brainerd Daily Dispatch*, 22nd April 1996
167 'calls for a lively sense . . .' Steve Waller, 'Fargo nominated for best picture Oscar' in the *Brainerd Daily Dispatch*, 14 February 1997
167 'We were born and grew up . . .' Joel, interview with Douglas J Rowe in the *Brainerd Daily Dispatch*, 14 March 1996
168 'What're you going to do . . .' Ethan, quoted in *The Big Lebowski: The Making of a Coen Brothers Film* by William Preston Robertson and Tricia Cooke

The Big Lebowski

171 '*Fargo*, which was allegedly based . . .' Ethan, quoted in *The Big Lebowski: The Making of a Coen Brothers Film* by William Preston Robertson and Tricia Cooke
172 'So, we complimented him on . . .' Ethan, quoted in *The Big Lebowski: The Making of a Coen Brothers Film* by William Preston Robertson and Tricia Cooke
172 'Pete is a Vietnam vet . . .' Ethan, quoted in *The Big Lebowski: The Making of a Coen Brothers Film* by William Preston Robertson and Tricia Cooke

172 'They had the homework in . . .' Ethan, quoted in *The Big Lebowski: The Making of a Coen Brothers Film* by William Preston Robertson and Tricia Cooke
172 'He's a really funny guy . . .' Ethan, quoted in *The Big Lebowski: The Making of a Coen Brothers Film* by William Preston Robertson and Tricia Cooke
172 'He was a member of . . .' Ethan, quoted in *The Big Lebowski: The Making of a Coen Brothers Film* by William Preston Robertson and Tricia Cooke
173 'a member of an amateur . . .' Joel, interview with *indieWIRE*
173 'It's a decidedly male sport . . .' Ethan, quoted in *The Big Lebowski: The Making of a Coen Brothers Film* by William Preston Robertson and Tricia Cooke
173 'We were really consciously thinking . . .' Ethan, interview with Nathan Rabin for *The Onion AV Club*, 19 July 2000
173 'I remember when Pete told . . .' Joel, quoted in *The Big Lebowski: The Making of a Coen Brothers Film* by William Preston Robertson and Tricia Cooke
173 'It moves episodically, and deals . . .' Joel, interview with *indieWIRE*
174 'The plot is sort of . . .' Joel, speaking on the VHS of *The Big Lebowski*
174 'The part of The Dude . . .' Joel, quoted in the production notes for *The Big Lebowski*
175 'We decided we wanted to . . .' Joel, quoted in *The Big Lebowski: The Making of a Coen Brothers Film* by William Preston Robertson and Tricia Cooke
175 'So we thought, well, let's . . .' Joel, quoted in *The Big Lebowski: The Making of a Coen Brothers Film* by William Preston Robertson and Tricia Cooke
175 'isn't specifically English – it's a . . .' Ethan, speaking on the VHS of *The Big Lebowski*
176 'They wanted a porn star . . .' Asia Carrera, interview with *The Unofficial Big Lebowski Homepage*
176 'That one! That's the one . . .' Asia Carrera, interview with *The Unofficial Big Lebowski Homepage*
176 'We really wrote that part . . .' Joel, quoted on the VHS of *The Big Lebowski*
176 '[Sam] would actually ask us . . .' Ethan, quoted on the VHS of *The Big Lebowski*
176 'is a weird mix. There . . .' Joel, quoted in *The Big Lebowski: The Making of a Coen Brothers Film* by William Preston Robertson and Tricia Cooke
177 'I'm not sure I ever . . .' Roger Deakins, quoted in *The Big Lebowski: The Making of a Coen Brothers Film* by William Preston Robertson and Tricia Cooke
177 'I decided early on that . . .' Roger Deakins, quoted in *The Big Lebowski: The Making of a Coen Brothers Film* by William Preston Robertson and Tricia Cooke

177 'It's damn well going back . . .' Roger Deakins, quoted in *The Big Lebowski: The Making of a Coen Brothers Film* by William Preston Robertson and Tricia Cooke

177 'Throughout, we wanted to reference . . .' Rick Heinrichs, quoted in the production notes for *The Big Lebowski*

177 'not only to establish the . . .' Rick Heinrichs, quoted in the production notes for *The Big Lebowski*

177 'Discussions were always framed with . . .' Ethan, quoted in *The Big Lebowski: The Making of a Coen Brothers Film* by William Preston Robertson and Tricia Cooke

177 'I personally am a Cheech . . .' Ethan, quoted in *The Big Lebowski: The Making of a Coen Brothers Film* by William Preston Robertson and Tricia Cooke

177 'we didn't want to overdo . . .' Rick Heinrichs, quoted in the production notes for *The Big Lebowski*

178 'in some of the clunky . . .' Rick Heinrichs, quoted in the production notes for *The Big Lebowski*

178 'At the Greystone Lebowski mansion . . .' Rick Heinrichs, quoted in the production notes for *The Big Lebowski*

178 'But since it grated on . . .' Rick Heinrichs, quoted in the production notes for *The Big Lebowski*

178 'We did a study of every . . .' Robert Graf, quoted in the production notes for *The Big Lebowski*

178 'Since the bowling alley is . . .' Ethan, quoted in *The Big Lebowski: The Making of a Coen Brothers Film* by William Preston Robertson and Tricia Cooke

179 'Stars are a very '50s . . .' Rick Heinrichs, quoted in *The Big Lebowski: The Making of a Coen Brothers Film* by William Preston Robertson and Tricia Cooke

179 'Both of the places we . . .' Rick Heinrichs, quoted in the production notes for *The Big Lebowski*

179 'Everyone likes to see a . . .' Joel, quoted in *The Big Lebowski: The Making of a Coen Brothers Film* by William Preston Robertson and Tricia Cooke

179 'And people whose houses we . . .' Ethan, quoted in *The Big Lebowski: The Making of a Coen Brothers Film* by William Preston Robertson and Tricia Cooke

180 'We wouldn't want to make . . .' The Coens, writing in the *Evening Standard*'s *Hot Tickets* magazine, 23 April 1998

180 'Why wouldn't it? It makes . . .' The Coens, writing in the *Evening Standard*'s *Hot Tickets* magazine, 23 April 1998

180 'We put together a tape . . .' Jacqui Landrum, quoted in the production notes for *The Big Lebowski*

180 'Jeff's a natural dancer. He's . . .' Jacqui Landrum, quoted in the production notes for *The Big Lebowski*

180 'We lit The Dude and . . .' Roger Deakins, quoted in the production notes for *The Big Lebowski*
180 'In Berkeley movies, the dancers . . .' Ethan, quoted in *The Big Lebowski: The Making of a Coen Brothers Film* by William Preston Robertson and Tricia Cooke
182 'The premise of the music . . .' Carter Burwell, interview with Doug Adams for *Film Score Monthly*, October/November 1998
182 'The pieces that I did . . .' Carter Burwell, interview with Doug Adams for *Film Score Monthly*, October/November 1998
182 'Few movies could equal that . . .' Roger Ebert, review of *The Big Lebowski* in the *Chicago Sun-Times*, March 1998
183 'Hot directors coming off major . . .' Todd McCarthy, review of *The Big Lebowski* in *Variety*, 20 January 1998
183 'Have the Coens gone feel-good . . .' J. Hoberman, review of *The Big Lebowski* in the *Village Voice*, 10 March 1998
183 'The Coens are after something . . .' Janet Maslin, review of *The Big Lebowski* in the *New York Times*, 6 March 1998
184 'Hollywood will be as perplexed . . .' Ian Nathan, review of *The Big Lebowski* in *Empire* issue #107, May 1998
184 'If it's possible to enjoy . . .' Alexander Walker, review of *The Big Lebowski* in the *Evening Standard*, 23 April 1998
184 'as rich, riotous and disorienting . . .' Quentin Curtis, review of *The Big Lebowski* in the *Daily Telegraph*, 24 April 1998
184 'There's no big idea in . . .' Matthew Sweet, review of *The Big Lebowski* in the *Independent on Sunday*, 26 April 1998
184 'It's almost impossible to think . . .' Geoff Andrew, review of *The Big Lebowski* in *Time Out*, 22 April 1998
186 'I remember going through it . . .' Jon Polito, interview with John H Richardson for US *Premiere*, October 1990
191 'It's a great movie, but . . .' Ethan, interview with Michel Ciment and Hubert Niogret in *Positif*, July/August 1987
193 'It's more attractive to make . . .' The Coens, interview with *indieWIRE*
193 'Even the things that don't . . .' Ethan, quoted in *The Big Lebowski: The Making of a Coen Brothers Film* by William Preston Robertson and Tricia Cooke

The Naked Man

197 'good intentions gone bad, and . . .' J Todd Anderson, interview with Rob Nelson for *City Pages (Minneapolis/St. Paul)*, 1 September 1999
197 'I worked six years of . . .' J Todd Anderson, interview with Rob Nelson for *City Pages (Minneapolis/St. Paul)*, 1 September 1999
198 'October definitely knew what they . . .' Ethan, interview with Rob Nelson for *City Pages (Minneapolis/St. Paul)*, 1 September 1999
198 'I'm just speculating here, but . . .' Ethan, interview with Rob Nelson for *City Pages (Minneapolis/St. Paul)*, 1 September 1999

198 'What this reflects more than . . .' Ethan, interview with Rob Nelson for *City Pages (Minneapolis/St. Paul)*, 1 September 1999
200 'I thought J Todd did . . .' Ethan, interview with Rob Nelson for *City Pages (Minneapolis/St. Paul)*, 1 September 1999

O Brother, Where Art Thou?
204 'We didn't start out with . . .' Ethan, interview with Simon Braund for *Empire* issue #136, October 2000
204 'We never actually read it . . .' Ethan, interview with Paul Fischer for *Dark Horizons*
204 'Scylla and Charybdis? Where were . . .' Ethan, interview with Jonathan Romney for the *Guardian*, 19 May 2000
204 'It's an endlessly re-interpretable story . . .' Joel, interview with Simon Braund for *Empire* issue #136, October 2000
204 'It's all stuff that to . . .' Joel, interview with Jonathan Romney for the *Guardian*, 19 May 2000
204 'It wasn't like we were . . .' Joel, interview with Jonathan Romney for the *Guardian*, 19 May 2000
205 'The political undercurrent of the . . .' Joel, interview with Jonathan Romney for the *Guardian*, 19 May 2000
205 'Because of the Depression-era setting . . .' Ethan, interview with Simon Braund for *Empire* issue #136, October 2000
205 'It pretends to be a . . .' Ethan, interview with Jonathan Romney for the *Guardian*, 19 May 2000
206 'We'd seen him in *Out* . . .' Joel, interview with Simon Braund for *Empire* issue #136, October 2000
206 'As an actor, you never . . .' Ethan, interview with Simon Braund for *Empire* issue #136, October 2000
206 'He looks like a movie . . .' Joel, interview with Simon Braund for *Empire* issue #136, October 2000
206 'I did *O Brother* for . . .' George Clooney, interview with Sally Vincent for the *Guardian*'s *Weekend* magazine, 15 February 2003
206 'We like working with John . . .' Joel, speaking on the *O Brother, Where Art Thou?* DVD
206 'Between the cast and us . . .' Ethan, interview with Jonathan Romney for the *Guardian*, 19 May 2000
207 'Before I read the script . . .' Roger Deakins, interview with Bob Fisher for *American Cinematographer*, October 2000
207 'I've worked in Louisiana . . .' Roger Deakins, interview with Bob Fisher for *American Cinematographer*, October 2000
207 'It's very garish in a . . .' Joel, interview with Simon Braund for *Empire* issue #136, October 2000
208 'give the images we were . . .' Roger Deakins, interview with Bob Fisher for *American Cinematographer*, October 2000

208 'They like to try new . . .' Roger Deakins, interview with Bob Fisher for *American Cinematographer*, October 2000
208 'didn't want glossy images . . .' Roger Deakins, interview with Bob Fisher for *American Cinematographer*, October 2000
209 'We were only rained out . . .' Roger Deakins, interview with Bob Fisher for *American Cinematographer*, October 2000
209 'Those moments aren't structurally necessary . . .' Roger Deakins, interview with Bob Fisher for *American Cinematographer*, October 2000
209 'Trying to track an Akela . . .' Roger Deakins, interview with Bob Fisher for *American Cinematographer*, October 2000
209 'That sequence posed quite a . . .' Roger Deakins, interview with Bob Fisher for *American Cinematographer*, October 2000
210 'The flashy science-fiction stuff . . .' Eric Nash, interview with Ron Magid for *American Cinematographer*, October 2000
210 'We told the Coens that . . .' Eric Nash, interview with Ron Magid for *American Cinematographer*, October 2000
210 'A banjo, a tyre swing . . .' Eric Nash, interview with Ron Magid for *American Cinematographer*, October 2000
211 'The real water only extended . . .' Eric Nash, interview with Ron Magid for *American Cinematographer*, October 2000
211 'All the cows around it . . .' Ethan, interview with Simon Braund for *Empire* issue #136, October 2000
211 'I guess once they've got . . .' Ethan, interview with Simon Braund for *Empire* issue #136, October 2000
211 'It's to do with idiosyncratic . . .' Joel, interview with Andrew Pulver for the *Guardian*'s *Weekend* magazine, 13 October 2001
211 'It was experimental in the . . .' Sarah Priestnall, interview with Bob Fisher for *American Cinematographer*, October 2000
212 'We found that the more . . .' Roger Deakins, interview with Bob Fisher for *American Cinematographer*, October 2000
212 'You can't take a cavalier . . .' Roger Deakins, interview with Bob Fisher for *American Cinematographer*, October 2000
212 'To my knowledge [it had] . . .' Joel, interview with Simon Braund for *Empire* issue #136, October 2000
212 'The salient difference between this . . .' Ethan, interview with Paul Fischer for *Dark Horizons*
212 'The songs all sort of . . .' Ethan, speaking on the *O Brother, Where Art Thou?* DVD
213 'Being so heavily involved in . . .' Ethan, quoted in 'O Brother, Why Art Thou So Popular?' on *BBC News Online*
213 'Both Ethan and I are . . .' Joel, quoted in 'O Brother, Why Art Thou So Popular?' on *BBC News Online*
213 'We'd get together with him . . .' Joel, interview with Paul Fischer for *Dark Horizons*

213 'He came in and had . . .' Ethan, interview with Simon Braund for *Empire* issue #136, October 2000

214 'Your voice coming out of . . .' Elsie Tyminski, quoted in 'O Brother, Why Art Thou So Popular?' on *BBC News Online*

215 '*O Brother, Where Art Thou?* has brio . . .' Peter Bradshaw, review of *O Brother, Where Art Thou?* in the *Guardian*, 15 September 2000

215 'There's no need to pinch . . .' Jason Caro, review of *O Brother, Where Art Thou?* in *Film Review Special* #34, November 2000

216 '*O Brother* certainly isn't as . . .' Kevin Jackson, review of *O Brother, Where Art Thou?* in *Sight and Sound*, October 2000

216 'Is it just uncool to . . .' Anthony Quinn, review of *O Brother, Where Art Thou?* in the *Independent*, 15 September 2000

216 '*O Brother* says everything about . . .' Alexander Walker, review of *O Brother, Where Art Thou?* in the *Evening Standard*, 14 September 2000

216 'As in many of the . . .' AO Scott, review of *O Brother, Where Art Thou?* in the *New York Times*, 22 December 2000

217 'In the same spirit, *O Brother* . . .' Roger Ebert, review of *O Brother, Where Art Thou?* in the *Chicago Sun-Times*, 29 December 2000

217 'A jab at anyone who . . .' J Huberman, review of *O Brother, Where Art Thou?* in the *Village Voice*, 26 December 2000

220 'It's absurd to think the . . .' Joel, interview with Matthew Hayes for the *Montreal Mirror*

221 'a full three happy endings . . .' Rob Content, review of *O Brother, Where Art Thou?* in *Film Quarterly*, Fall 2001

223 'that the natural solidarity of . . .' Rob Content, review of *O Brother, Where Art Thou?* in *Film Quarterly*, Fall 2001

224 'As we were making this . . .' Joel, speaking on the *O Brother, Where Art Thou?* DVD

The Man Who Wasn't There

227 'We started thinking about the . . .' Ethan, speaking on *The Man Who Wasn't There* DVD

227 'The barber thing is really just . . .' Ethan, speaking on *The Man Who Wasn't There* DVD

228 'This movie is heavily influenced . . .' Joel, quoted in the production notes for *The Man Who Wasn't There*

228 'Cain was interested in people's . . .' Ethan, quoted in the production notes for *The Man Who Wasn't There*

228 'Even though there is a . . .' Ethan, quoted in the production notes for *The Man Who Wasn't There*

229 'With this one, we wrote . . .' Joel, interview with Andrew Pulver for the *Guardian*'s *Weekend* magazine, 13 October 2001

229 'I don't know why [Thornton] . . .' Joel, interview with Andrew Pulver for the *Guardian*'s *Weekend* magazine, 13 October 2001

229 'I was on the phone . . .' Billy Bob Thornton, interview with Stuart Jeffries for the *Guardian*, 14 May 2001
230 'He certainly has the confidence . . .' Joel, interview with Andrew Pulver for the *Guardian*'s *Weekend* magazine, 13 October 2001
230 'Ed says very little, he's very . . .' Joel, interview with Andrew Pulver for the *Guardian*'s *Weekend* magazine, 13 October 2001
230 'If this movie was being . . .' Ethan, quoted in the production notes for *The Man Who Wasn't There*
230 'I know that when Joel . . .' Frances McDormand, quoted in the production notes for *The Man Who Wasn't There*
230 'an actor who fills the . . .' Ethan, quoted in the production notes for *The Man Who Wasn't There*
230 'He'd been working a lot . . .' Joel, quoted in the production notes for *The Man Who Wasn't There*
231 'For a lot of intangible . . .' Joel, quoted in the production notes for *The Man Who Wasn't There*
231 'Black and white is a . . .' Joel, quoted in the production notes for *The Man Who Wasn't There*
231 'I love the process. I'd . . .' Roger Deakins, quoted in the production notes for *The Man Who Wasn't There*
232 'We aimed for less contrast . . .' Roger Deakins, quoted in the production notes for *The Man Who Wasn't There*
232 'In many ways it's easier . . .' Roger Deakins, speaking on *The Man Who Wasn't There* DVD
232 'Black and white is about . . .' Roger Deakins, speaking on *The Man Who Wasn't There* DVD
232 'The decision to shoot on . . .' Roger Deakins, speaking on *The Man Who Wasn't There* DVD
232 'It's a compromise we had . . .' Joel, interview with Sheila Johnston for the *Daily Telegraph*, 13 October 2001
233 'I made sure that we . . .' Roger Deakins, interview with Jay Holbern for *American Cinematographer*, October 2001
233 'For some reason it's an . . .' Ethan, speaking on *The Man Who Wasn't There* DVD
233 'science fiction films from the 50s . . .' Joel, interview with Andrew Pulver for the *Guardian*'s *Weekend* magazine, 13 October 2001
233 'It even manifests itself into . . .' Dennis Gassner, quoted in the production notes for *The Man Who Wasn't There*
233 'the hardest scene to get . . .' Roger Deakins, speaking on *The Man Who Wasn't There* DVD
234 'We had to retrofit it . . .' Dennis Gassner, quoted in the production notes for *The Man Who Wasn't There*
234 'Once we dressed the space . . .' Dennis Gassner, quoted in the production notes for *The Man Who Wasn't There*

234 'arranged the pianos with their . . .' Roger Deakins, interview with Jay Holbern for *American Cinematographer*, October 2001
235 'The Craftsman bungalow was pretty . . .' Dennis Gassner, quoted in the production notes for *The Man Who Wasn't There*
235 'The sense that the space . . .' Dennis Gassner, quoted in the production notes for *The Man Who Wasn't There*
235 'The sad thing is that . . .' Ethan, quoted in the production notes for *The Man Who Wasn't There*
235 'I was still smoking at . . .' Billy Bob Thornton, quoted in the *Evening Standard's Hot Tickets* magazine, 25 October 2001
235 'After the movie I quit . . .' Billy Bob Thornton, quoted in the *Evening Standard's Hot Tickets* magazine, 25 October 2001
236 'theramin classic fifties flying saucer . . .' Ethan, speaking on *The Man Who Wasn't There* DVD
236 'It's one of those scenes that's . . .' Billy Bob Thornton, speaking on *The Man Who Wasn't There* DVD
237 'The first time I saw it at . . .' Roger Ebert, review of *The Man Who Wasn't There* in the *Chicago Sun-Times*, 2 November 2001
237 'Beautifully made picture is one . . .' Todd McCarthy, review of *The Man Who Wasn't There* in *Variety*, 13 May 2001
237 'A tediously sub-Lynchian UFO subplot . . .' J Huberman, review of *The Man Who Wasn't There* in the *Village Voice*, 6 November 2001
238 'Slowly paced for a thriller and . . .' Kim Newman, review of *The Man Who Wasn't There* in *Empire*, November 2001
238 'What a stunning, mesmeric movie this is . . .' Peter Bradshaw, review of *The Man Who Wasn't There* in the *Guardian*, 26 October 2001
238 '*The Man Who Wasn't There* is . . .' Phillip French, 'The Coens Raise Cain' in the *Observer*, 28 October 2001
238 'A brave, mostly very successful . . .' Geoff Andrew, review of *The Man Who Wasn't There* in *Time Out*, 24 October 2001
238 'easily [the Coens'] most unique . . .' Jason Caro, review of *The Man Who Wasn't There* in *Film Review*
239 'it is a perfectly executed . . .' Tim Robey, review of *The Man Who Wasn't There* in the *Daily Telegraph*, 26 October 2001
239 'Whilst the film is technically . . .' Phillip Kerr, review of *The Man Who Wasn't There* in the *New Statesman*, 22 October 2001
240 'to let people know how . . .' Joel, quoted in *Uncut* #50, July 2001
241 'Sometimes I would ask . . .' Billy Bob Thornton, quoted in the production notes for *The Man Who Wasn't There*
242 'You wouldn't believe how much . . .' Ethan, quoted in *The Big Lebowski: The Making of a Coen Brothers Film* by William Preston Robertson and Tricia Cooke
243 'There are ways in which . . .' Joel, interview with Andrew Pulver for the *Guardian*'s *Weekend* magazine, 13 October 2001

243 'If I in the third person faltered and . . .' James M Cain, from *The Five Great Novels of James M Cain*
245 'It'll be more than he . . .' from *Double Indemnity* by James M Cain
245 'Oh, Chambers, you did me . . .' from *The Postman Always Rings Twice* by James M Cain
247 'We set the film [in . . .]' Joel, interview with Sheila Johnston for the *Daily Telegraph*, 13 October 2001
247 'It's like he stands outside . . .' Ethan, interview with Geoff Andrew for *Time Out*, 29 August 2001
248 'We've never really thought about . . .' Ethan, interview with Paul Zimmerman for *FilmZone*, 1996
249 'The film distributor doesn't want us to . . .' Ethan, interview with Joanne Latimer for *Softimage.com*, 15 May 2001

Intolerable Cruelty
254 'Because it's one of the . . .' 'Mean Mr Mustard', review of *Intolerable Cruelty* for *Ain't It Cool*, 22 January 2003

Still in the Drawer
255 'We never really did anything with it . . .' Joel, interview with Hal Hinson for *Film Comment*, March/April 1985
255 'It had 28 Einsteins in it . . .' Ethan, interview with Hal Hinson for *Film Comment*, March/April 1985
255 'It was a small part . . .' George Clooney, interview with Jann Carl for *Entertainment Tonight*, December 2000
256 'Without any jokes at all . . .' The Coens, quoted in *Uncut* issue #50, July 2001
257 'It's hard for someone to lose money . . .' Joel, interview with Andrew Pulver for the *Guardian*'s *Weekend* magazine, 13 October 2001
257 'I think it's dead.' Joel, interview with Smriti Mundhra for *IGN FilmForce*, 2 November 2001
258 'No sound, except for an . . .' Extract of *The Ladykillers* script, quoted in *FilmJerk.com*
258 '*The Ladykillers* could easily become . . .' Edward Havens, review of *The Ladykillers* script in *FilmJerk.com*
258 'we've both talked about . . .' Ethan, interview with Nathan Rabin for *The Onion AV Club*, 19 July 2000
259 'be an interesting exercise . . .' Ethan, interview with Nathan Rabin for *The Onion AV Club*, 19 July 2000
259 'Like *Old Yeller*.' Joel, interview with Nathan Rabin for *The Onion AV Club*, 19 July 2000
259 'We keep arguing . . .' Ethan, interview with Nathan Rabin for *The Onion AV Club*, 19 July 2000

Bibliography

Books

Bergan, Robert, *The Coen Brothers*, Phoenix, London, 2000

Cain, James M, *The Five Great Novels of James M Cain*, Picador, London, 1985

Cheshire, Ellen and Ashbrook, John, *The Pocket Essential Joel and Ethan Coen*, Pocket Essentials, Harpenden, 2002

Coen, Joel and Coen, Ethan, *Barton Fink & Miller's Crossing*, Faber & Faber, London, 1991

Coen, Joel and Coen, Ethan, *The Man Who Wasn't There*, Faber & Faber, London, 2001

Curtis, James, *Between Flops: A Biography of Preston Sturges*, Limelight, New York, 1991

Halliwell, Leslie and Walker, John (ed), *Halliwell's Film & Video Guide 2000*, HarperCollins Entertainment, London, 1999

Halliwell, Leslie and Walker, John (ed), *Halliwell's Film & Video Guide 2003*, HarperCollins Entertainment, London, 2002

Halliwell, Leslie and Walker, John (ed), *Halliwell's Who's Who in the Movies*, HarperCollins Entertainment, London, 1999

Hammett, Dashiell, *The Glass Key*, Orion Books, London, 2002

Korte, Peter and Seessien, Georg, *Joel & Ethan Coen*, Titan Books, London, 1999

Lowenstein, Stephen (ed), *My First Movie*, Faber and Faber, London, 2000

Markham-Smith, Ian and Hodgson, Liz, *Nicolas Cage: The Unauthorised Biography*, Blake, London, 2001

Robertson, William Preston and Cooke, Tricia, *The Big Lebowski: The Making of a Coen Brothers Film*, Norton, New York, 1998

Woods, Paul A (ed), *Joel & Ethan Coen: Blood Siblings*, Plexus, London, 2000

Articles

Adams, Doug, 'Composition Theory' in *Film Score Monthly*, October/November 1998

Altman, Rachel, 'Dennis Gassner' in US *Premiere*, April 1990

Andrew, Geoff, 'The Coen Brothers and *Barton Fink*' in *Time Out*, 5 February 1992

Andrew, Geoff, 'Barton Fink' in *Time Out*, 12 February 1992

Andrew, Geoff, 'The Big Lebowski' in *Time Out*, 22 April 1998

Andrew, Geoff, interview with the Coens in *Time Out*, 29 August 2001

Andrew, Geoff, 'The Man Who Wasn't There' in *Time Out*, 24 October 2001

Anonymous, production notes for *Miller's Crossing*, copyright 20th Century Fox

Anonymous, production notes for *Barton Fink*, copyright 20th Century Fox

Anonymous, production notes for *The Hudsucker Proxy*, copyright Warner Brothers
Anonymous, production notes for *Fargo*, copyright PolyGram
Anonymous, production notes for *The Big Lebowski*, copyright PolyGram
Anonymous, production notes for *The Man Who Wasn't There*, copyright PolyGram
Anonymous, 'Miller's Crossing' in *Empire* issue #21, March 1991
Anonymous, 'Blood Simple' in the *People*, 4 February 1985
Anonymous, 'Fargo' in *Newsday*, 14 March 1996
Anonymous, 'Blood Simple' in *Variety*, 23 May 1984
Anonymous, 'Crimewave' in *Variety*, 22 May 1985
Anonymous, 'Raising Arizona' in *Variety*, 4 March 1987
Anonymous, 'Barton Fink' in *Variety*, 27 March 1991
Anonymous, 'Miller's Crossing' in *Variety*, 3 September 1990
Anonymous, 'Bruce Campbell: The Man Who Was Ash' in *Insound* http://www.insound.com/zinestand/cash/feature.cfm?aid=3019
Anonymous, Cannes festival report in *Empire* issue #25, July 1991
Anonymous, front page of the *Brainerd Daily Dispatch*'s *Fargo* site, http://www.brainerddespatch.com/fargo
Anonymous, editorial in the *Brainerd Daily Dispatch*, 22 April 1996
Anonymous, 'The Coen Brothers' in *indieWIRE*, http://www.geocities.com/Hollywood/7042/interviewlebow.html
Anonymous, 'An Interview with Asia Carrera' in *The Unofficial Big Lebowski Homepage*, http://www.geocities.com/Hollywood/Boulevard/9284/lebowski 2.htm
Anonymous, 'O Brother, Why Art Thou So Popular?' in *BBC News Online*
Anonymous, 'A DVD Talk with Kenneth Loring' in *DVD Talk*, http://www.dvdtalk.com/bloodsimpleinterview.html
Anonymous, Cannes festival report in *Uncut* issue #50, July 2001
Barth, Jack, 'Praising *Arizona*' in *Film Comment*, March/April 1987
Benson, Sheila, 'Raising Arizona' in the *Los Angeles Times*, March 1987
Bergson, Phillip, 'Finks Ain't What They Used to Be' in *What's On in London*, 10 February 1992
Bilbow, Marjorie, 'Crimewave' in *Screen International* issue #546, May 1986
Biskind, Peter, 'Joel and Ethan Coen' in US *Premiere*, March 1996
Bradshaw, Peter, 'O Brother, Where Art Thou?' in the *Guardian*, 15 September 2000
Bradshaw, Peter, 'The Man Who Wasn't There' in the *Guardian*, 26 October 2001
Braund, Simon, 'Empire One on One: The Coen Brothers' for *Empire* issue #136, October 2000
Braunschweig, Stephané, 'Blood Simple' in *Cahiers du Cinema*, July/August 1985
Breitbart, Eric, 'New York Independents' in *American Film*, May 1985
Brown, Geoff, 'Miller's Crossing' in *The Times*, 14 February 1991

Brown, Geoff, 'The Hudsucker Proxy' in *The Times*, 1 September 1994
Brown, Geoff, 'Fargo' in *The Times*, 30 May 1996
Brown, Georgia, 'The Hudsucker Proxy' in the *Village Voice*, 22 March 1994
Brown, Georgia, 'Fargo' in the *Village Voice*, 12 March 1996
Canby, Vincent, 'And Baby Makes 3' in the *New York Times*, 11 March 1987
Canby, Vincent, 'Miller's Crossing' in the *New York Times*, September 21 1990
Canby, Vincent, 'Barton Fink' in the *New York Times*, 20 May 1991
Canby, Vincent, 'Barton Fink' in the *New York Times*, 18 August 1991
Carl, Jann, interview with George Clooney in *Entertainment Tonight*, December 2000
Caro, Jason, 'O Brother, Where Art Thou?' in *Film Review Special* #34, November 2000
Caro, Jason, 'The Man Who Wasn't There' in *Film Review Special* #38, November 2001
Ciment, Michel and Niogret, Hubert, 'Interview with Joel and Ethan Coen' in *Positif*, July/August 1987
Ciment, Michel and Niogret, Hubert, 'A Rock on the Beach' in *Positif*, September 1991
Ciment, Michel and Niogret, Hubert, 'Closer to Life than the Conventions of Cinema' in *Positif*, September 1996
Clark, John, 'Strange Bedfellows' in US *Premiere*, April 1994
Coen, Joel and Ethan, 'On *The Big Lebowski*' in the *Evening Standard*'s *Hot Tickets* magazine, 23 April 1998
Content, Rob, 'O Brother, Where Art Thou?' in *Film Quarterly*, Fall 2001
Coursodon, Jean-Pierre, 'A Hat Blown on the Wind' in *Positif*, February 1991
Curtis, Quentin, 'The Big Lebowski' in the *Daily Telegraph*, 24 April 1998
Dunne, Michael, 'Barton Fink, Intertextuality, and the (Almost) Unbearable Richness of Viewing' in *Literature/Film Quarterly* volume 28 number 4, 2000
Ebert, Roger, 'Blood Simple' in the *Chicago Sun-Times*, February 1985
Ebert, Roger, 'Raising Arizona' in the *Chicago Sun-Times*, 20 March 1987
Ebert, Roger, 'Miller's Crossing' in the *Chicago Sun-Times*, 5 October 1990
Ebert, Roger, 'Barton Fink' in the *Chicago Sun-Times*, 23 August 1991
Ebert, Roger, 'The Hudsucker Proxy' in the *Chicago Sun-Times*, 25 May 1994
Ebert, Roger, 'The Big Lebowski' in the *Chicago Sun-Times*, March 1998
Ebert, Roger, 'O Brother, Where Art Thou?' in the *Chicago Sun-Times*, 29 December 2000
Ebert, Roger, 'The Man Who Wasn't There' in the *Chicago Sun-Times*, 2 November 2001
Edelstein, David, 'Invasion of the Baby Snatchers' in *American Film*, April 1987
Emerson, Jim, 'That Barton Fink Feeling' in *Cinepad*, 1991, www.cinepad.com/coens.htm
Errigo, Angie, 'If you want to get ahead . . .' in *Empire* issue #21, March 1991
Errigo, Angie, 'Barton Fink' in *Empire* issue #33, March 1992
Ferrante, Anthony C, 'The Coen Proxy' in *IF Magazine*, 7 July 2000, http://www.ifmagazine.com/common/article.asp?articleID=734

Fischer, Paul, 'Nothing's Simple for These Brothers Coen' in *Dark Horizons*, 2000, http://www.darkhorizons.com/news6/coen.htm
Fischer, Paul, 'The Coens' Odyssey' in *Dark Horizons*, 2000, http://www.darkhorizons.com/news8/coen2.htm
Fisher, Bob, 'Escaping from Chains' in *American Cinematographer*, October 2000
Francke, Lizzie, 'Hell Freezes Over' in *Sight and Sound*, May 1996
French, Phillip, 'The Coens Raise Cain' in the *Observer*, 28 October 2001
Fuller, Graham, 'Do Not Miss *Fargo*' in *Interview*, March 1996
Giddins, Gary, 'Miller's Crossing' in the *Village Voice*, 25 September 1990
Goodridge, Mike, 'The Big Lebowski' in *Screen International*, 30 January 1998
Grant, Edmond, 'Barton Fink' in *Films in Review*, November/December 1991
Harkness, John, 'The Sphinx Without a Riddle' in *Sight and Sound*, August 1994
Havens, Edward, 'The Ladykillers' in *FilmJerk.com*, 18 January 2003, http://www.filmjerk.com/archives/0301/030119coens.html
Hays, Matthew, 'The Coen Code' in the *Montreal Mirror*, 26 February 1998
Hinson, Hal, 'Bloodlines' in *Film Comment*, March/April 1985
Hoberman, J, 'The Big Lebowski' in the *Village Voice*, 10 March 1998
Hoberman, J, 'O Brother, Where Art Thou?' in the *Village Voice*, 26 December 2000
Hoberman, J, 'The Man Who Wasn't There' in the *Village Voice*, 6 November 2001
Holbern, Jay, 'The Root(s) of All Evil' in *American Cinematographer*, October 2001
Howe, Desson, 'Fargo' in the *Washington Post*, 14 March 1996
Jackson, Kevin, 'O Brother, Where Art Thou?' in *Sight and Sound*, October 2000
Jameson, Richard T, 'What's in the Box?' in *Film Comment*, September/October 1991
Jeffries, Stuart, 'Smoke Amid Silence' in the *Guardian*, 14 May 2001
Jenkins, Steve, 'Blood Simple' in *Monthly Film Bulletin*, January 1985
Jenkins, Steve, 'Crimewave' in *Monthly Film Bulletin*, April 1986
Jenkins, Steve, 'Raising Arizona' in *Monthly Film Bulletin*, July 1987
Jenkins, Steve, 'Miller's Crossing' in *Monthly Film Bulletin*, February 1991
Jenkins, Steve, 'Barton Fink' in *Sight and Sound*, February 1992
Johnston, Sheila, 'Double Fink' in the *Independent*, 22 May 1991
Johnston, Sheila, 'Cutting Edge Coens' in the *Daily Telegraph*, 13 October 2001
Kael, Pauline, 'Blood Simple' in the *New Yorker*, 25 February 1985
Kael, Pauline, 'Raising Arizona' in the *New Yorker*, March 1987
Kemply, Rita, 'Raising Arizona' in the *Washington Post*, 20 March 1987
Kerr, Phillip, 'The Man Who Wasn't There' in the *New Statesman*, 22 October 2001
Klady, Leonard, 'Fargo' in *Variety*, 12 February 1996
Latimer, Joanne, 'The Coens – Cannes' in *Softimage.com*, 15 May 2001, http://www.softimage.com/Community/Xsi/Mag/Features/Cannes 2001/3/

Levy, Steven, 'Shot by Shot' in US *Premiere*, March 1990

Lyttle, John, 'The Hudsucker Proxy' in the *Independent* London Supplement, September 1994

Mackenzie, Suzie, 'Someone to Lean On' in the *Guardian*, 2 September 2000

Magid, Ron, 'A New High-Water Mark' in *American Cinematographer*, October 2000

Malcolm, Derek, 'Fargo' in the *Guardian*, 30 May 1996

Malcolm, Derek, 'The Hudsucker Proxy' in the *Guardian*, 1 September 1994

Maslin, Janet, 'Fargo' in the *New York Times*, 8 March 1996

Maslin, Janet, 'The Big Lebowski' in the *New York Times*, 6 March 1998

Mathews, Jack, 'Holly Hunter' in *American Film*, December 1989

Maxford, Howard, 'The Coen Brothers' in *What's On in London*, 7 September 1994

McCarthy, Todd, 'The Hudsucker Proxy' in *Variety*, 31 January 1994

McCarthy, Todd, 'The Big Lebowski' in *Variety*, 20 January 1998

McCarthy, Todd, 'The Man Who Wasn't There' in *Variety*, 13 May 2001

'Mean Mr Mustard', 'Intolerable Cruelty' in *Ain't It Cool*, 22 January 2003, http://www.aintitcool.com/display.cgi?id=14269

Miller, Arthur, 'Barton Fink' in US *Premiere*, October 1991

Milne, Tom, 'Hard on Little Things' in *Sight and Sound*, Summer 1987

Mottesheard, Ryan, 'Shooting Coens' in *indieWIRE*, http://www.indiewire.com/film/interviews/int_Deakins_Roger_011030.html

Mottram, James, 'Frances McDormand' in *BBC News Online*, 22 October 2001, http://www.bbc.co.uk/films/2001/10/17/francis_mcdormand_2001_interview.shtml

Mundhra, Smriti, 'Interview with Joel Coen' in *IGN FilmForce*, 2 November 2001, http://filmforce.ign.com/articles/315/315734p1.html

Nathan, Ian, 'Fargo' in *Empire* issue #84, June 1996

Nathan, Ian, 'The Big Lebowski' in *Empire* issue #107, May 1998

Naughton, John, 'Double Vision' in UK *Premiere*, September 1994

Nelson, Rob, 'Good Touch, Bad Touch' in *City Pages (Minneapolis/St. Paul)*, 1 September 1999

Newman, Kim, 'Goose Bumps' in *City Limits*, 25 January 1985

Newman, Kim, 'The Hudsucker Proxy' in *Empire* issue #64, October 1994

Newman, Kim, 'The Hudsucker Proxy' in *Sight and Sound*, September 1994

Newman, Kim, 'The Man Who Wasn't There' in *Empire*, November 2001

Odien, WC, 'The Rise and Fall of Norville Barnes' in *Cinefex* issue #58, June 1994

Probst, Chris, 'Cold-Blooded Scheming' in *American Cinematographer*, March 1996

Pulleine, Tim, 'Crimewave' in *Films and Filming* issue #379, April 1986

Pulver, Andrew, 'Pictures That Do the Talking' in the *Guardian*'s *Weekend* magazine, 13 October 2001

Quinn, Anthony, 'O Brother, Where Art Thou?' in the *Independent*, 15 September 2000

Rabin, Nathan, 'Joel and Ethan Coen' in *The Onion AV Club*, 19 July 2000, http://www.theavclub.com/avclub3624/avfeature823624.html

Richardson, John H, 'The Joel and Ethan Story' in US *Premiere*, October 1990

Robey, Tim, 'The Man Who Wasn't There' in the *Daily Telegraph*, 26 October 2001

Romney, Jonathan, 'Myth America' in the *Guardian*, 25 August 1994

Romney, Jonathan, 'Double Vision' in the *Guardian*, 19 May 2000

Rowe, Douglas J, 'The Coen Brothers, *Fargo* and Foregoing Boundaries' in the *Brainerd Daily Dispatch*, 14 March 1996

San, Helen, 'Carter Burwell: Passion Under Pressure' in *Cinemusic*, http://www.cinemusic.net/spotlight/1999/cb-interview.html

Scott, AO, 'O Brother, Where Art Thou?' in the *New York Times*, 22 December 2000

Sessions, Kevin, 'Ethan and Joel Coen' in *Interview*, April 1987

Sonnenfeld, Barry, 'Shadows and Shivers for *Blood Simple*' in *American Cinematographer*, July 1985

Sweet, Matthew, 'The Big Lebowski' in the *Independent on Sunday*, 26 April 1998

Thornton, Billy Bob, 'On *The Man Who Wasn't There*' in the *Evening Standard*'s *Hot Tickets* magazine, 25 October 2001

Tookey, Christopher, 'Barton Fink' in the *Sunday Telegraph*, 16 February 1992

Tookey, Christopher, 'The Hudsucker Proxy' in the *Daily Mail*, 2 September 1994

Tookey, Christopher, 'Fargo' in the *Daily Mail*, 31 May 1996

Usher, Shaun, 'Barton Fink' in the *Daily Mail*, 14 February 1992

Vincent, Sally, 'Pretty Boys Can Think' in the *Guardian*'s *Weekend* magazine, 15 February 2003

Walker, Alexander, 'The Hudsucker Proxy' in the *Evening Standard*, 1 September 1994

Walker, Alexander, 'The Big Lebowski' in the *Evening Standard*, 23rd April 1998

Walker, Alexander, 'O Brother, Where Art Thou?' in the *Evening Standard*, 14 September 2000

Waller, Steve, 'Fargo nominated for best picture Oscar' in the *Brainerd Daily Dispatch*, 14 February 1997

Wise, Damon, interview with the Coens in *Filmfestivals.com*, 2001, http://www.filmfestivals.com/cannes_2000/official/brother.htm

Wright, Timothy, 'Hope in the Midst of the Nuclear Threat: A Critical Examination of the Imagery in *Raising Arizona*', http://www.regent.edu/acad/schcom/rojc/wright.html

Zimmerman, Paul, interview with the Coens in *FilmZone*, 1996, http://www.independentproject.com/oldWFH/disk05/FilmZone/Interviews/coens.html

Index